THE CHINESE PATH
What Has the Rise of China Contributed to the World?

THE CHINESE PATH
What Has the Rise of China Contributed to the World?

CHEN Xueming

Translate by Gao Wei, May Carl, Gin Jiang

Portico Publishing Company

Portico Publishing Company

B&R Book Program

The Chinese Path: What Has the Rise of China Contributed to the World?
by CHEN Xueming

The Chinese Path: What Has the Rise of China Contributed to the World?

by CHEN Xueming
Translate by Gao Wei, May Carl, Gin Jiang

Published in The United States by
Portico Publishing Company
2109-2 Dublin Lane
Diamond Bar California 91765
USA

ISBN 978-1-60633-569-7

CONTENTS

CONTENTS

INTRODUCTION

The Global Significance of the Chinese Path

Nowadays, Chinese people call the path they chose "the path of socialism with Chinese characteristics", because it is considered "socialistic" and is also "adapted to the specific conditions of China". Although based on "Chinese characteristics", its significance for mankind has been increasingly emerging. It has profoundly changed the course of China's historical development, and at the same time, has also greatly impacted world history. The Chinese path lays emphasis on China's own national "characteristics", which does not imply narrow nationalism. Quite the reverse, it denies and transcends national narrowness, and signifies the full play of intra-national cohesion so as to form an advantage of itself. So in this sense, it is inevitable for the Chinese path to exert a worldwide influence. Being a cosmopolitan historical event, the initiation of the Chinese path has both domestic and international significance. Its global significance is hereinafter described in four aspects.

I. Exploring a New Development Model for Human Civilization

Stepping into the stage of civilization out from the age of barbarism, human beings have experienced periods of primitive civilization, feudal civilization and capitalist civilization, which have brought great progress for mankind. Capitalism, in particular, has pushed this progress to an unparalleled degree. While at the same time, these forms of civilization have also wracked mankind, especially capitalism, which has brought about unprecedented challenges. The reality shows that human civilization is now at an inflection point in its own history, and it is not unlikely that humanity itself will fall with the decay of civilization if we cannot rise to the present challenges which are mainly manifested in the aggravation of "three major contradictions". The first contradiction is growing human inequality. Capitalist civilization is based on exploitation and pillage which, in the era of globalization, have become more and more severe, thus increasing inequality among people. The second contradiction is intensified conflicts between humans and nature, and nature's ecological capacity for mankind is close to saturation. Thirdly, unbalanced needs of human beings have gradually made people "one-dimensional" consuming machines. Therefore, the world and historical significance of the Chinese path hinges on whether it could successfully deal with these challenges and resolve the increasingly fierce contradictions, on whether it could become a new path for mankind's progress towards civilization, and on whether it could seek out a new state of being for mankind.

It is quite superficial to attribute the contributions of the Chinese path to China's intention of becoming the world's second largest economy. During the Asian and world financial crises, the large Chinese economy stood out as a Gold Anchor to maintain global economic stability, clearly demonstrating the contributions of the Chinese path. Nonetheless, the contributions of the Chinese path include but are not limited to the economic sphere. Defining China's development only in terms of GDP growth is not necessarily good for the whole world.

The truth is that the Chinese path has not only brought about the rapid growth of GDP, but more importantly, has explored a new development model on this land with a long history. Within this model, Chinese people are creating a novel state of being, which together shape a new form of civilization. The Chinese path is led by socialistic theories with its own characteristics, and China is pursuing peaceful and sustainable development in an all-round coordinated way. The true essence of the Chinese path lies in the fact that as China has become the second largest economy in the world, it still endeavors to minimize the costs which are common in the industrial development of the Western world; when China is trying to make the pie bigger, it distributes the pie to everyone by every means; when China is focusing on economic development, it does not ignore the improvement of people's livelihood, social stability and people's all-round development; when China sticks to its economic construction, political, cultural, social and Eco-civilization constructions are also made to follow along closely; when China is building a moderately prosperous society, it still attaches a high priority to the great development and flourishing of socialist culture; when China is satisfying people's material needs, it still tries to cultivate the new generation through building up a socialist core value system. Though it cannot be affirmed that a new development model and a new human state of being have already been shaped in China, we can confidently claim that we are stepping decisively towards this goal. It is fair to say that China's socialistic path with its own characteristics represents the pursuit of a genuine state of being human, of humanity, and a revolution against the Western-dominated state of being that is now in crisis. From this point of view, it is never possible to overstate the significance of the Chinese path for human civilization and world history.

II.Setting a Positive Model in Poverty Relief for Developing Countries

An urgent issue for human society at present is to alleviate poverty of the broad masses of developing countries in the Third World and lead them to a wealthy life. China, also a Third World country, has been viewed by many as a model in eliminating poverty and backwardness. The international significance of the Chinese path lies to a great degree in how it provides lessons for poverty relief in many poor Third World nations, and whether its specific path to creating "world history" sets a positive example for other developing countries who wishes to choose their own development path.

It is undeniable that the great achievements of the Chinese path are now receiving attention from many developing countries, implying that a highly positive model has already been established among them. Socialism with Chinese characteristics has helped China step from localization to globalization, develop the diachronic and synchronic unification of world history, and thereby demonstrate its true nature and power in unlimited time and space. In this very progress, this path has presented a vast number of developing countries with referential development ideas and methods.

China's socialistic path is distinct from the African Model, the Latin American Model or the East Asian Model, but still has a universal significance in guiding Third World countries out of poverty. China's conditions, although unique to China itself, can to a certain extent also be generalized to Third World countries, and thereby providing a referential development model for the latter. As is purported by some foreign scholars and politicians, especially those from the Third World, the Chinese path is a model different from what the Western countries, the World Bank and the International Monetary Fund have been advocating. It is not there for indiscriminate copy, but is perhaps the best model for drawing many important instructive lessons.

The vast number of Third World countries attach particular importance to the gradualness, orderliness and steadiness of the Chinese path. To be more specific, all the following strategies and policies that are presently in effect have raised great concerns of the Third World. In regard to the ownership of property, as opposed to full privatization, China adopts mixed ownership in which public ownership is the main component. Public ownership still controls the national economic lifeline. In terms of resource allocation, compared to Western countries, China has stronger government regulation and intervention on the economy although it is market-oriented. Politically, China does not adopt a multi-party or parliamentary system, or the separation of powers of the executive, legislature and judiciary, while at the same time, it keeps broadening the scope of socialist democracy. Ideologically, China welcomes the coexistence of different ideas with the policy of "letting a hundred schools of thought contend" while maintaining the leadership of Marxism in the ideological sphere.

Indeed, it is by no means accidental that the Chinese path has provided a successful experience for the Third World countries to pay attention to and follow, for the experience has greatly broadened the pathway to Third World modernization, enriched mankind's knowledge of how to develop towards more civilized societies, and encouraged the diversity of human civilization in the globalized age.

III. Bringing Vitality and Hope to the International Communist Movement

The international Communist movement is an indispensable part of the history of human civilization because the future of mankind is closely related to the future of the Communist movement, and therefore the global significance of researching the Chinese path includes how it has influenced the international Communist movement. Ever since the end of 1980s and the beginning of 1990s, after the collapse of socialistic regimes in the Eastern Europe, the international Communist movement has entered a low ebb, thereby posing an urgent problem of how to build socialism within the newly established socialist regimes in undeveloped countries.

Marx proposed the hypothesis of "Caudine Forks", that is, Eastern undeveloped countries passing through the capitalist stage to go straight into socialism. Though no detailed explication of the hypothesis was found in Marx's works, the October Revolution led by Lenin had put it into practice, and the success of the Chinese revolution once again proved its feasibility. Retrospectively looking at the history of the international Communist movement, it is easy to see whether undeveloped countries could leap over the Caudine Fork and establish socialist regimes or not. The real problem, however, lies in the fact that some leaders in the socialist Soviet Union and China made no distinction between the socialism which was built based on passing over Caudine Forks, needing to further "appropriate capitalism's positive acquisitions", and the socialism which is caused by the basic contradictions of capitalism and built upon "capitalism's positive acquisitions". Even worse, they built the former type of socialism as though it was the latter one, which was a major cause of the setback of Chinese socialist construction after the collapse of socialist regimes in Eastern Europe. This suggests that although it is clear that undeveloped countries could overpass Caudine Forks and build socialist regimes, it is still unclear how the regimes could thus construct socialism well. In this case, we could put it this way: Marx's hypothesis in his late years of the achievement of socialism in Eastern undeveloped countries was only half implemented by Lenin and Mao Zedong. That is, the Soviet Union and China had only established socialist regimes by passing through the Caudine Forks of capitalism. The other half of the hypothesis, i.e. to construct socialism successfully, which is probably of more importance, remains to be fulfilled by future generations.

The major principle of theories of socialism with Chinese characteristics is to distinguish the above-mentioned two types of socialism. The chief architect of China's reform and opening-up policy, Deng Xiaoping, emphasized that at present Chinese socialism is still at the "primary stage", just in order to distinguish it from the kind of socialism described in Marx's *Capital* and to let Chinese people build socialism based on the "Caudine Forks" hypothesis rather than on the intensification of capitalist contradictions. Socialistic theories in China, whether in terms of the developmental path, phase, fundamental task and driving force of socialism, or in terms of its external conditions, strategy, leading force or supporting power, are all based on "incorporating the positive acquisitions of capitalism". China's reform and opening-up, the socialistic market economy, and the mixed ownership with public ownership as the leading force are all endowed with legitimacy and reasonableness. Of course, the Chinese path, suited to China's own conditions, is not merely an achievement in theory, but also a success in practice.

The temporal problem of how to consolidate, construct and develop a socialistic system, which had been bothering the international Communist movement ever since Lenin's establishment of a socialist regime in USSR was solved by the birth of the Chinese path. The breaking through of the problem has put the international Communist movement in a new starting point. Despite the fact that Chinese socialism has to coexist and compete with world capitalism which is fully matured and rich-experienced, and that the world Communist movement has not yet come out of its most difficult and intricate period, the contemporary world Communist movement will definitely get renewed vitality and hope with the rise of Chinese socialism. This is exactly the true meaning of the Chinese path for the international Communist movement, and its great contribution for human history.

VI. Exploring New Pathways for Marxism to Show Reality and Develop

Marxism remains the most influential school of thought in the world today. The future of humanity, in some sense, depends on the future of Marxism. Thus in order to discern the significance of the Chinese path for the world, we have to study its significance for Marxism. A key aspect of the global significance of the Chinese path is manifested in its importance for Marxism, and the other aspects are also closely related to Marxism.

The significance of the Chinese path for Marxism is generally reflected in the following three facets. Firstly, it proves that the fundamental theories of Marxism are not out of date, and further verifies that Marxism is the banner under which mankind can march forward. Secondly, it overthrows some untimely theories of Marxism with practice, which has further purified Marxism. Lastly, it propels Marxism forward and thereby keeps the vigor of Marxism by making it more suited to the needs of time. The "verification", "falsification" and "promotion" of Marxism constitute the entire meaning of the Chinese path, which can be elaborated from the following five points in a more specific way.

(1) The Chinese path proves that Marxist theory of socially basic contradiction is an irrefutable truth, makes Marxist ideology of dialectical materialism shine with radiance, testifies to the correctness of Marx's judgment that capitalism would be replaced by socialism, shows the validity of his conclusion that the liberation of mankind cannot be attained without the leadership of the proletarian party, and reveals the reality of Marxist theory of oriental society.

(2) The great significance of the Chinese path for Marxism is not only manifested in a series of basic theories of "verifying" Marxism in its own practice, but also, at the same time, "falsifying" some of the original outdated conclusions of Marxism. The truth is very clear: the Chinese path proves that Marxist socialist market-free judgments are untenable, that the Marxist "philosophy of social conflict" has become outdated, and indicates that Marxist "material ontology" is flawed, meaning that we must re-examine Marx's proposal of "the most radical rupture with traditional ideas". But it must be clarified that some of the original conclusions and views of Marxism, which are referred to here as "falsified" by the Chinese path, are not only the propositions of the Marxist founders, Marx and Engels, under their historical conditions, but are also the ideas of Marx and Engel's "successors" that were written in the name of Marxism.

The process of "verifying" and "falsifying" Marxism by the Chinese path is also the process of developing Marxism. The development of Marxism in China is comprehensive and holistic. That is to say, the Chinese path has made remarkable development on three components: Marxist philosophy, Marxist political economy, and scientific socialism theory.

(3) The development of Marxist philosophy is mainly embodied in the following facts. The Chinese path has developed the Marxist philosophy of "material ontology" to "material-practice ontology" by holding the banner of "putting people first". The Chinese path is a path for peaceful development, and China's building of a harmonious socialist society has shifted Marxist philosophy from focusing on "conflict" to "unity". The Chinese path dares to face and is good at dealing with intricate affairs, which highlights the status of the complexity of contradictions in Marxist philosophy. The Chinese path sticks to progressive reform, which guarantees the irreplaceable legal status of reforms in the Marxist theory of social revolution.

(4) The development of a Marxist political economy is elucidated as follows. By creating a socialist market economic system, the Chinese path has for the first time in the history of Marxist political economy integrated market and socialism. Persisting in utilizing and developing capital, the Chinese path has established the role of capital in creating values in the system of Marxist political economy. Establishing and perfecting the economic system in which public ownership is in a dominant position and diverse forms of ownership develop side by side, the Chinese path has broadened the scope of Marxist political economy by bringing non-public ownership into a socialist ownership structure. Rising to the challenges in the age of "virtual economy", the Chinese path has filled in the "blank" of developing and supervising the virtual economy for Marxist political economy. Taking the promotion of economic growth as its primary task, the Chinese path unwaveringly adheres to the strategic thinking that "only development counts" and thereby makes Marxist political economy "development-centered".

(5) The most important development of scientific socialism

includes the following aspects. Confirming that China is now at the primary stage of socialism, the Chinese path has made a significant contribution to the theory of the stages of socialist development. Comprehensively defining the essence of socialism, the Chinese path has given the most incisive and complete answer in the history of scientific socialism to the question of what socialism is. Exploring the driving force of socialism, the Chinese path has brought the scientific socialist spirit of innovation to a whole new level. Through strengthening the party's class foundation and expanding its mass foundation, the Chinese path has enriched and developed the scientific socialist theory of party-building. Through reshaping the relationship between socialism and capitalism, the Chinese path has changed the scientific socialist theory of setting socialism against capitalism.

Indeed, Marxism, which has been "verified", "falsified" and "promoted" by the Chinese path, is no longer entirely Marxism in its original sense. The drastic changes in Eastern Europe were undoubtedly a great frustration to Marxism, but after a period of silence in the early 1990s, Marxism began to "revive". Looking at the prosperity of Marxism in today's world, we cannot but admit that it is closely related to the Chinese path which has created tremendous "positive energy" for it. When Marxism was going through its most difficult times, Deng Xiaoping told people to stay calm, and not to have the idea that Marxism had disappeared, gone, or failed. Nothing of the sort! It is fair to say that Deng Xiaoping had enough confidence to say that, and that "confidence" comes from China's successful advancement of the great cause of socialism with Chinese characteristics.

We have revealed the historical significance of the socialist path with Chinese characteristics from the aforementioned five internally related aspects. This is actually intended for further "defining" and "positioning" the Chinese path in order to locate it in world history. We believe that as long as we truly see the position of the Chinese path in world history, and understand its far-reaching significance for human society, we can be more conscious in upholding and enriching the theoretical system of socialism with Chinese characteristics, and can be more responsible in unswervingly following the path of socialism with Chinese characteristics.

Part I

The Chinese Path and Human Civilization

The path of socialism with Chinese characteristics, initiated by Chinese people under the leadership of the Communist Party of China (CPC), has not only changed Chinese history, but also altered the progress of human development, and therefore bears a far-reaching significance for world history. The Chinese path, in this case, is not merely a part of the history of China, but also of the whole world. Its importance could be approached from several aspects. Here we discuss what the Chinese path has brought for human civilization, or to put in another way, how to make sense of the events that took place in China during all these years from the interrelationship between the Chinese path and human civilization.

Chapter One

Consolidating the Material Base for Human Civilization

After stepping out from the historical stage of barbarism into the civilized age, human beings has successively experienced primitive civilization, feudal civilization and capitalist civilization. It has always been the production of material goods that drives the transformation of civilization. In this sense, strong economic power and a solid material base used to be and still is the necessary foundation of human civilization. In *The Communist Manifesto*, Marx and Engels incisively pointed out for the first time that "in every historical epoch, the prevailing mode of economic production and exchange, and the social organization necessarily following from it, form the basis upon which it is built up"[1]. Marx and Engels not only illustrated the objective rule that relations of production are determined by productive forces and superstructure determined by economic base, but also indicated that economic power is the ultimate foundation of civilized human society. From this, it is fair to say that whether and to what extent a development model contributes to civilized human society depends mostly on whether and to what extent it helps increase material wealth and economic power. So now, when we are positioning the Chinese path in the history of human civilization and determining its contributions to the latter, the primary standard is to see how it contributed to the increase of the material base and of economic power. During a visit to Russia, responding to a question from a local student, President Xi Jinping said, "China, with a population of over

1 *Marx and Engels Collected Works* (Vol.2), Chin.ed., Beijing: People's Publishing House, 2009, p.9.

1.3 billion people, has brought the whole world genuine benefits with its prosperity. If, on the contrary, China had been enduring long-standing impoverishment and weakness, it would have become a serious problem that the whole world has to worry about." Just as Xi said, the whole world and human civilization have profited from the prosperity and strength of China, which is primarily manifested in the improvement of world economic power and the material wealth of human civilization.

China is a large integral part of civilized human society, and therefore its prosperity and mightiness constitute the material base for mankind's civilization. The growth of China's comprehensive national strength means an increase in economic power of human society in some sense. In the aggregate volume of the world's economy, the enlargement of "China's part" is decisive, as it could add to the economic aggregate and make up for the deficiency in other parts of the world. The foremost achievement of the path with Chinese characteristics chosen by Chinese people is the persistent and rapid development of the economy. On this path, over 0.6 billion people have been lifted out of poverty and over 1.3 billion people have shifted to a modern lifestyle. Comprising about one fifth of the global population, all Chinese people have not only solved the problems of poverty and poor living conditions, but have been gradually stepping into an affluent life. The report to the 18th National Congress of CPC summarized China's economic achievements from two perspectives:

> The economy has developed steadily and rapidly. China's overall national strength has grown considerably. The gross domestic product (GDP) reached 47.3 trillion yuan in 2011, and government revenue increased by a wide margin. The overall agricultural production capacity has increased and grain output has gone up year after year. Fresh progress has been made in adjusting the industrial structure, and the infrastructure has been extensively upgraded. Urbanization has been steadily advanced, and development between urban and rural areas and between regions has become better balanced. Notable progress has been made in making China an innovative

> country, and major breakthroughs have been made in manned spaceflights, the lunar exploration program, and in the development of a manned deep-sea submersible, supercomputers and high-speed railways. Solid steps have been taken to promote ecological progress, and comprehensive progress has been made in resource conservation and environmental protection....[2]
>
> Over the past ten years, we have achieved new historic successes and laid a solid foundation for completing the building of a moderately prosperous society in all respects. China's economy has risen from the sixth to the second place in the world. The country has undergone new historic changes: Its productive forces and economic, scientific and technological strength have increased considerably, living standards, individual income and social security have improved significantly, and its overall national strength and international competitiveness and influence have been enhanced substantially.[3]

The above quoted passages reflect China's economic success on the path of socialism with Chinese characteristics, and this success has greatly consolidated the material base of human civilization. The following specific data explicates these contributions in detail. From 1978 to 2010, China's GDP has risen from 362.4 billion yuan to 39.8 trillion yuan, comprising 9.5% of the total GDP of the whole world, up from 1.8%, and moving up to the second place from tenth. China's total imports and exports increased from US$ 20.6 billion to US$2.9728 trillion. Occupying 9.6% of the world exports share, China has become the largest exporter contributing 50% of world trade growth. China's foreign exchange reserve reached US$25 trillion, up from US$16.7 billion, contributing to one third of the world's total foreign exchange reserves.[4] All these actual figures remind us that not only has China's comprehensive national strength been enhanced, but also the material base for the whole of civilized human society has

2 Hu Jintao, *Firmly March on the Path of Socialism with Chinese Characteristics and Strive to Complete the Building of a Moderately Prosperous Society in All Respects—Report to the Eighteenth National Congress of the Communist Party of China*, Beijing: People's Publishing House, 2012, pp.2-3.

3 Ibid., pp.6-7.

4 Cf. Xu Chongwen, The socialism with Chinese characteristics is the greatest creation in the history of human civilization, *Journal of CPC Yunnan Provincial Party School*, 2012(5).

been reinforced.

The Chinese path contributes to the material base of human civilization not merely in terms of growing stronger itself, but also in terms of driving and promoting the economic growth of human society. The large economy with great vitality under the lead of the Chinese path has become a key factor for stabilizing and developing the economy of the entire human society. In the age of globalization, the world economy is getting more and more integrated. Material, capital and personnel exchanges among China and other countries have been accelerated by the invention of new transportation vehicles, the liberalization of international trade and the promotion by international organizations such as WTO. The Chinese economy, under such circumstances, not only brings challenges and competition for human society with its rapid development, but also opportunities. On the one hand, China has taken the whole world as its market; on the other hand, China has created new markets for other countries and regions, thus establishing win-win relations in economic development.

A number of overseas intellectuals have reached a consensus that China's giant economy has already become the major engine of the world economy. Three examples are illustrated here. First, in the book China, Inc., American journalist Ted Fishman divides China's reform and opening-up into three phases. Phase one is the world stepping into China; Phase two is China stepping out to the world; Phase three is China influencing the world. It is introduced in the book that by the year 2011, China's trade had reached US$ 3.64 trillion, its actual use of foreign capital had reached US$116 billion, and its FDI was US$60.1 billion, through which innumerable jobs and investment opportunities have been created for China's trading partners all over the world. The second example is the article "China's 10-year ascent to trading powerhouse" that appeared in *The New York Times* on Dec.9, 2011. It was pointed out that after China joined the W.T.O., it became a highly desirable trading partner. Companies and consumers worldwide have benefited from China's emergence as a top trading partner. From this example we can see that today's China has become one of the most eligible members in the W.T.O. Through participating in upgrading global economic governance mechanisms, such as International Macroeconomic Policy Coordination and the G20, it endeavors to reform and promote the international monetary system, the international trade system and commodity pricing mechanism, and tries to facilitate economic globalization and regional economic integration, thus becoming an important enabler in transforming world economy.[5] The third example is Fareed Zakaria's article "The rise of a fierce yet fragile superpower" in Newsweek on Dec. 22nd, 2007. In this article, China is described as having become the second most important country on the planet. In 2007 China contributed more to global growth than the United States, the first time another country had done so since at least the 1930s. It also became the world's largest consumer, eclipsing the United States in four of the five basic food, energy and industrial commodities.[6] Although it is believed that a massive economic boom of China relies heavily on the support of the whole world, it is clearly notable that China's development will give more positive feedback to the world.

When observing a country's foreign economic cooperation and exchange, people usually attach primary importance to its Outward Direct Investment (ODI), which is a normal criterion for a country's contribution to the economic growth of human society. Let us look at how Thomson Reuters, the world's largest multimedia provider for financial news, reported the prosperity of China's ODI in 2009. From January to mid-February, when the global cross-boarder Mergers and acquisitions (M&A) dropped by 35% on a year-on-year basis, China's overseas acquisitions rose by 40% reaching a total of US$

5 Cf. Yan Xu, The significance of a thorough understanding of socialism with Chinese Characteristics for the world civilization evolution, *Party Construction*, 2012(4).

6 Cf. Xin Xiangyang, *The socialism with Chinese characteristics and the development of world civilization*, http://www.wenming.cn,Oct. 12th, 2010.

21.8 billion, second place after Germany. After February, Chinese enterprises' overseas acquisitions were even more upsurging:Valin Iron&Steel Group purchased 17.34% of the stake of Fortescue Metals Group (FMG), the world's fourth largest iron ore producer, and becoming FMG's second largest shareholder. China's Minmetals Corporation purchased most of the Australian Oz Minerals' assets for about $1.386 billion. Geely Automobile completed its acquisition of Australian transmission supplier Drivetrain Systems International (DSI). PetroChina acquired 45.51% of the total issued share capital of Singapore Petroleum Company Limited (SPC). Sinopec Group launched China's biggest-ever foreign oil acquisition to buy Addax Petroleum Corp (AXC.TO) for about C$8.27 billion (US$7.242 billion). Suning Appliance Co. raised its stake in Laox Co., a Japanese home appliance chain, to 51%, and became the first Chinese company to hold proprietary in a Japanese firm. In fact, this report is not the full picture of China's ODI in 2009. For example, according to a report by the China National Development and Innovation Committee (NDIC), PetroChina secured government approval to acquire 49% of the Osaka refinery of Japanese producer Nippon Oil in June.[7] The statistics is just a snapshot of China's ODI in 2009. It has been basically the same since then.

While promoting international economic cooperation and exchange, thus facilitating the stability and development of the world economy, China is fulfilling its international obligations as a big and responsible nation. Sharing its economic achievements with other developing countries has directly consolidated the material base for civilized human society. From 2001 to Oct. 2011, China has provided over 170 billion Yuan for various kinds of foreign assistance, relieved due debt of nearly 30 billion Yuan from heavily indebted poor countries and least developed countries, has pledged zero tariff treatment to 97% of the tax items from the least developed countries

---

7 Cf. Xin Xiangyang, *The socialism with Chinese characteristics and the development of world civilization*, http://www.wenming.cn,Oct. 12th, 2010.

that have diplomatic relations with China, and has trained over 60,000 people in various professions for 173 developing countries and 13 regional international organizations.[8]

In fact, looking around global markets, it is easy to see how much China has enriched the physical goods of the world and therefore contributed to the material base of human society. Anybody who has been abroad, especially to Western countries, will find it hard to buy a product that is locally manufactured, for almost every product is labeled "Made in China". A shop assistant would probably shake his/her head if asked to help the customer get a souvenir produced locally other than in China. Former Premier Zhu Rongji has referred to this with pride several times. For example, on Sep.4th, 2001, during his speech and answers to questions at a business breakfast hosted by Enterprise Ireland, he said: "You can find a lot of products labeled 'Made in China' in the supermarkets of the USA." Also, on April 22nd, 2002, in his response to a Hong Kong journalist in Egypt, he said: "Last year (note: Sep. 2001) when I was in Russia, the Prime Minister (note: Mikhail Kasyanov) said he bought his jacket in America, but it was made in China and was of very high quality."[9]

The size and vitality of the Chinese economy that has developed on the Chinese path has made an extraordinary contribution to the material base of civilized human society during the periods of both the Asian and global financial crises. China, in these times when the fate of human society hung in the balance, acted literally as the mainstay of the world economy. It is said that "when the Asian economy and the world economy fell into crisis, China was a stable Gold Anchor"[10]. This is surely true. Think about how the ferocious Asian financial crisis in 1997 swept over Asia. China played a key role in helping

---

8 Cf. Yan Xu, The significance of a thorough understanding of socialism with Chinese Characteristics for the world civilization evolution, *Party Construction*, 2012(4).

9 *Zhu Rongji Meets the Press*, Beijing: People's Publishing House, 2009, pp327/430.

10 Xin Xiangyang, *The socialism with Chinese characteristics and the development of world civilization*, http://www.wenming.cn,Oct. 12th, 2010.

various other Asian countries avoid the catastrophe. For example, when the crisis broke out, China helped Thailand with an aid package of over US$4 billion in total, and provided Indonesia with credit and emergency pharmaceutical drug assistance. Particularly when running the risk of getting caught in the crisis, China gave a promise not to devalue the RMB, which shows its significant role in stabilizing and facilitating the economy of Asia, even of the world. The U.S. financial credit crisis, the financial crisis and debt crisis that started from the beginning of the 21st century are still lingering. However, China's role cannot be belittled in preventing these crises from wrecking the capitalist world. At the end of 2008, China had introduced ten measures of about 4 trillion Yuan to stimulate economic expansion, which not only increased domestic demand in China, but also balanced global economic growth. Some foreign media has reported that what China has done is a "bailout" for itself as well as for the whole world[11]. If there had been no great economic success brought by the Chinese path with own characteristics and if China had not made use of such success to combat the worldwide economic crisis, the crisis would have become increasingly fierce and the material base for human civilization would have been devastated accordingly. It is obvious, therefore, that the Chinese path has greatly contributed to the consolidation of the material base for human civilization.

11 Ibid.

CHAPTER TWO

Highlighting the Diversity of Human Civilization Development

Cultures in the world are diversified, and so should be mankind's pathways to civilizations. An important point made by Marxist historical materialism is that the development of civilized human society should be unified as well as diversified. Marx believes that on the one hand, the development of civilization is a natural historical process, and will always have a universal trend in accordance with inherent laws. On the other hand, as long as human society develops under particular historical conditions, different nations and countries will show various forms and details that constitute the diversity of human civilization. Marx once referred to the diversity as "showing infinite variations and graduations in appearance"[1]. But under the shadow of "Western-centrism", Western civilization seems to be the one and only form of human civilization. Western-centrism interprets Western civilization as the universal and only form of human civilization, takes the Western modernization process as the "model" for all men, and describes the Western cultural value as the common value for mankind.[2] Western-centrism was further encouraged by the drastic changes in the Soviet Union and Eastern Europe. The once fashionable chorus of "there is no alternative", namely human beings have no choice other than resorting to the "Western" way to realize civilization, was once worshiped as indisputable. Western hegemonists boast that Western civilization is the only ideal form

1 *Marx and Engels Collected Works* (Vol.7), Chin.ed., Beijing: People's Publishing House, 2009, p.894.

2 Cf. Yuan Yinchuan, *On the historical significance of the socialism with Chinese characteristics*, Huxiang Forum, 2012(2).

in the world, and try every means to undermine or destroy the validity of other civilizations. A Japanese-American scholar, Francis Fukuyama, expresses this kind of viewpoint with his declaration of "*the end of history*". He arrogantly asserts that Western civilization, namely liberal democracy, constitutes "the end point of mankind's ideological evolution" and is the "final form of human government", and as such constitutes the "end of history" as it becomes the system of government throughout the world.[3] Another important contribution of the Chinese path for human civilization, therefore, lies in its demolition of Western-centric thoughts and speeches, and in its demonstration of the diversity of human civilization.

The Chinese path is not a deviation from the mainstream of human civilizations. From the very beginning, it has adhered to the viewpoint of global history, and drawing on all great cultural achievements created by human society, including those from Western countries. Deng Xiaoping clearly pointed out "if we want socialism to achieve superiority over capitalism, we should not hesitate to draw on the achievements of all cultures and to learn from other countries, including the developed capitalist countries, and all advanced methods of operation and techniques of management that reflect the laws governing modern socialized production."[4] Jiang Zemin also dissected acutely that "China's development and progress cannot do without the cultural achievements of other countries in the world. Our socialist modernization needs to draw upon and carry forward the fine cultural traditions of the Chinese nation and also study and absorb the outstanding cultural achievements created by other people, including those under capitalism."[5] However, when we are drawing lessons from the achievements of other cultures, neither do we blindly follow them, nor equate modernization with westernization. Instead,

3 Francis Hukuyama, *The End of History and the Last Man*, New York: The Free Press, 1992, p.1.

4 *Selected Works of Deng Xiaoping* (Vol.III), Chin. ed., Beijing: People's Publishing House, 1993, p.373.

5 *Selected Works of Jiang Zemin* (Vol.I), Chin. ed., Beijing: People's Publishing House, 2006, p.124.

we learn from others' experiences, especially outstanding cultural achievements of Western countries, in a creative way according to China's social conditions. Deng Xiaoping also pointed out, "In carrying out our modernization programme we must proceed from Chinese realities. Both in revolution and in construction we should also learn from foreign countries and draw on their experience, but mechanical application of foreign experience and copying of foreign models will get us nowhere. We have had many lessons in this respect. We must integrate the universal truth of Marxism with the concrete realities of China, blaze a path of our own and build a socialism with Chinese characteristics— that is the basic conclusion we have reached after reviewing our long history."[6] Some people misunderstand our learning from Western cultures as wholesale copy and mechanical acceptance. Jiang Zemin specifically stressed that "the diversity of national cultures is a basic characteristic of human society and a driving force behind progress of human civilization"[7], and that "there cannot be only one civilization, one social system, one development model or one set of values in the world."[8] Hu Jintao has been reiterating the co-existence of multi-cultures and multi-models for progress. In the United Nations Summit for the commemoration of the 60th anniversary, he stated: "In the course of human history, all civilizations have, in their own way, made a positive contribution to the overall human progress. It is their differences that allow them to learn from one another and grow stronger together. Uniformity, if imposed on them, can only take away their vitality and cause them to become rigid and decline. The world's civilizations may differ in age, but none is better or more superior to others."[9] In his report to

6 *Selected Works of Deng Xiaoping* (Vol.III), Chin. ed., Beijing: People's Publishing House, 1993, pp.2-3.

7 *Selected Works of Jiang Zemin* (Vol.III), Chin. ed., Beijing: People's Publishing House, 2006, p.298.

8 Ibid., p.110.

9 Hu Jintao, *Build Towards a Harmonious World of Lasting Peace and Common Prosperity—Statement by Hu Jintao at the United Nations Summit*, People's Daily, Sep. 15th, 2005.

the 17th National Congress of CPC, he said: "Culturally, they should learn from each other in the spirit of seeking common ground while shelving differences, respect the diversity of the world, and make joint efforts to advance human civilization."[10] Sticking to the premise that there are diverse forms of cultures and different pathways to civilizations, Chinese people have been drawing on the Western culture selectively, creatively and complementarily, and have finally established a path of itself, i.e. the path with Chinese characteristics.[11]

The establishment of the Chinese path signifies the birth of a new form of human civilization which has made the Western form come down from on high, and protects human civilization from becoming entirely westernized. Some scholars have noticed that the appearance of Chinese civilization is a challenge to the West. Kristin Forbes, a former member of the White House's Council of Economic Advisers, once said: "China is the West's greatest hope and greatest fear." She regards the rise of China as the hope of mankind from the perspective of the human civilization, whereas viewing it as a source of fear from the standpoint of Western culture. George Yeo, former Singaporean Foreign Minister, commented on China's rise in an interview from *The Christian Science Monitor*: "With the world in turmoil... For the first time in a long time, the Western model has a serious competitor." Here, Yeo not only distinguishes Chinese civilization from Western civilization, but also regards the former as a "serious competitor" to the latter. The American Scholar Stefan Halper mentioned "globalization is shrinking the world", while "China is shrinking the west" in ways that "progressively limit the projection of Western influence and values...." It is implied that by competing with the value system of Western civilization, the Chinese path has weakened its influence in a time that globalization has made the world more and more integrated.

---

10 Hu Jintao, *Hold High the Great Banner of Socialism with Chinese Characteristics and Strive for New Victories in Building a Moderately Prosperous Society in all respects*, People's Daily, Oct. 16th, 2007.

11 Cf. Zhou Jianchao, *On the diversity of social development and the socialism with Chinese characteristics*, Theory Guide, 2012 (4).

Another American scholar, James Mann, published his article "A Shining Model of Wealth without Liberty" in *The Washington Post*. He wrote: "Above all, we should approach China through the lens of our national interest. That includes not just security and prosperity but our interest in a world with open political systems and the freedom to dissent. If we don't take China's new model as seriously as the rest of the world does, we could find that we're the ones on the wrong side of history." His definition of the Chinese path as "wealth without liberty" is obviously a misunderstanding, or even slander. But his worries are right in that the success of the Chinese path would be a heavy blow to the American model.[12]

In the diversified array of human cultures, the Chinese path, with its own characteristics, is a "miracle" which is also referred to by some Western scholars as the "Beijing Consensus". The "Beijing Consensus", a counterpart of the "Washington Consensus", is a description of China's progress to modernization from a global perspective. In some sense, the differences between the "Beijing Consensus" and the "Washington Consensus" represent the distinctions between Chinese and Western ways to modernization. In the end of the 1980s and beginning of the 1990s, most countries in the world were experiencing social transformations. Latin American countries, Russia and Eastern Europe transformed according to the "Washington Consensus", based on "neoliberal-centered" reform policies proposed by neoclassical economists in the light of the theories which were thought to suit the West. But it turns out that these policies did not bring success to these countries. In recent years, international researchers have been concerned with explaining why the "Washington Consensus" has not yielded any expected results, namely, why hasn't it helped these countries realize modern civilizations. Hence, there is talk of "beyond the Washington Consensus" or "Post-Washington Consensus", which mainly implies that the "Washington Consensus" can neither solve

12 Cf. Sun Zhonliang, *The global significance of the Chinese model in the post-crisis era. Scientific Socialism*, 2012(1). Statements of the foreign scholars in this paragraph are all quoted from Sun's article.

the problem of poverty, nor bring prosperity to the whole world, and that the socially transforming countries can no longer stick to the old path of neo-liberalism, but rather to a path beyond the "Washington Consensus", i.e. a new path beyond "neo-liberalism".

When Latin America, Russia, and Eastern Europe were socially transforming according to the "Washington Consensus", China was endeavoring to explore a new way for itself. In the article "The Beijing Consensus: Notes on the New Physics of Chinese Power", Joshua Cooper Ramo describes the development path unique to China, i.e. "Beijing Consensus" or "Chinese path", as not driven by the wishes of bankers, but by a desire to have equitable, peaceful high-quality growth. He thinks that the basic strategy of "Beijing Consensus" is turning traditional ideas like privatisation and free trade on their heads. It is defined by a ruthless willingness to innovate and experiment, by a lively defense of national borders and interests and by the increasingly thoughtful accumulation of tools of asymmetric power projection. Its primary goal is to assure growth as well as the independence of action. "Beijing Consensus" begins its analysis of the problem from the individual, whereas "Washington Consensus" is written to be a banker's list of dream conditions for development.[13] In the opinion of G. A. Zyuganov, Chairman of the Russian Communist Party's Central Committee, "Beijing Consensus" can be represented by the following formula: China's success= socialism+ century-long traditions of Confucianism+ government's command of the economy and market mechanism+ implementation of highly advanced technologies.[14] Ramo and Zyuganov depict "Beijing Consensus" from different angles which exactly constitute the major points of China's progress towards modernization and are virtually the "magic" of the "miracle" of Chinese path in the diversified human civilizations.

---

13 Cf. Zhou Jianjun, et al., *The significance of China's transformation: from Washington consensus to Beijing Consensus*, Forum of World Economics and Politics, 2015 (1).

14 Cf. Chang Zongyao, *On the global significance of the socialism with Chinese characteristics*, Theoretical Exploration, 2008(4).

Some Chinese scholars use "Civilization Type Theory" to show the diversity of human civilizations in today's world, and try to identify the Chinese path in such circumstances. Present world's civilizations could be classified into three types according to the dominant factors: religion-dominated civilization, such as India; economy-dominated civilization, such as Western countries; and politics-dominated civilization, such as China. These three different types rely on the leading roles of religious beliefs, capital assets and political powers in social life. Ever since the end of primitive society, religion-dominated countries and regions have experienced the social patterns and periods of "uni-religious society— multi-religious society— pan-religious society"; economy-dominated countries and regions have experienced "slave society— feudal society— capitalist society"; politics-dominated countries and regions have experienced "patriarchal society— dictatorial society— socialist society". Based on Civilization Type Theory, researchers have reached a consensus that China's socialism is practically at the same stage of development with Western capitalism, and hence the statements about the inferiority of Chinese civilization to Western civilization cannot hold water. Considering traditional cultures, and history and stage of development, China's socialism is characterized as a "politics-dominated civilization with a modern socialist-party system" with the basic characteristics of "the people-oriented leadership of CPC", "the market-oriented economy under the regulation of government" and "the politic-ethic-scientific culture type". Chinese socialism explores a new possibility for civilization, and provides a vivid example for the poor and undeveloped countries to advance economy and eliminate poverty. The superiority of the Chinese path will become more and more obvious as human civilizations shifts from an industry-based stage to an ecology-based stage.[15]

The initiation of the Chinese path is also an act to diversify human

15 Cf. Xu Jinyun, *The Civilization Type Theory and the socialism with Chinese Characteristic*, Exploration, 2011(1).

civilizations in the globalized age. During the process, Chinese people have deepened their understanding of social developmental laws and modes. Choosing a path unique to themselves, they bring forth innovations within the bi-directional interactions between theory and practice. Giving up the ossified and closed-door planned economy and refusing the wrong way of "westernization" or "transformation from socialism into capitalism", they unswervingly stick to the socialist road with Chinese characteristics. The Chinese path has made it clear that the world history is both diachronic and synchronic. "The transformation of history into world history" is invariably the ultimate same goal of all countries and nations, of course, by different ways. Human civilization has never been and will never be realized through a single path. Rather, it is the product of various conflicting cultural forces which was once referred to by Engels as the "resultant" of "an infinite number of parallelograms of forces". He stressed that each force contributes to the resultant and is, to that extent, part and parcel of it. Based on the deep understanding of social development, Chinese people confidently take the path with Chinese characteristics which literally shows the diversity of human civilizations.

Chapter Three
Blazing a New Way for Peaceful Development

A country which has gained power would possibly pose a threat to the existence and development of other countries or even to the peace of the world in the following three ways.

Firstly, by abusing the power to impose its social system and societal values on other nations, it would plunge the world into turmoil.

Secondly, in order to attain a high level of material affluence, energy and resources are consumed excessively, and GDP is taken as the only criterion for the country's development. When running out of domestic energy and resources, it desperately pillages these from other countries, which supports its own growth but sets itself against the others.

Thirdly, when the development of the productive forces is not benefiting all the people but widening the gap between rich and poor, severe domestic social disruption will occur and negatively impact other nations and areas. Gradually, the country will become a dangerous destabilization to a broad region or even the world.

Will the rise of China bring about any or all of the possibilities? The answer is for sure: NO!

Many people think that traditional Chinese philosophies, such as "Nothing is more precious than peace (yǐ hé wéi guì)" and "Inner Sage and Outer King (wài shèng nèi wáng)", would be the reason for China's preference for peace. This may be true but it is only part of the story. It is not convincing enough to attribute China's peaceful co-existence with other nations to its centuries-long love for peace.

Aside from its traditional philosophies, the impacts of China's rise on the world depend more on the ideological base of the present social system. As a matter of fact, it is exactly the Chinese socialism and its ideological base, namely Marxism, that ensures no China Treat to the world, for socialism is intrinsically linked with peace, peaceful coexistence, and common development.

I. Statements on "Peace" by Marx, Engels and Lenin

As the first and the most influential socialist country in the world, the Soviet Union pursued socialist imperialism through competing with America, intervening in other countries' internal affairs with military force, and infringing on other countries' sovereignty. Since the Soviet Union had been controlling the right to interpret Marxist theories for a long time, people got used to relating Marxism with everything done by the Soviet government, thus considering Marxism as a synonym for violence, revolution, war and antagonism, regarding it as the opposite of peace, and holding the misconception that the major attempt of socialist foreign policies is to impose its social system and societal values on other parts of the whole world.

As a matter of fact, these are all dogmatic and false understandings of Marxism. Since the very first day it stepped into the international political arena, Marxism has been holding "peace" as its guiding principle, and the advocacy of peace has been its most prominent value orientation and theoretical tradition. Viewed from this standpoint, it is impossible and unnecessary for a socialist country to impose its social system and societal values on others. As long as the "imperialist" diplomacies of Stalin and successive Soviet governments are not mistaken for real socialist foreign policies as described by James Dougherty and Robert Pfaltzgraff, one can hardly doubt that peace has always been the cornerstone of socialism.[1]

To make this point clear, let us have a review of the statements by Marx, Engels and Lenin, the founders of Marxism and leaders of the proletarian revolution.

1. Relevant Statements by Marx

In the *Inaugural Address of the International Working Men's Association* (First International), he wrote:

> The immense and unresisted encroachments of that barbarous power, whose head is in St. Petersburg, and whose hands are in every cabinet of Europe, have taught the working classes the duty to master themselves the mysteries of international politics; to watch the diplomatic acts of their respective governments; to counteract them, if necessary, by all means in their power; when unable to prevent, to combine in simultaneous denunciations, and to vindicate the simple laws of morals and justice, which ought to govern the relations of private individuals, as the rules paramount of the intercourse of nations.
>
> The fight for such a foreign policy forms part of the general struggle for the emancipation of the working classes.[2]

This statement not only tells us that the proletariat has to counteract and denunciate the government's barbarous foreign intrusions, but also puts forward the general rules of handling international relationships. The laws of morals and justice which ought to govern the relations of private individuals should be vindicated as the rules paramount of the intercourse of nations.

In *First Address of the General Council on The Franco-Prussian War*, Marx quoted from *Manifesto to the Workmen of all Nations* that "on the pretext of European equilibrium, of national honor, the people of the world is menaced by political ambitions. French, German,

1 James E. Dougherty & Robert L. Pfaltzgraff, Jr., *Contending Theories of International Relations*, Philadelphia/New York/Toronto: J. B. Lippincott Company.

2 *Selected Works of Marx and Engels* (Vol.II), Chin.ed., Beijing: People's Publishing House, 1995, p.607.

Spanish workmen! Let our voices unite in one cry of reprobation against war! ...War for a question of preponderance or a dynasty can, in the eyes of workmen, be nothing but a criminal absurdity. In answer to the warlike proclamations of those who exempt themselves from the blood tax, and find in public misfortunes a source of fresh speculations, we protest, we who want peace, labor, and liberty."[3]

In this address, Marx also said meaningfully: "The very fact that while official France and Germany are rushing into a fratricidal feud, the workmen of France and Germany send each other messages of peace and goodwill;... It proves that in contrast to old society, with its economical miseries and its political delirium, a new society is spring up, whose International rule will be Peace, because its national ruler will be everywhere the same— Labour!"[4] It is clearly showed that the international rule of the new socialist society, in contrast to the old capitalist society, will be peace. Although he himself did not build up the society, the peace-oriented guiding principle had already been established.

There are also some famous quotes from Marx's works, such as "Any people that oppresses another people forges its own chains."[5] Is there any other statement which denounces foreign intrusion and oppression more forcefully like this? Marx, the founder of Marxism, said it out of hatred against war, for according to him, warfare is the monster to make people kill each other. "...it (war) would certainly produce a useless exhaustion of forces for some longer or shorter interval."[6] These words clearly show his hatred against aggressive wars! Also, he opposed any act that breaches international law. He criticized the British foreign policies like this: "The *Blue Book* on the

---

3 *Selected Works of Marx and Engels* (Vol.III), Chin.ed., Beijing: People's Publishing House, 1995, p.16.

4 Ibid. p. 19.

5 *Selected Works of Marx and Engels* (Vol.II), Chin.ed., Beijing: People's Publishing House, 1972, p.312.

6 *Marx and Engels Collected Works* (Vol.34), Chin.ed., Beijing: People's Publishing House, 1972, p.440.

intervention in Mexico, just published, contains the most damning exposure of modern English diplomacy with all its hypocritical cant, ferocity against the weak, crawling before the strong, and utter disregard of international law."[7]

2. Relevant Statements by Engels

Engels had foreseen the destructive power of the two world wars in the 20th-century capitalist world by pointing out that: "...the only war left form Prussia-Germany to wage will be a world war, a world war, more over, of an extent and violent hitherto unimagined. Eight to ten million soldiers will be at each other's throats and in the process they will strip Europe barer than a swarm of locust."[8] This clearly indicates that he had not only anticipated the extreme cruelty of warfare, but was also strongly against it.

Similar to Marx's statements, there are many extraordinary remarks opposing foreign oppressions in Engels' works. For instance, "A people that oppresses others cannot emancipate itself. The power it needs to oppress others is ultimately always turned against itself."[9] He even asserted "the time has passed forever where one nation can claim to lead all the rest".[10]

Engels warned that a proletariat, having gained victory, should never impose its boon on any other countries. He stated: "Only one thing is certain, namely that a victorious proletariat cannot forcibly confer any boon whatever on another country without undermining its own victory in the process."[11] What he said shows his clear

7 *Marx and Engels Collected Works* (Vol.15), Chin.ed., Beijing: People's Publishing House, 1965, p.499.

8 *Marx and Engels Collected Works* (Vol.21), Chin.ed., Beijing: People's Publishing House, 1965, p.401.

9 *Selected Works of Marx and Engels* (Vol.III), Chin.ed., Beijing: People's Publishing House, 1995, p.242.

10 *Marx and Engels Collected Works* (Vol.38), Chin.ed., Beijing: People's Publishing House, 1972, p.494.

11 *Marx and Engels Collected Works* (Vol.35), Chin.ed., Beijing: People's Publishing House, 1971, p.353.

and unconditional position against "conferring" the proletarian "boon", because its own victory would be undermined. In regard to international relations, Engels expounded his views very clearly:

> The proletariat in the various countries was left to organize itself in its own forms. This happened, and the International is now much stronger than before. In accordance with this we must continue to work on common ground. We must permit discussion in order not to become a sect, but the common standpoint must be retained. The loose association, the voluntary bond which is furthered by congresses, is sufficient to win us the victory which no power in the world can snatch from us again.[12]

Here, the principles of international relations are proposed as follows: to work on common ground, to retain a common standpoint, to permit discussion, and to allow the proletariat in various countries organize in its own forms.

The following remark could also be regarded as Engels' definition of international relations. "Any international action must have as a necessary premise a previous agreement both as to the basis and as to the form. It strikes me as inadmissible that one nationality should take the initiative publicly and then invite the others to fall in.... But for mercy's sake don't spoil it by openly taking the initiative without preliminary consultation with the others."[13]

He was firmly against forcing down the throat of other nationalities things which they will not certainly swallow. According to him, it is harmful for us to try to manipulate others against their will, which will destroy the trust we gained in this internationalized era. So he said to his socialist followers: "Now, mind you don't go and do the same yourselves by appearing to want to lay down the law for the

12 *Marx and Engels Collected Works* (Vol.22), Chin.ed., Beijing: People's Publishing House, 1965, pp.479-480.

13 *Marx and Engels Collected Works* (Vol.39), Chin.ed., Beijing: People's Publishing House, 1974, pp.185-187.

Socialists of other nations."[14]

He added:

> ...that international co-operation is possible only among equals, and even a primus inter pares at most for immediate action. So long as Poland remains partitioned and subjugated, therefore, there can be no development either of a powerful socialist party within the country itself or of genuine international intercourse between Poles other than émigrés and the rest of the proletarian parties in Germany, etc.... It is in no way our business to restrain the efforts of the Poles to attain living conditions essential to their further development, or to persuade them that, from the international standpoint, national independence is a very secondary matter when it is in fact the basis of all international cooperation.[15]

What is emphasized in the above-quoted paragraph is the principles of equality and independence in international cooperation.

Another relevant statement in Engels' work is: "There could, indeed, be no two opinions as to the right of every one of the great national subdivisions of Europe to dispose of itself, independently of its neighbours, in all internal matters, so long as it did not encroach upon the liberty of the others. This right was, in fact, one of the fundamental conditions of the internal liberty of all."[16] According to him, a nation's right to dispose of itself is of paramount importance.

Engels precisely underlined the significance of mutual understanding and equality in international communication: "To sum up: a little more reciprocity could do no harm— equality between nations is as necessary as that between individuals."[17]

---

14 *Marx and Engels Collected Works* (Vol.37), Chin.ed., Beijing: People's Publishing House, 1971, p.157.

15 *Selected Works of Marx and Engels* (Vol.IV), Chin.ed., Beijing: People's Publishing House, 1972, p.428.

16 *Marx and Engels Collected Works* (Vol.16), Chin.ed., Beijing: People's Publishing House, 1965, p.174.

17 *Marx and Engels Collected Works* (Vol.39), Chin.ed., Beijing: People's Publishing House, 1974, p.89.

3. Relevant Statements by Lenin

After the victorious October Revolution, Lenin had been holding high the banner of peace. In the well-known *The Peace Programme*, he pointed out that peace is the general principle of USSR countries' foreign policies. He said: "...that having started on our work of peaceful development we shall exert every effort to continue it without interruption" and " we shall do our utmost to preserve peace in the future."[18]

In his opinion, Marxism is fundamentally against bullying. "Marx, mindful in the first place of the interests of the proletarian class struggle in the advanced countries, put the fundamental principle of internationalism and socialism in the foreground—namely, that no nation can be free if it oppresses other nations."[19] Here, Lenin regards the opposition against oppression as the fundamental principle of socialism and internationalism. He also made the famous remark that "communism cannot be imposed by force"[20], implying that a real communist country would never be a threat to other countries.

From Lenin's perspective, the reason why a socialist country would never threat other countries with different social systems is that Marxists always believe in the diverse ways to approach socialism, and therefore would not force their own way on others. He said:

> The same variety will manifest itself also in the path mankind will follow from the imperialism of today to the socialist revolution of tomorrow. All nations will arrive at socialism—this is inevitable, but all will do so in not exactly the same way, each will contribute something of its own to some form of democracy, to some variety of the dictatorship of the proletariat, to the varying rate of socialist transformations in the different aspects of social life.[21]

---

18 *Lenin Collected Works* (Vol. 44), Chin.ed., Beijing: People's Publishing House, 1987, pp.326/328.

19 *Selected Works of Lenin* (Vol.II), Chin.ed., Beijing: People's Publishing House, 1976, p.722.

20 *Selected Works of Lenin* (Vol. III), Chin.ed., Beijing: People's Publishing House, 1976, p.781.

21 *Lenin Collected Works* (Vol. 28), Chin.ed., Beijing: People's Publishing House, 1991, p.163.

Lenin declared that peace would be the starting point of any foreign policy of the USSR:

> The Russian Socialist Federative Soviet Republic wishes to live in peace with all peoples and devote all its efforts to internal development so as to put production, transport and government affairs in order on the basis of the Soviet system.[22]

In order to further assure the weak nationalities that the Soviet Union would maintain peaceful relationships with them, he made an impassioned pledge in a meeting:

> As long as no nationalities engage in intrigues against us which bind them to the imperialist oppression, as long as they do not help to crush us, we shall not be deterred by formalities. We shall not forget that we are revolutionaries. (Applause.) But there are facts incontrovertibly and indisputably showing that in Russia, that has defeated the Mensheviks and Socialist-Revolutionaries, the smallest, completely unarmed nationality, however weak it may be, may and must absolutely rest assured that we have nothing but peaceful intentions towards it, that our propaganda about the criminality of the old policy of the old governments is not weakening, and that we are as firm as ever in our desire at all costs, and at the price of enormous sacrifices and concessions, to maintain peace with all nationalities that belonged to the former Russian Empire, but who did not wish to remain with us. We have proved this. And we shall prove this no matter how great the curses rained on us from all sides. It seems to us that we have given excellent proof of it, and we declare to the meeting of representatives of the workers and peasants of Russia, to the many millions of workers and peasants, that we shall do our utmost to preserve peace in the future, that we shall not shrink from great sacrifices and concessions in order to safeguard this peace.[23]

According to him, as long as it was for the sake of peace, the Soviet Union was willing to make concessions. So after finishing a democratic peace with Estonia, he said:

---

22 *Lenin Collected Works* (Vol. 37), Chin.ed., Beijing: People's Publishing House, 1996, p.354.

23 *Lenin Collected Works* (Vol. 42), Chin.ed., Beijing: People's Publishing House, 1987, p.326.

> Furthermore, the terms of the peace treaty provide for a number of territorial concessions on our part which do not completely correspond to the strict observance of the principle of self-determination of nations, and prove in practice that the question of frontiers is of secondary importance to us, the question of peaceful relations, however, the question of our ability to await the development of the conditions of life of each nation, is not only an important question of principle, it is also a matter in which we have succeeded in winning the confidence of nations hostile to us. It is no accident that we have achieved this in relation to Estonia; it is evidence that the weak proletarian republic, existing in isolation and apparently helpless, has begun to win to its side countries dependent on the imperialist states—and they constitute the vast majority. That is why our peace with Estonia is of such great historical significance.[24]

He stressed that doing is better than saying. It does not suffice to just talk about peace. We should strive for it in a real way. He took a strong position against those who started wars under the banner of peace.

> It must be remembered that all over the world there has been an inordinate amount of pacifist talk, an unusual number of pacifist phrases and assurances, and even vows against war and against peace, although there is usually little preparedness on the part of the majority of states, especially on the part of the modern civilised states, to take any realistic steps, even the most simple, to ensure peace. On this, and on similar questions, we should like to see a minimum of general assurances, solemn promises and grandiloquent formulas, and the greatest possible number of the simplest and most obvious decisions and measures that would certainly lead to peace, if not to the complete elimination of the war danger.[25]

Peace in our age is not only a way for survival or a struggle strategy, but more importantly, it is the essence of socialism, which means that only socialism can lead to real peace. He stressed:

---

24 *Lenin Collected Works* (Vol. 38), Chin.ed., Beijing: People's Publishing House, 1986, pp.102-103.

25 *Lenin Collected Works* (Vol. 43), Chin.ed., Beijing: People's Publishing House, 1987, p.240.

> Our "peace programme" must explain that the imperialist powers and the imperialist bourgeoisie cannot grant a democratic peace. Such a peace must be sought for and fought for, not in the past, not in a reactionary utopia of a non-imperialist capitalism, not in a league of equal nations under capitalism, but in the future, in the socialist revolution of the proletariat. Not a single fundamental democratic demand can be achieved to any considerable extent, or with any degree of permanency, in the advanced imperialist states, except through revolutionary battles under the banner of socialism.[26]

The above quotations from works of Marx, Engels and Lenin illustrate that if we follow their instructions, the socialist China, no matter how powerful it becomes, will never try to force its social system and societal values on other countries.

After the Third Plenary Session of the 11th Central Committee of CPC was held in Beijing, China has been starting to build up a socialist path with its own characteristics. During this time, the government has been unswervingly pursuing a peaceful foreign policy of independence and self-determination, having no intentions to work its will on others or to seek hegemony. This is exactly in accord with the Marxist theory of peace and the diplomacy based on it.

Conforming to the historical trend of the time, Deng Xiaoping was especially aware of the coordination between peace and socialism, and thus had been endeavoring to "pursue a peaceful environment" for socialist modernization. Based on the works of Marx, Engels, and Lenin, Deng Xiaoping officially put forward the scientific argument that "socialism with Chinese characteristics stands for peace", in other words, "the socialism we are building is a socialism that is adapted to our own conditions, a socialism that helps to constantly develop the productive forces and that favours peace." This argument not only realized a significant historical transition from "war and revolution"

26 *Lenin Collected Works* (Vol. 27), Chin.ed., Beijing: People's Publishing House, 1990, pp.288-289.

to "peace and development"[27], but also drew the line between the diplomacy of socialist China and that of the Stalinist socialism.

"The Principles of Peaceful Coexistence" should not be taken as an expedient under specific circumstances, according to Deng Xiaoping. Quite the reverse, China, pursuing the socialism with its own characteristics, is bound to follow a foreign policy of peace. He explicated: "Socialism is opposite to hegemony, and is basically incompatible to imperialist wars or any acts of expansion and aggression. A socialist country, once starting seeking hegemony or undermining the sovereignty of another nation, will damage its own international image, weaken its moral force, and spoil its socialist cause."[28] Deng had made it completely clear here why a socialist country should adhere to a foreign policy of peace, which is viewed as a key factor determining the failure or success of socialist cause from a strategic height.

Deng further emphasized that China, when dealing with foreign affairs, would give no thought to differences in social systems or ideologies. Instead, it would follow the tide of history to proceed from the long-term strategic interests of itself and of the mankind. So he stated repeatedly that China would never serve as a leader or a head, would never be aligned, would never seek hegemony, would never be the "center of world revolution", and would never "export revolution".

From the remarks of Deng Xiaoping and all the other leaders of China, and from the foreign policies that China has always been following, it is hard for one with an unbiased mind to believe that China, under the guidance of Marxism, will threat the world by forcefully imposing its social systems and societal values on other nations out of its own interests. In today's world, the United States and the Western world are controlling almost every aspect of the "soft

27 *Selected Works of Deng Xiaoping* (Vol. III), Chin. ed., Beijing: People's Publishing House, 1993, p.328.

28 Cited from: Wang Qinping, *Deng Xiaoping's Thoughts on Diplomacy*, Beijing: World Affairs Press, 1996, p.49.

power" such as freedom, equality, democracy, human rights and the rule of law and so on. The socialist China, of course, is also promoting its own soft power, but will not willfully force it on other nations.

II. All-round Development of Humanity and Society: the Cardinal Direction of Socialism

According to Li Junru, a key variable for China's peaceful rise is its strategies in the rivalry for resources with other countries. In other words, whether China's rise would be threatening or peaceful depends largely on whether it would vie for global resources aggressively or not.[29] He is right in that although China will never thrust its "soft power", such as the social system or ideologies, upon others, it will definitely plunder resources with other countries if sticking to the Western model of development. In this case, the China Threat is not a matter of subjective wants but an inevitable consequence. John Mearsheimer, a professor from the University of Chicago, once offered a prediction that a rising China will become "an aggressive state determined to achieve regional hegemony", not due to any "wicked motives", but rather and nothing more than as the best way to maximize the prospects for China's survival, development and prosperity. Mearsheimer's view is quite representative, for it echoes many similar worries that China is going to aggressively fight for resources for the purpose of developing itself without any "wicked motives". In this case, Marxism alone is not enough to convince people that China has no wicked motives. It is more important to show that China will never fight for resources thus worsening the global problem of resource-shortage.

This raises the questions of whether the socialist China is different from the capitalist countries in its needs for resources, and if any, what they are.

29 Cf. "*China's peaceful rise will not pose any threat to the world*", http://www.chinanews.com, March 8th, 2004.

Why did Marx build up the socialist system to transcend the existing capitalist system? Obviously, the reason is that the two systems are radically different, the former being by far superior to the latter. This superiority will help people lead a more humanistic lifestyle which is closely related to how resources are consumed.

As Erich Fromm has argued, among all the misunderstandings about Marxism, there is probably none more widespread than the idea of Marx's "historical materialism".[30] For example, there are misunderstandings that Marx is supposed to have believed that the paramount psychological motive in man is his wish for monetary gain and comfort, and that this striving for maximum profit constitutes the main incentive in his personal life and in the life of the human race. The majority of people are motivated by a wish for greater material gain, for comfort and gadgets, and this wish is restricted only by the desire for security and the avoidance of risks. "Historical materialism is believed to be a philosophy claiming that man's material interest, his wish for ever-increasing material gain and comforts, are his main motivation.

The misunderstandings of the concept of historical materialism hurdle a proper understanding of Marx's philosophy for building up a socialist society, and also distort Marx's original intention into its opposite. "This view of Marx then goes on to discuss his socialist paradise as one of millions of people who submit to an all-powerful state bureaucracy, people who have surrendered their freedom, even though they might have achieved equality; these materially satisfied 'individuals' have lost their individuality and have been successfully transformed into millions of uniform robots and automatons, led by a small elite of better-fed leaders."[31] If a socialist society is just like what Fromm describes here, the present Western world has already become "socialist" for the majority of people are motivated by a

30 Erich Fromm, *Marx's Concept of Man*, New York: Frederick Ungar Publishing Co., 1961.

31 Ibid., p.3.

wish for greater material gain. They are increasingly satisfied with a life regulated and manipulated, both in the sphere of production and of consumption, by the state and the big corporations and their respective bureaucracies; they have reached a degree of conformity which has wiped out individuality to a remarkable extent. They are, quoting Marx's term, impotent "commodity men" serving virile machines.

Criticizing the distortions of Marx's concepts of historical materialism and socialism, Fromm also offered his own understandings, which are undoubtedly the most accurate. According to him, the popular view assuming that in Marx's opinion the strongest psychological motive in man is to have more material comfort is a fundamental misunderstanding of historical materialism as a psychological theory of man's drives and passions. In fact, historical materialism is not at all a psychological theory; it claims that the way man produces determines his thinking and his desires, and not that his main desires are those for maximal material gain. Certain economic conditions, like those of capitalism, produce as a chief incentive of the desire for money and property; other economic conditions can produce exactly the opposite desires. The passion for money and property, according to Marx, is just as much economically conditioned as the opposite passions. "Marx's 'materialistic' or 'economic' interpretation of history has nothing whatsoever to do with an alleged 'materialistic' or 'economic' striving as the most fundamental drive in man."[32] "Marx's aim was that of the spiritual emancipation of man, of his liberation from the chains of economic determination, of restituting him in his human wholeness, of enabling him to find unity and harmony with his fellow man and with nature."[33] "The central theme of Marx is the transformation of alienated, meaningless labor into productive, free labor, not the better payment of alienated labor

32 Ibid., p.13.

33 Ibid., p.3.

by a private or 'abstract' state capitalism."[34] "Marx's aim is not limited to the emancipation of the working class, but the emancipation of the human being through the restitution of the unalienated and hence free activity of all men, and a society in which man, and not the production of things, is the aim, in which man ceases to be a 'crippled monstrosity', and becomes a fully developed human being."[35]

If historical materialism is as Fromm phrases above, the socialist prospects will be quite different from those misconceptions. Again, let us have a look at what Fromm has said: "Marx's whole criticism of capitalism is exactly that it has made interest in money and material gain the main motive in man, and his concept of socialism is precisely that of a society in which this material interest would cease to be the dominant one."[36] According to him, the essence of Marx's concept lies in that "material interest would cease to be the dominant one". There is supporting evidence in Marx's works that proves the validity of Fromm's claim. In the *Economic and Philosophical Manuscripts of 1844*, Marx wrote:

> *Communism* as the *positive* transcendence of *private property human self-estrangement*, and therefore as the real appropriation of the human essence by and for man; communism therefore as the complete return of man to himself as a social (i.e., human) being—a return accomplished consciously and embracing the entire wealth of previous development. This communism, as fully developed naturalism, equals humanism, and as fully developed humanism equals naturalism; it is the genuine resolution of the conflict between man and nature and between man and man — the true resolution of the strife between existence and essence, between objectification and self-confirmation, between freedom and necessity, between the individual and the species. Communism is the riddle of history solved, and it knows itself to be this solution.[37]

---

34 Ibid.,p.42

35 Ibid.,p.50

36 Ibid., p. 14.

37 Marx, *Manuscript of Economics and Philosophy in 1844*, Chin. ed. (Translated by Liu Pikun et al.), Beijing: People's Publishing House, 1979, p.73.

Marx illustrates his understanding of *communism* here. Socialism, as the primary stage of communism, cannot be as perfect as communism as mentioned above, yet it is getting closer and closer to it. Obviously what Marx has highlighted here is man's return to himself and realization of his essence in the process of production. The nature of individuals thus depends on the material conditions determining their production.

Another less quoted argument in Marx's *Capital Volume III* also supports Fromm's claims:

> In fact, the realm of freedom actually begins only where labour which is determined by necessity and mundane considerations ceases; thus in the very nature of things it lies beyond the sphere of actual material production. Just as the savage must wrestle with Nature to satisfy his wants, to maintain and reproduce life, so must civilised man, and he must do so in all social formations and under all possible modes of production. With his development this realm of physical necessity expands as a result of his wants; but, at the same time, the forces of production which satisfy these wants also increase. Freedom in this field can only consist in socialised man, the associated producers, rationally regulating their interchange with Nature, bringing it under their common control, instead of being ruled by it as by the blind forces of Nature; and achieving this with the least expenditure of energy and under conditions most favourable to, and worthy of, their human nature. But it nonetheless still remains a realm of necessity. Beyond it begins that development of human energy which is an end in itself, the true realm of freedom, which, however, can blossom forth only with this realm of necessity as its basis. The shortening of the working day is its basic prerequisite.[38]

According to Marx, a communist society as the realm of freedom can only be built on the basis of former socialist and communist societies which are realms of necessity. But it is of entirely different nature with the latter, for it lies beyond the sphere of actual material production

38 *Marx and Engels Collected Works* (Vol. 25), Chin.ed., Beijing: People's Publishing House, 1974, pp.926-927.

and beyond the satisfaction of the needs to maintain and reproduce life.

Based on a deep understanding of human nature, Marx never explained his concept of socialism in terms of man's unlimited desire for material comfort. Marx takes self-activity, namely the free and conscious activity, as the species-character of human beings. Through the self-activity, man can fulfill its value as living beings. Goethe gave the most poetic and powerful expression to a similar idea in his *Faust*. Neither possession, nor power, nor sensuous satisfaction, Faust teaches, can fulfill man's desire for meaning in his life; he remains in all this separate from the whole, hence unhappy. Only in being productively active can man make sense of his life, and while he thus enjoys life, he is not greedily holding on to it. He has given up the greed for having, and is fulfilled by being; he is filled because he is empty; he is much, because he has little.

From this concept of human essence, Marx has arrived at a new understanding of wealth and poverty. He expressed in the following:

> It will be seen how in place of the wealth and poverty of political economy come the *rich human being* and the rich *human* need. The rich human being is simultaneously the human being *in need of* a totality of human manifestations of life—the man in whom his own realisation exists as an inner necessity, as *need*. Not only *wealth*, but likewise the *poverty* of man—under the assumption of socialism—receives in equal measure a *human* and therefore social significance.[39]

Here, it is proposed to understand the concepts of wealth and poverty from a man's self-realization as an inner necessity. In the political economy, people used to distinguish wealth from poverty based on private property and material satisfaction, but Marx suggested replacing them with a new concept of richness as related to the man's self-realization. In a capitalist perspective, a wealthy man is

39 Marx, *Manuscript of Economics and Philosophy in 1844*, Chin. ed. (Translated by Liu Pikun et al.), Beijing: People's Publishing House, 1979, p.82.

not necessarily a rich man; whereas in a socialist perspective, a man may not possess material wealth but still be a rich man. Fromm emphasized: "It is particularly important to understand this position of Marx today, when both the Communist, and most of the Socialist parties, with some notable exceptions like the Indian, also Burmese and a number of European and American socialists, have accepted the principle which underlies all capitalist systems, namely, that maximum production and consumption are the unquestionable goals of society."[40] He did not forget to add that: "One must of course not confuse the aim of overcoming the abysmal poverty which interferes with a dignified life, with the aim of an ever-increasing consumption, which has become the supreme value for both Capitalism and Krushchevism. Marx's position was quite clearly on the side of the conquest of poverty, and equally against consumption as a supreme end."

After figuring out the real aim and concept of socialism, it should be clear by now why Marx was strongly discontented with the capitalist system and tried to transcend it with socialism. There is a false assumption that the purpose of transcending capitalism is to gain economic improvement of the working class, and the reason for the abolition of private property is to help working class own what the capitalist now has. As a matter of fact, it is not the injustice in wealth distribution that was condemned by Marx, but the forced, alienated and meaningless labour that turns man into "a crippled monstrosity". In Fromm's words:

> It is believed that Marx spoke primarily of the economic exploitation of the worker, and the fact that his share of the product was not as large as it should be, or that the product should belong to him, instead of to the capitalist. But as I have shown before, the state as a capitalist, as in the Soviet Union, would not have been any more welcome to Marx than the private capitalist. He is not concerned primarily with the equalization of

40 Erich Fromm, *Marx's Concept of Man*, New York: Frederick Ungar Publishing Co., 1961, p.37.

income. He is concerned with the liberation of man from a kind of work which destroys his individuality, which transforms him into a thing, and which makes him into the slave of things.[41]

In the alienated world of capitalism, Marx has recognized what becomes of human needs. Needs are not expressions of man's latent powers, that is, they are not human needs. He wrote:

Each tries to establish over the other an *alien* power, so as thereby to find satisfaction of his own selfish need. The increase in the quantity of objects is therefore accompanied by an extension of the realm of the alien powers to which man is subjected, and every new product represents a new *potentiality* of mutual swindling and mutual plundering.... Subjectively, this appears partly in the fact that the extension of products and needs becomes a *contriving and ever-calculating* subservience to inhuman, sophisticated, unnatural and imaginary appetites. Private property does not know how to change crude need into *human* need.... He puts himself at the service of the other's most depraved fancies, plays the pimp between him and his need, excites in him morbid appetites, and lies in wait for each of his weaknesses— all so that he can then demand the cash for this service of love.[42]

In the above-quoted passage, Marx provides a profound understanding of alienation from the perspective of how people find satisfaction of their own needs and turn the material needs into genuine human needs in the capitalist world.

Marx went still further on the distortion of human needs. "As a result, therefore, man (the worker) only feels himself freely active in his animal functions—eating, drinking, procreating, or at most in his dwelling and in dressing-up, etc.; and in his human functions he no longer feels himself to be anything but an animal. What is

41 Ibid., p.49.

42 Marx, *Manuscript of Economics and Philosophy in 1844*, Chin. ed. (Translated by Liu Pikun et al.), Beijing: People's Publishing House, 1979, pp.85-86.

animal becomes human and what is human becomes animal."[43] The problem of capitalism, according to Marx, is that it has turned human needs into animal needs, and vice versa. Man is only active in his animal functions, such as eating and drinking, as if they are his sole functions; whereas labour is only for making a living, thus ceasing to be a part of workers' nature and making man work like animals. But man, having evolved from animal, has both animality and humanity. The misery of man in the capitalist world is that the activation of his animal functions is misunderstood as his true nature, whereas labour, supposedly a self-expression of man's individual physical and mental powers, is treated to be part of animal nature.

Following Fromm's understanding of Marx's concepts, and reviewing Marx's relevant statements, one can easily see that for Marx, the aim of socialism is not to improve people's economic life and make them live in luxury and extravagance just as the capitalists do today. Socialism is basically in opposition to capitalism, defining people's lifestyle in an entirely different way. It will never take the maximization of production and consumption as its ultimate goal. It aims to overcome the abysmal poverty which interferes with a dignified life, but this is not to be confused with the aim of gaining material property. Unlike capitalism, socialism will never transform man into an "economic animal" who only satisfies his material needs. Therefore, it is not aimed for the continuation of the capitalist way of life, but for a whole new one.

Nowadays, more and more intellectuals have reached consensus on this point. "Eco-Marxism", a new development of Marxist theories in the end of the 20th century, seeks moderate consumption and man's all-round development as the main part in socialist construction.

A famous proposition put forward by eco-Marxists is that an individual's satisfaction of needs is oriented from production activities rather than consumption activities. In *The Limits to Satisfaction*, Leiss

43 *Marx and Engels Collected Works* (Vol. 42), Chin.ed., Beijing: People's Publishing House, 1979, p.94.

criticizes the idea of equating satisfaction with unlimited material consumption in the modern industrial economy. He points out that the "ideal type" for existing social policy is a population which is concentrated in urban high-rise dwellings and is dependent upon massive, complex systems for its energy supply, food and other necessities, and waste disposal. At the same time, there is some evidence to show that individuals are aware of the fact that increasing rates of consumption are supposed to compensate for frustrations experienced in other domains of social life. Under these circumstances individuals could choose, for example, to trade off at diverse levels the satisfactions gained by personal activity in the production of everyday requirements against the satisfactions of consumption in a generalized market setting, and thus the enjoyment of activities is associated with ever-larger sets of commodities. In other words, the individuals' satisfaction and happiness are measured by the rates of consumption, which according to Leiss, is the very proof of alienation of modern industrialism.

Leiss stresses that one should stop associating satisfaction with consumption. In the works of earlier thinkers such as Fourier, Marx and Marcuse, it can be found that an individual's satisfaction should be oriented from the activities that he is engaged in; that is to say, satisfaction is ultimately determined by production activities. Leiss writes: "the possibility of satisfaction would be primarily a function of the organization of productive activity, and not— as in our society today— primarily a function of consumption".[44] If we are clear with the fact that increasing rates of consumption will by no means compensate for frustrations experiences in other domains of social life, then we have reason to believe that the possibilities for progressive social change are dependent upon identifying other spheres of activity apart from the consumption process, in which the sense of satisfaction and well-being also may be grounded.

44 William Leiss, *The Limits to Satisfaction: an Essay on the Problem of Needs and Commodities*, Canada: McGill-Queen's University Press, 1988, p. 106.

He further argues that individuals' needs and the means to satisfy these needs are diversified, and therefore no extremely specialized goods and services will be needed. "On the level of individual activity, the possibilities of satisfaction in an alternative setting would be related to overcoming the extreme specialization of work in the provisioning of goods and services (especially the methodical separation of mental and manual labour) and a consequent limitation of the sphere of commodity exchange."[45] People have a native capacity for healing, consoling, moving, learning, building their houses, and burying the dead. Each of these capacities meets a need.

He points out that to focus attention on the sphere of production rather than consumption is not only a transfer of attention, but to create an environment in which people are directly involved in the activities that are related to the satisfaction of their needs. The process of creating this environment is the process and also the most effective way of solving the ecological crisis. Satisfaction of people's needs is now negatively impacting the ecosystem, and therefore should be considered as a interactive and integral part of ecological problems. In this case, it is of great significance to relate the reduction of consumption needs and the change of the high-consumption lifestyle with both the labour activities and the free time of all individuals. Human satisfaction must be rooted in production activities.

He concludes that the key factors for an individual to get genuine satisfaction in the sphere of production are the following. Firstly, through engaging directly in productive activities, an individual could achieve self-fulfillment and enjoyment, so as to lead a creative and flourishing life. Secondly, since this kind of production is not oriented toward satisfying abnormal consumption needs, production and consumption are kept separate. The capitalist productivity will shrink, and therefore, human establishes a harmonious instead of a confronting relationship with nature which brings supreme happiness

45 Ibid.

and satisfaction.

Another renowned eco-Marxist, André Gorz, distinguishes economic rationality from ecological rationality as related to the satisfaction in consumption and that in production. Among the various features of economic rationality, according to him, the most prominent one is that the whole society and people's activities are dominated by consumption, thus demanding an unlimited maximum of economic productivity. Accurate counting and calculating of labour costs is quested for the maximization of efficiency and profit.

Gorz writes: "To be guided by economic rationality, production must not only be intended for commodity exchange; it must be intended for exchange on a free market where unconnected producers find themselves in competition facing similarly unconnected purchasers."[46] Since production is basically intended for exchange, it will be the more the better. Therefore, the category of "sufficiency" is no longer a cultural category but an economic one. The traditional principle of "enough is enough" is substituted by "the more the better" passion. In Gorz's words:

> In place of the certainty of experience that 'enough is enough' it gave rise to an objective measure of the efficiency of effort and of its success: the size of profits. Success was no longer therefore a matter for personal assessment and a question of the 'quality of life', it was measureable by the amount of money earned, by accumulated wealth. Quantification gave rise to an indisputable criterion and a hierarchical scale which had no need of validation by any authority, any norm, any scale of values. Efficiency was measurable and, through it, an individual's ability and virtue: more was better than less, those who succeed in earning more are better than those who earn less.[47]

He means that under the guidance of economic rationality, profit is of paramount importance, and the only criterion for measuring an

46 Andre Gorz, *Critique of Economic Reason* (Translated by Gillian Handyside and Chris Turner), London/New York: VERSO, 1988, p.111.

47 Ibid., p.113.

individual's scale of happiness is his consumption of commodity and possession of material wealth.

Marx's criticism of the capitalist mode of production, according to Gorz, is mainly on the economic rationality which is concentrated on the sphere of consumption. So Gorz quotes Marx's statements to reveal the negatives impacts of economic rationality. He intends that in Marx's and Engels' viewpoints, the economic rationality characterizing capitalism "would have potentially emancipatory implications, in that it swept away all values and purposes that were irrational from an economic point of view, leaving nothing but money relations between individuals, nothing but power relations between classes, nothing but an instrumental relation between Man and Nature, thus giving birth to a class of completely dispossessed worker proletarians, reduced to nothing more than an indefinitely interchangeable labour power and divested of any particular interest."[48] According to the Marxian view, "this self-same process of rationalization which, on the one hand, engenders a demiurgic, poietic relationship between Man and Nature as a result of mechanization and, on the other, bases the 'colossal' power of the forces of production on an organization of labour which strips both work and worker of all their human qualities."[49] "As a result of capitalist rationalization, work ceases to be an individual activity and a submission to basic necessities; but at the precise point at which it is stripped of its limitations and servility to become poiesis, the affirmation of universal strength, it dehumanizes those who perform it."[50] What Gorz stresses here is that according to Marx, the harm of economic rationality lies in the fact that it has made interpersonal relations money-oriented, and has left nothing but an instrumental relation between man and nature which dehumanizes the workers.

From the point of view of Gorz, the transformation from economic

48 Ibid., p. 19.

49 Ibid., p. 20.

50 Ibid., p. 20.

rationality to ecological rationality is a process of gradually seeking satisfaction in the sphere of production rather than consumption. Only when individuals are free from the grip of economic rationality and when the whole society seeks satisfaction from production, a large area of free time could be possible for people in the modernized society. People's lives cease to be occupied by consumption or any other activities which are intended for obtaining means of livelihood. Values are no longer quantifiable in this sphere of autonomous living. The progressive diminution of work for economic ends will have made it possible for autonomous activities to become preponderant in that society. Economic rationality should be kept away from free time, thus making leisure no longer simply be rest or compensation, but essential living time and the reason for living. Leisure should gain the upper hand over work, and free time over unfree time. This free time will be the bearer of all common values, that is, creativity, conviviality, aesthetics and play will come to predominate over the values of efficiency and profitability involved in work. Gorz also points out that when work has been reduced to the status of a mere means and free time being the bearer of all common values, a vision of a possible other society will emerge. In his words : "What is involved is the transition from a productivist work-based society to a society of liberated time in which the cultural and the societal are accorded greater importance than the economic: in a word, a transition to what the Germans call a '*Kulturgesellschaft*'."[51]

The fundamental difference between socialism and capitalism, according to eco-Marxists, is that the former seeks satisfaction in the sphere of production whilst the latter in consumption. They are not proposing to completely abandon consumption activities, but to drastically change the present mode of consumption with the help of new conceptions. This is related to how we understand consumption and how to consume in a socialist society. As pointed out incisively by

51 Ibid., p. 183.

eco-Marxists, a basic requirement is to break the connection between "the more" and "the better", and to establish a link between "the less" and "the better".

Gorz proposes that as long as we create more durable and environment-friendly objects, or more objects which are accessible to everyone, it is possible to live a better life with less consumption. In his words:

> In particular they might even escape the grip of economic rationality by discovering that more is not necessarily better, that earning and consuming more do not necessarily lead to a better life, and that there can, therefore, *be more important demands than wage demands*. ... 'The market-based order' is fundamentally challenged when people find out that not all values are quantifiable, that money cannot but everything and that what it cannot buy is something essential, or is even the essential thing.[52]

It is important to properly interpret the concept of *sufficiency*, according to Gorz. As a matter of fact, "the category of *the sufficient* is not an economic category: it is a cultural or existential category. To say that what is enough is enough is to imply that no good would be served by having more, that more would not be better. 'Enough is as good as a feast' as the English say."[53]

He further indicates that the ideal socialist lifestyle is "working less and living better", which is based on the disconnection between "the more" and "the better", and the connection between "the better" and "the less". "Working less" means meeting one's needs by working according to one's natural rhythm, that is, the economic standard of maximal production and profit is subject to the standard of society-ecology[54]. In this way, people can live in a new realm where the market disappears, everyone is satisfied and people gather together to plan for their own life.

52 Ibid., p. 116.

53 Ibid., p. 112.

54 Andre Gorz, *Capitalism, Socialism, Ecology*, London, 1994, p. 32.

In Gorz's mind, a socialist society is one with absolute equality on the basis of "working less and living better". Economic growth brought by the capitalist mode of production helps a growing mass of people enjoy the privileges that was once reserved for a small group of professional elite, but excludes them from more new opportunities. In a modern capitalist society, it is generally believed that there is no point in having something that everyone owns, so it is better to own something that everyone desires. That is to say, an object loses its value as soon as it is accessible to everybody, and it becomes precious only when it is rare. This is exactly why the ruling class keeps producing new material needs in order to maintain inequality and manipulate people. In a society of "working less and living better", we no longer need be endowed with any privileges and cannot be deprived of any opportunities, because what we produce is what is really in need. Equality emerges in such a society, just as Marx once said, where the free development of each is the condition for the free development of all.

Leiss holds that it is actually "a turn from quantitative to qualitative criteria" when we break the link between "the more" and "the better", and relate "the better" with "the less" in the sphere of consumption. He reminds us of John Stuart Mill's statements in the chapter "Of the Stationary State" in the book *Principles of Political Economy* in which a stabilization of economic progress and population growth is mentioned. Mill has proposed the audacious notion that the productive capacities and population level existing at that time need not expand any further. Of course he has recognized the gross inequities in the distribution of life's amenities and the opportunities for self-fulfillment among the population, but he contends that these could only be remedied by more rational forms of social organization. In Leiss eyes, Mill has maintained - correctly, as it turned out - that quantitative increases would not necessarily improve the lot of mankind as a whole. He highly appreciates Mill's argument that "a turn from quantitative to qualitative criteria was the primary desideratum for further social progress"[55].

Facing increasingly worse ecological situation, Mill's theory has been finally brought up for discussion in Western countries. "This recent discussion, however, only tends to confirm Mill's fear that the idea of the stationary state would be taken seriously only in response to pressing necessity, rather than being freely adopted as a desirable framework for qualitative improvement."[56] Leiss would never agree with taking Mill's theory as a expedient measure to solve matters of urgency, rather than as an constantly effective way to an ideal society. For him, if there is one basic proposition that forms the cornerstone of this tradition, it is the idea that the possibilities of human satisfaction must be rooted in the creation of a well-functioning sphere of shared activity and decision-making within which individuals would forge the means for satisfying their needs. He writes: "what is most important for this tradition is a change in the mode of expressing and satisfying needs, not a definition or predetermination of an alternative set of needs as such".[57] The key point is to reform the framework for the satisfaction of needs, that is, to establish a framework which is based on the quality of consumption and living.

Some people may be concerned about returning to the harshness of circumstances which in the past often characterized life in the hinterland. Leiss explains that modern civilization and wealth of people are to a large extent correlated with commodity and market exchanges. Therefore, whether the alternative eco-Marxist social policy in Mill's theory would cause poverty or not depends primarily on our perception of commodity and market exchanges. In his words:

> We may assume that the degree of significance of commodity production will vary widely according to specific historical circumstances and

55 William Leiss, *The Limits to Satisfaction: an Essay on the Problem of Needs and Commodities*, Toronto, 1976, p. 104.

56 Ibid., p.104.

57 Ibid., p.105.

> variations in social organization and personal desires. There need not be any uniform pattern even within a particular society, if that society is sufficiently decentralized to allow wide variations in the choices available to its members. The simple rule governing such choices may be stated as follows: reliance on access to complex manufactured objects through market exchanges is inversely related to the degree of local, direct control over the means of satisfying needs.[58]

In eco-Marxists' vision, according to Leiss, people's happiness and wealth are ensured by the increasing control over the means of satisfying needs as well as the decreasing reliance on the access to complex manufactured objects through market exchanges.

From all the foregoing analyses, it is obvious that socialism does not promote a high-consumption lifestyle. In other words, satisfaction is not derived from consumption but from work. When the link between "the more" and "the better" is broken, and "the better" is associated with "the less", a turn from quantitative to qualitative criteria takes place, and ways to express and satisfy individual needs are changed. "Working less and living better" is exactly the socialist lifestyle.

Now we may return to the differences between socialism and capitalism in their demands for resources. With the detailed elaboration above, we can see that socialism is not a high-consumption society and therefore it does not promote the kind of capitalist lifestyle which is associated with material extravagance and endless needs. The features of profit-seeking and consumption-centeredness have made capitalism highly demanding for resources, whereas in socialist society, the ultimate goal of achieving all-round development has reduced its needs for resources to a moderate extent. More specifically it means the following. Firstly, socialism has integrated "the less" with "the better". Attaching a high priority to quality rather than quantity, it is less demanding for resources. Secondly, an essential prerequisite for individual self-fulfillment in socialist society is the harmony between man and nature. So it will consciously regulate the amount and means

58 Ibid., 106.

of exploitation and utilization of resources when disturbing the nature. If our argument for the connotation and purpose of socialism is clear and convincing, then our conclusion about the demand for resources is also self-evident.

Now let us talk about the present-day China. China is a socialist country, but it must be made clear that China's socialist system today is very different from the socialist system of the Stalin model of the year. An important point is that today's China is no longer centered on consumption, that is, the capitalist way of life. The current practices of how to deal with material consumption and how to build and develop itself are gradually conforming to the Marxist definition of socialism. Let us take a brief look at the relevant expositions of leaders of China including Deng Xiaoping, Jiang Zemin and Hu Jintao and Xi Jinping, and see how China has been promoting all-round development without concentrating on consumption.

Deng Xiaoping proposed a ruling strategy of centering on economic construction, which can be interpreted from the following three respects. Firstly, the strategy was brought forth in the time of taking class struggle as the key link. Shifting focus from class struggle to economic construction was obviously the right choice under that circumstance. Secondly, since elimination of poverty was the momentous task and prerequisite for people to live with dignity, development of productive forces could not be put aside in the pursuit of a new lifestyle. So it is understandable that Deng Xiaoping took economic construction as the starting point of building socialism with Chinese characteristics. Thirdly, taking economic construction as the center, he also repeatedly cautioned that the all-round socialist construction should be achieved from economic, political and cultural perspectives. He stated, "Alongside the expansion of our productive forces, we should also reform and improve our socialist economic and political structures, build a highly-developed socialist democracy and perfect the socialist legal system. While working for a socialist civilization which is materially advanced, we should build one which is culturally and ideologically advanced by raising the scientific and cultural level of the whole nation and promoting a rich and diversified cultural life inspired by high ideals."[59] But, unfortunately, people always tend to remember his statements about economy and ignore his ideas on the all-round development of society and humanity.

In leading the construction of socialism with Chinese characteristics, Jiang Zemin has gradually recognized that socialism must hold high the banner of social and human development in an all-round way. Inheriting and developing Deng Xiaoping's related ideas, he not only reaffirmed comprehensive socialist construction from economic, political and cultural aspects, but also coined a new concept of "promoting all-round social progress". His outstanding contribution is turning this concept into the party's program, strategy and policy, and making it the operational guide to direct the whole party and the people. In the time of Deng Xiaoping, due to the historical limitations, the Marxian socialism that frees people from the grip of material needs had not fully emerged. In the period of Jiang Zemin, nonetheless, it has clearly presented itself. In the keynote speech at a Grand Gathering Marking the 80th Founding Anniversary of CPC, Jiang explicitly stated that we should regard the all-round development of society and humanity as the essence of socialist construction. He said: "All our work to build socialism with Chinese characteristics, and in fact, everything we do, should be aimed both at meeting the people's immediate material and cultural needs and at improving their quality, that is, stimulating their all-round personal development."[60] On how to achieve the all-round development of society and people, he specifically stressed the harmonious development of man and nature. "In the modernization drive, it is necessary to make sustainable development an important strategy. Controlling population growth, conserving resources

59 *Selected Works of Deng Xiaoping* (Vol.II), Chin. ed., Beijing: People's Publishing House, 1994, p. 208.

60 *Selected Works of Jiang Zemin* (Vol.III), Chin. ed., Beijing: People's Publishing House, 2006, p.294.

and protecting the environment must all receive priority in order to bring population growth in line with the development of the productive forces, coordinate economic development with resources and the environment, and bring about a virtuous cycle."[61] "Economic development must be considered in conjunction with the population, resources and the environment. We cannot just make plans for current development, but must also consider future generations and create better conditions for future development. We absolutely cannot squander resources and cause pollution that has to be cleaned up later. It would be even worse to squander our heritage, leaving our future generations with nothing."[62] "We must never forget that faster development cannot come at the price of wasting resources and sacrificing the environment. Economic development in any locality must focus on improving quality and performance and optimizing structure, and be based on a virtuous ecological cycle. This is the only way for development to become sound and sustainable."[63]

All-round development of man and society has become the most impressive guideline of the central government led by Hu Jintao, which has made Marx's concept and basic requirements of socialism take root and blossom in China. The socialist model of development that was once insightfully revealed by Marx and explicated by Deng Xiaoping and Jiang Zemin was, for the first time, described as the "Scientific Outlook on Development" in the Third Plenary Session of the 16th CPC Central Committee. In the *Decision of the Central Committee of the Communist Party of China on Some Issues Concerning the Improvement of the Socialist Market Economy* adopted in this session, the Scientific Outlook on Development means to "uphold the principle of 'man first' and form the concept of overall, coordinated and sustainable development so as to promote the overall economic,

61 *Jiang Zemin's Remarks on the Socialism with Chinese Characteristics*, Beijing: CCCPC Party Literature Research Office, 2002, p. 279.

62 Ibid., pp. 279-280.

63 Ibid., p. 292.

social and human development" and to "coordinate the development of urban and rural areas, of different regions, of economic and social sectors and of man and nature, and of coordinating the national development and the opening-up to the outside world". Since then, Hu Jintao has repeatedly stressed this concept on many different occasions from all aspects. From the Decision and a series of Hu's speeches, we can see that the socialist development model of CPC has been greatly enriched and improved by the central government, which is mainly reflected in the following two aspects. Firstly, "putting people first" is the core of the Scientific Outlook on Development. Opposite to material-centeredness, it takes the satisfaction of man's real needs as the starting point and ultimate goal of social development. Social activities should center on people instead of materials. Secondly, comprehensive, balanced and sustainable development is highlighted. Development is not just economic growth. It balances the growth of economy, politics, culture and society. It coordinates growth rate with the economic structure, and quality with efficiency for further sustainable development. It harmonizes man and nature, so that our people will live under sound ecological and environmental conditions

Xi Jinping proposes to realize the Chinese dream, the content of which is definitely not limited to material wealth. It refers to the pleasure that is based on the all-rounded development which has been and will continue to be pursued by Chinese people. Although we are still far away from this goal, we are steadfastly marching towards it. This is exactly the process of tackling the central problem of man becoming one-dimensional in modern civilization.

Now that the socialist construction under the leadership of CPC has moved to the correct track of putting people first and promoting the all-round development of society and mankind, China will have its own basic strategy in the development and utilization of resources accordingly. That is, we must more fully and more consciously depend on our own structural innovation, on constantly expanding the domestic market, on converting the huge savings of the citizens into investment, and on improving the quality of the population and scientific and technological progress to solve the problems of resources and the environment. China is committed to improving the efficiency of resource use and is committed to the development of new energy sources. Leaders of China are soberly aware that if we rely heavily on the consumption of resources and on the external market and external resources ideas, we are bound to conflict with other countries. So we are determined to adopt a restrained attitude and to achieve specialized and internal development. The above-mentioned strategy proposed by leaders of China is clearly not only a response to the temporary situation, but is an objective requirement for the implementation of the Scientific Outlook on Development in accordance with the present situation, and is an inevitable outcome of the correct understanding of socialist values. Although at present the strategy has yet to be perfected, it is for sure that the general direction and the basic outline has been set and will never change.

Will China's development pose a threat to the world when its strategy in utilizing resources is fully commensurate with the title of socialism? It is obvious that, with regard to the development and use of the most sensitive resources, China and other countries are building a new type of cooperative relationship of mutual promotion, mutual benefit, mutual assistance and complementarity, and are establishing win-win or multi-win relationships. At the meantime, China puts forward the concepts of the "Scientific Outlook on Development" and "Peaceful Rise", which are the two different components of a complete set of ideas. The inner connection between the two concepts is the strategy of developing and utilizing resources. The implementation of Scientific Outlook on Development depends on our adherence to the strategy, which will further lead to China's peaceful rise. Jiang Zemin once pointed out: "The earth, on which human beings co-exist, and the sky, under which we live, are an integral whole that can not be divided. The protection of them requires the concerted action of all countries"[64]. With such awareness and sense of responsibility, leaders and people would never let China come into conflict for resources with other countries. The socialist lifestyle we are promoting makes the conflict unnecessary.

III.Key Words for the Chinese Path: Peaceful Development and Harmonious World

In the Western world, there has always been talk of Yellow Peril, which suggests that if China is thrust into turmoil with serious wealth polarization, the whole world will be affected and numerous Chinese refugees fleeing to other parts of the world will be a source of danger. In this sense, whether China's rise will be a threat to the world depends on whether the society could remain stable, and the stability of the society depends on whether the broad masses of people can benefit from the development of productive forces and achieve common prosperity. No matter how economically developed a society is, the seeds of unrest will be sown and the exploited will finally stand up fighting if the development makes the rich richer and the poor poorer. This will become a source of destabilization for the whole world and will naturally raise concerns of everyone. In this case, whether China will become a threat to the world is directly related to whether it could maintain social justice and equality, lead people onto a path of common prosperity, and gradually eliminate exploitation. In a review, Engels related Russia's foreign relations with its domestic conflicts. He said:

> The contest that has now broken out in Russia between the ruling and the oppressed classes of the rural population is already undermining the entire system of Russian foreign policy. That system was only possible so long as Russia had no internal political development. But that time is past. Industrial and agricultural development fostered in every way by the

64 Ibid., p. 295.

> government and the nobility, has reached a point where the existing social conditions can no longer be endured. Elimination of these conditions is a necessity, on the one hand, but impossibility without violent change, on the other. With the Russia that existed from Peter the Great to Nicholas, the foreign policy of that Russia collapses as well.[65]

As a socialist country, China has to answer the question of whether its socialist system and related ideological values could guarantee the fairness and equality, help Chinese people achieve common prosperity, and gradually eliminate exploitation. If the answer is NO, the world peace is not for sure after China's rise. If the answer is YES, we can firmly assure the rest of the world that the socialist China will never become a "Yellow Peril".

Here, two issues must be clarified. Is socialism a system that ensures social justice and equality in its essence? If it is, is the Chinese socialism exactly the same? The first question is a prerequisite, for it deals with the nature of socialism. The answer is supposed to be obvious, but remains unsettled due to various reasons.

Adam Schaff, a Polish Marxist philosopher, questioned the so-called "Marxism" which was held as a governing ideology by the ruling party, viz., KPP (Komunistyczna Partia Polski) at that time, and he was severely criticized and oppressed as a dissident. After KPP fell out of power, when many orthodox Marxists changed their sides and turned to attack Marxism, Schaff stuck to his position as a Marxist and made more and more profound research into the essence of Marxism and socialism, among which the most important is his understanding of the essence of socialism.

Without a clear understanding of socialism, it is hard to determine whether countries of "real socialism" are really socialist. Schaff pointed out that the political right did not deny the socialist character of these countries, and therefore the problems of these countries are the problems of socialism. He said: "from its point of view the

65 *Marx and Engels Collected Works* (Vol.13), Chin. ed., Beijing: People's Publishing House, 1965, pp. 679-680.

deformations which occurred in those countries were only what could be expected from socialism". But the left were worried about the nature of these countries. They "felt irritated by those political deformities which contradicted the vision of the *ideal* socialism". Schaff criticized the political left that "some of them are trying to reject the socialist society that has been established, ignoring the fact that the whole world has been considering it real socialist and a different system from capitalism. This simplistic act is naïve, even politically wrong"[66]. Schaff showed his attitude towards the Soviet Union socialist pattern:

> Without defending their deformities, I continue to hold the position that according to a Marxist view regarding the nature of the ownership of the means of production, the basic economic form of these countries was socialist. But, at the same time, the superstructure that they built was incompatible with the generally understood ideals of a socialist society. Precisely from this contradiction emerges an important warning for the supporters of socialism: the revolution in the sphere of the ownership of the means of production and the consequent liquidation of the capitalist class which it entails, are not sufficient conditions for building a socialist society, which encompasses attributes such as freedom, equality and fraternity. Under certain circumstances there can even arise a society with a communo-fascist superstructure based on the nationalisation of the means of production.[67]

In Schaff's opinion, if societies could be classified according to the form of property ownership as Marx suggested, the Soviet Union was surely socialist. But in fact, the superstructure that it built was incompatible with the generally understood ideals of a socialist society, and therefore it was not really socialist. So Schaff concluded that to liquidate private property is the necessary but not sufficient condition for building a socialist regime.

---

66 Adam Schaff, *Unexplored areas of present-day socialism*, In Socialism of the Future, Chin. ed. (Edited and translated by the Central Compilation and Translation Bureau of China), Beijing: Central Compilation and Translation Press, 1994, pp. 79-80.

67 Ibid., p.79.

From the above statements of Schaff, it seems that he did not deny that public ownership of the means of production is the major character of socialism. But he did emphasize the multiple meanings of socialism by saying:

> Given the experience we have had, I consider that this warning is very important. We have to abandon the Marxist concept of classifying societies only according to the form of property ownership that exists within them. It is not enough merely to examine the base of the society; we must also examine its superstructure. But when we begin to analyse this matter, we have to recognise that there are various notions of socialism (as a system), and this explains the variety of political movements - frequently at loggerheads - which call themselves "socialist". [68]

Schaff reminded people to recognize the multiple meanings of the concept of socialism and he was opposed to the rupture among groups who held different views of socialism. This rupture, he mentioned, would benefit no one but our foe. He said:

> The history of the idea of socialism shows us this, as well as the present situation of the socialist movement, affected sometimes by animosities which can even be fratricidal. If the rupture between communists and socialists in the Weimar Republic had not happened, Hitler would not have come to power. General Franco would not have triumphed in the Spanish Civil War if the battles between communists, socialists, anarchists and Trotskyists had not taken place.[69]

He listed a good deal of arguments in the socialist movements to support the multiple meanings of "socialism". The arguments are, in a clear sense, "entirely 'unexplored areas' without any evident or obvious answers", including the distinctions between *state socialism*[70] and

68 Ibid., p.80.

69 Ibid., pp.80-81.

70 Marx and Engels predicted the gradual disappearance of the state under socialism as a form of exercising power, as an instrument of oppression, but also the continuation of the state as an administrator of property.

socialism without a state[71], *democratic socialism*[72] and *the socialism of the dictatorship of the proletariat*[73], *bureaucratic socialism*[74] and *the socialism of popular self-management*[75], *socialism of the planned economy* and *market socialism*[76], and *One-party socialism* and *pluralist socialism*[77].

Are there any similarities among the different groups of socialism? If they have nothing in common, how could they all be labeled as socialist movement? In other words, how to gather the supporters under the banner of socialism? Schaff not only discussed the varieties of socialism, but also stressed their commonality which plays the key role in understanding his concept of socialism.

> Or what is it that enables the supporters of socialism to gather under one banner, despite the sometimes very deep differences which separate them? We can respond, on the basis of the history of the socialist movement around the world, that it is the conviction that the main goal of socialism (as a social regime) is the abolition of all kinds of human exploitation. The slogans of 'liberty, equality and solidarity' are incorporated into this conviction. The rest is secondary.[78]

It is, as Schaff pointed out, the abolition of all kinds of human exploitation that becomes the shared goal of all socialist supporters. This is how they are united.

---

71 Anarchism as conceived by Bakunin and Kropotkin and their supporters.

72 The version of the present-day socialists and social democrats which can be traced back partly to Engels and his position regarding parliamentarism and its role.

73 Lenin's version, which may have referred to certain ideas of Marx, but which was interpreted by the Bolsheviks and accepted by the Comintern, and applied according to national conditions.

74 A generalization of the experience of the countries with 'real socialism'.

75 Based mainly on the example of Yugoslavia after its break with the Cominform, but supported by many adversaries of Stalinism, headed by the Trotskyist movement of the Fourth International.

76 Including the complicated problem of the ownership of the means of production.

77 Adam Schaff, *Unexplored areas of present-day socialism*, In Socialism of the Future (Chinese version edited and translated by the Central Compilation and Translation Bureau of China), Beijing: Central Compilation and Translation Press, 1994, p.81.

78 Adam Schaff, *Unexplored areas of present-day socialism*, In Socialism of the Future, Chin. ed. (Edited and translated by the Central Compilation and Translation Bureau of China), Beijing: Central Compilation and Translation Press, 1994, p. 82.

"Can we call a person socialist if he takes a stand on the principle of eliminating exploitation? Yes. This is, actually, a universal and profound principle that serves as the cornerstone of the unification of all socialist supporters."[79] Schaff admitted that he was enlightened by Wladyslaw Gomulka who formed this thought when he was a prisoner of the Stalinists. Schaff said: "Honestly speaking, when I first heard about his thought, I realized that I had been short of understanding of the dispute on how to define socialism. After deeper research, I strongly believe Gomulka is right, and the other viewpoints, no matter of their source or nature, no matter how important they are claimed to be, are only secondary. This tells us that the socialist supporters are in conformity despite their different opinions."[80] No matter who inspired Schaff, one thing is for sure, he believed that all socialists generally agree with a universal and standard definition of socialism— elimination of human exploitation in all forms.

Schaff is right to define the essence of socialism as "abolishing all forms of human exploitation". The establishment of a society without human exploitation, that is, the establishment of a fair and equitable society with common prosperity is fully consistent with the original vision of socialism of Marx and Engels who had very prudent predictions on the future socialism. Although their theories have been constantly developing, the role of common prosperity has never been downplayed. The key difference between socialism and capitalism, according to them, consists in the organisation of production on the basis of common ownership, initially by the nation, of all means of production. At the meantime, they emphasize that the goal of common ownership is people's common prosperity. In some sense, public ownership is the institutional guarantee and highly developed productive power is the material base for people's wealth. In *Outlines of the Critique of Political Economy*, Marx asserted that "production will

79 Ibid.

80 Ibid.

now be calculated to provide wealth for all".

To build a socialist society with common prosperity is a basic standpoint of all Marxists and a strong wish of all intellectuals and civilians. A society that is with liberty, equality and wealth of all people and without exploitation is an ideal socialist society in the eyes of everybody. Besides Marx, Engels and Schaff, many other scholars have also echoed people's wishes in their works. For instance, Alec Nove, a British scholar, thinks that socialism is "where most citizens have a reasonable degree of control over their lives and their work, where excessive power is not exercised by extremely rich owners or vast faceless corporations". According to Ota Sik, a Czech scholar, socialism "as meant to obviate its fundamental opposite, capitalism, by substituting social ownership of the means of production for their private ownership." [81] John Roemer, an American economist, finds it useful to define socialism a system in which "there are institutional guarantees that aggregate profits are distributed more or less equally in the population".[82]

Socialist values of justice, equality and common prosperity are in sharp contrast with capitalism. Facts have proven that even when capitalism brings about advanced productive powers and enhances productive efficiency, still it cannot create a just, equitable and commonly prosperous society for its productivity is based on inequality. As a matter of fact, this fundamental defect of capitalism has been revealed by Marx, Engels and even some utopian socialists. Fourier once pointed out that if there is no sign of equality in the legislation of a civilized system, people will get poorer with the development of productivity. The first sign of equality should be a guarantee for people's minimal standard of living. In such a society where the industrial development cannot provide a job for the poor,

---

81 Ota Sik (Ed), *Socialism Today: The Changing Meaning of Socialism*, London: MacMillan Academic and Professional LTD., pp. 3/87.

82 John.E.Roemer, Can there be socialism after communism? In Pranab K. Bardhan and John. E.Roemer (eds.) *Market Socialism: The Current Debate*, New York: Oxford University Press, 1993, p. 90.

how could we possibly find justice?[83] For some socialists, market fundamentalism of the capitalist world is intended for personal interests. Inequality, social division or even social disruption is possible under this premise. Unbalanced ownership is the base for capitalistic commodity economy and will continue to play its role in the rapid development of capitalist economy. The ruling class has been pledging fairness, but the reality was just the other way round. Fair competition has always been a disingenuous concept, for it is inconceivable for ordinary people to enjoy the same privileges as monopolies. They are limited by who they are, how rich they are, and how well-educated they are.

Capitalism relies on efficiency not fairness. The problem is how long it can last if the basic contradiction remains unresolved. The capitalist system determines that efficiency cannot co-exist with fairness, and that the latter has to be sacrificed. When talking about his society, Samuelson admitted that "[The conflict] between equality and efficiency [is] our biggest socioeconomic tradeoff, and it plagues us in dozens of dimensions of social policy. We can't have our cake of market efficiency and share it equally."[84] It has been revealed that the huge amount of wealth and abnormally high productive efficiency has made a sharp contrast between economic efficiency and equality. In the capitalist world where the degree of socialization of production is getting higher and the property ownerships lag far behind, there will be two inevitable results: economic efficiency will get abnormally high, and social equality will be very unlikely. The sharp contrast between high efficiency and inequality is reaching the limits of tolerance. Extreme polarization will definitely bring about extreme domestic disruption and will further lead to worldwide chaos. From social inequality to polarization between the rich and the poor and

83 *Selected Works of Fourier* (Vol.II), Chin. ed. (translated by Zhao Junxin et al.), Beijing: The Commercial Press, 1982, p. 232.

84 Samuelson, Paul A. & Nordhaus, William D. Economics (19th Edition), McGraw-Hill/Irwin, 2010, page 323.

from polarization to social disturbance will be the only possible route for capitalism which will lead to a dead end. In some well-developed capitalist countries, this problem has just started to show itself. But in some less developed capitalist countries which have been trying to follow suit, the problem has got serious. Here again, we have to restate our basic viewpoint in this section: if a country cannot achieve common prosperity, it will still pose a threat to the world no matter how economically advanced it is.

Hitherto some people may come up with the following question. If capitalism is doomed for chaos and crisis because of its pursuit of efficiency without paying attention to equality, then what about the Soviet Union which attached great importance to equality but still fell apart? Let us reflect carefully whether the Soviet Union was really a society of justice and equality. The Soviet model of socialism was actually not the kind of socialism in Marx's eyes because it took material well-being as the main goal of social development. There were actually severe social injustice, inequality and polarization in the Soviet Union. However, people always tend to blame its low efficiency and ignore its inequality which was exactly the root for the chaos and collapse of the Soviet Union.

After a visit in Russia, John Maynard Keynes raised three questions concerning the Soviet model of socialism in his book *A Short View of Russia*: Is the new religion partly true, or sympathetic to the souls of modern men? Is it on the material side so inefficient as to render it incapable to survive? Will it, in the course of time, with sufficient dilution and added impurity, catch the multitude? "Impurity" in Keynes words means social inequality or injustice. For him, at the time, the economy of Soviet Union was able to prevent people from starving to death and could even provide them with a little comfort, but the Soviet socialism could not last long with such economic inefficiency. However, the problem of "impurity" was not able to put an end to the Soviet Union very soon because it used "equality" to catch the people. He wrote: "But as a religion what are its forces?

Perhaps they are considerable. The exaltation of the common man is a dogma which has caught the multitude before now."[85] Nevertheless, it turned out that Keynes' prediction was wrong. Twelve years after Keynes' visit, it was exposed how "impure" the Soviet socialism was! In *The End of Socialism in Russia*, Max Eastman gives some information from official Russian sources which suggest that the difference between the highest and the lowest salaries paid in Russia is of the same order of magnitude (about 50 to 1) as in the United States.[86] It was also estimated as late as 1939 that the upper 11 or 12 percent of the Soviet population now receives approximately 50 percent of the national income.[87] The situation got worse after the World War II, especially when Khrushchev was in office. The gap between the poor and the rich was extremely large and reached a peak in 1970s and 1980s. The truth is that in the Soviet Union at that time, special-interest groups were protected by political dictatorship, which led to the social instability in late 1980s and 1990s and finally brought about the Soviet transition from socialism to capitalism.

We reveal the problems of injustice in capitalist countries and the Soviet Union in order to provide supporting evidence for the importance of socialist values of depolarization, common prosperity and social justice, which are the base for social stability. Under this premise, we have to think about whether the Chinese socialism is what we are expecting for? Whether it can achieve the goal of depolarization, common prosperity and social justice?

Just as Deng Xiaoping suggested, we should work hard to build socialism not only because socialism provides conditions for faster development of the productive forces than capitalism, but also because it is the only social system can eliminate the greed, corruption and injustice that are inherent in capitalism and other

85 John M. Keynes, *Essays in Persuasion*. London: Macmillan, 1931(1st edition).

86 F.A. Hayek, *The Road to Serfdom*, London and New York: Routledge, 1944(reprinted in 2006).

87 Ibid.

systems of exploitation. In his speeches during the Southern Tour, he summarized the essence of socialism as "liberation and development of the productive forces, elimination of exploitation and polarization, and the ultimate achievement of prosperity for all"[88]. He also mentioned, in some other occasions, that "Wealth in a socialist society belongs to the people. To get rich in a socialist society means prosperity for the entire people. The principles of socialism are: first, development of production and second, common prosperity."[89] However, there have been some misunderstandings and misinterpretations of Deng Xiaoping's statements.

Firstly, some people tend to ignore his statements on the essence of socialism and his stresses on common prosperity and elimination of exploitation, while at the same time taking the principle of liberating and developing productive forces as the only characteristic of socialism. Deng Xiaoping did make such statements as "... that poverty is not socialism, that socialism means eliminating poverty"[90], "They (note:the tasks set in the socialist stage) are legion, but the fundamental one is to develop the productive forces so as to demonstrate the superiority of socialism over capitalism and provide the material basis for communism"[91], and so on. But in his words, the liberation and development of productive forces are always related to common prosperity. It is obviously a deliberate misinterpretation of his ideas when talking about development of production out of the context.

Secondly, some people are confused with the relationship between liberating and developing productive powers and common prosperity. It is hard for them to tell which is the means and which is the end. In fact, according to Deng, "liberation and development of productive

88 *Selected Works of Deng Xiaoping* (Vol.III), Chin. ed., Beijing: People's Publishing House, 1993, p. 373.

89 Ibid., p.172.

90 Ibid., p. 116.

91 Ibid., p. 137.

forces", "elimination of exploitation and polarization" and "the ultimate achievement of prosperity for all" do not go side by side. They are actually going progressively. "Elimination of exploitation and polarization" acts as the end of the "liberation and development of productive forces" and as the means of "the ultimate achievement of prosperity for all". So obviously, "the ultimate achievement of prosperity for all" is the goal for the "liberation and development of productive forces" and "elimination of exploitation and polarization". Only when the latter two are fully incorporated, people can achieve common prosperity. With only the liberation and development of productive forces, prosperity will not be for all people. The most important thing is not to confuse the means with the tasks and goals set in the present stage. Deng Xiaoping's theory of the essence of socialism has well related the values of social justice, equality and common prosperity with present-day tasks and means, signifying an integration of the goals and means.

If the aforementioned two misunderstandings are cleared up, it is easy to see that Deng has defined the essence of socialism as the elimination of exploitation and polarization and the ultimate achievement of prosperity for all. In other words, common prosperity is the essence of socialism with Chinese characteristics proposed by Deng and is now practiced by billions of Chinese people. Just as Deng explicitly stated, "the aim of socialism is to make all our people prosperous"[92] and "the greatest superiority of socialism is that it enables all the people to prosper, and common prosperity is the essence of socialism"[93]. In this sense, the Chinese socialism is not only opposite to capitalism, but is also totally different from the Soviet socialism although it was originally derived from the latter.

Without doubt, today's China still has problems such as income inequality and even exploitation to some extent. These problems have

92 Ibid., pp. 110-111.

93 Ibid., p. 364.

been recorded in a large amount of authoritative data which need not be listed in detail here. But as long as we carefully study and analyze how leaders of China deal with these problems, it cannot be denied that the Chinese socialism is intended for the ultimate goal of eliminating exploitation and polarization and achieving prosperity for all.

The leaders of China are soberly aware of the fact that China is now in the primary stage of socialism. In this stage, it is incapable of entirely eliminating exploitation and polarization and achieving common prosperity for all people. In this case, it is important to bear the following two principles in mind.

The first principle is to keep income inequality to an acceptable degree. In the present stage, moderate income gap can serve as a material and moral incentive for people to acquire wealth and develop productive powers. Although acknowledging and encouraging inequality in income is an unavoidable process for common prosperity, leaders of China have been trying to control this inequality within a moderate degree. For one thing, the public sector of economy is strengthened through constant reforms. So long as the public sector plays a predominant role in China's economy, workers' interests can be guaranteed. For another thing, the income gap has been controlled to a reasonable degree by drawing up relevant laws, statutes and policies, and by regulating income distributing and monitoring systems. The private sector is only allowed to expand moderately because it gains profits mainly from investments and stocks other than labour and there is certain kind of exploitation in the private sector, which is inevitable in the primary stage of socialism. Being well aware of this problem, leaders of China have been trying to prevent the private sector from expanding to be universal and predominant. In other words, a small private sector is allowed develop but is restricted so that it would not weaken the predominant position of the public sector which is a basic feature of the economy as a whole, nor would it be involved in some of the vital economic sectors related to the national economy and industry.

The second principle is to take the present problems of income gap and exploitation as a driving force towards the ultimate goal of eliminating inequality and exploitation. Moderate income gap is allowed, as long as how it is formed and who it benefits are restricted by socialist policies. Tolerance of exploitation to some extent is the prerequisite for promoting social wealth, which further creates conditions for eliminating exploitation in the end. Therefore, private ownership and exploitation in present-day China are significant for achieving the ultimate goal of exploitation elimination and common prosperity, and are also regulated by the latter in turn. Putting the elimination of exploitation and achievement of common prosperity as the final goal of socialism is not only the task of socialism in the present stage, but will also be our pursuit in later stages. This final goal, however, should never be viewed as a pie in the sky. It should be realized with our practices in creating economic and social preconditions. Being aware of the long-term and arduous task, we have to regulate the existing income gap and exploitation more carefully and work hard to achieve this goal.

For the above-mentioned reasons, we can assert that now China is a society which aims at eliminating polarization and exploitation, achieving common prosperity and maintaining social justice. It is taking great strides towards this goal.

While leading people to achieve socialist modernization, leaders of China are putting extreme emphases on social stability and unity while pursuing the final goal. Deng Xiaoping was the first of them to put forward the idea of "stability is of overriding importance". Later on, Jiang Zemin cautioned to properly deal with the relationship of reform, development and stability. He pointed out that we should firmly "seize opportunities to deepen reform, open wider to the outside world, promote development and maintain stability". With the concepts of "Scientific Outlook on Development" and "harmonious world", Hu Jintao has not only brought Deng and Jiang's thoughts to a new level of socialist goals, but has also put them into practice. If leaders of China do not take the elimination of exploitation and polarization and the ultimate achievement of prosperity for all as the goal of socialist construction, their thoughts on maintaining social stability will be a castle in the air and futile. With this goal in mind, they have been focusing on leading a large amount of labourers into a comparatively just and equitable society that is moderately prosperous and harmonious, which is a solid foundation for social stability. At present, China's domestic stability and unity are ensured by the goal of eliminating exploitation and polarization and achieving common prosperity. In this respect, China is now effectively removing every single factor that may cause turmoil and destabilization. From Deng Xiaoping to Xi Jinping, with increasing emphasis on the final goal, their confidence in maintaining the social stability has been strengthened. In China, a socialist country with such stability, harmony and unity, there is no reason to worry about any turmoil, much less any negative impact or even threat to the world.

The history of human civilization is a history of struggles. Any progress of civilization was achieved through struggles between accumulated labour and direct labour, and among different social classes. The evolution of different forms of human civilization on the one hand marks the development of material civilization and spiritual civilization, and on the other hand indicates that conflicts and confrontations are under way in a new form. Stepping into the stage of civilization out from the age of barbarism, human beings have experienced periods of primitive civilization, feudal civilization and capitalist civilization. Compared to previous civilization forms, the capitalist civilization, viz., modern industrial civilization, is the most advanced form. But the conflicts and confrontations embraced in capitalism are also the fiercest. As Marx stated, the capitalist civilization "is written in the annals of mankind in letters of blood and fire". It is based on exploiting domestic workers and farmers, and invading and robbing other countries. It is hard for us to forget the British Enclosure Movement when "sheep devoured people" and the slaughter of more than 70 million North American indigenous Indians by Western colonists. In the 20th century, capitalist used military power to manipulate market, so the existence of New Imperialism means endless wars. Under such a background, Samuel P. Huntington published his book *The Clash of Civilizations*, in which he suggested that the world has not been in peace ever since the cold war, and that modern civilization is inundated with conflicts (although the author's definition of the conflicts as those between non-western nations and western countries is still the subject of debate). Is the human civilization doomed for such conflicts, contradictions and crises? Are struggles and confrontations inevitable in the progress of civilization? The answers could only be "yes" before the initiation of the Chinese path, after which the situation has changed. The Chinese path is a path for peaceful development, whose major significance for human civilization is replacing monopoly and domination with sharing and win-win. It has, therefore, explored a new way for human civilization, a new way that is neither based on expansionism nor hegemonism.

Deng Xiaoping, the general designer of the Chinese path, repeatedly emphasized the peaceful development of China. Keeping his finger on the pulse of the time, he explicitly integrated socialism with peace and sought for a "peaceful environment" for socialist modernization. He proposed a socialism that favours peace: "The socialism we are building is a socialism that is adapted to our own conditions, a socialism that helps to constantly develop the productive forces and that favours peace."[94] Based on his profound understanding of the interrelationship between socialist system and peaceful environment, he proposed a comprehensive independent foreign policy, the core of which is making China an importance force for safeguarding world peace. He said: "From the political point

94 Ibid., p. 328.

of view, there is one thing that I can state clearly and positively, and that is that China seeks to preserve world peace and stability, not to destroy them. The stronger China grows, the better the chances are for preserving world peace".[95]

Jiang Zemin stoutly announced to the world that China will never seek hegemony and will make unremitting efforts to safeguard regional and world peace. He said: "China will always stand firm as a strong force upholding world peace. It will never enter into an alliance with any country or group of countries and will not join any military bloc. China will never seek hegemony or expansion; it is opposed to hegemonism, power politics, aggression and expansion in whatever form."[96]

The central leadership with Hu Jintao as general secretary had also been unswervingly pursuing the independent foreign policy of peace, which is mainly manifested in the strategy of "China's peaceful rise". "Peaceful rise" is a strong and precise conclusion of China's principles on domestic politics and diplomacy, highlighting China's strategy for development in the new century. In the speech at the 110th birth anniversary of Mao Zedong, Hu Jintao said: "China is committed to growing friendship and cooperation in all fields with other countries on the basis of the Five Principles of Peaceful Coexistence. We need to carry out exchanges and cooperation with other others on the basis of equality and mutual benefit, and make our contributions to the noble cause of peace and development of all humankind."

In the speech at opening ceremony of Boao Forum in 2013, Xi Jinping held high the banner of peace and said:

> Peace, like air and sunshine, is hardly noticed when people are benefiting from it. But none of us can live without it. Without peace, development is out of the question. Countries, whether big or small, strong or weak, rich or

95 Ibid., p. 104.

96 *Collection of Important Literature since the 14th CPC National Congress* (Vol.I), Beijing: People's Publishing House, 1999, pp. 35-36.

> poor, should all contribute their share to maintaining and enhancing peace. Rather than undercutting each other's efforts, countries should complement each other and work for joint progress. The international community should advocate the vision of comprehensive security, common security and cooperative security so as to turn our global village into a big stage for common development, rather than an arena where gladiators fight each other. And no one should be allowed to throw a region and even the whole world into chaos for selfish gains.
>
> ...
>
> We are firm in our resolve to uphold peace and stability in Asia and the world. Knowing too well the agonizing sufferings inflicted by war and turbulence, the Chinese people deeply cherish peace. China will continue to develop itself by securing a peaceful international environment and, at the same time, uphold and promote world peace through its own development.[97]

The remarks of Deng Xiaoping, Jiang Zemin, Hu Jintao and Xi Jinping have clearly shown that Chinese people are desperate for peace and the Chinese path is a peaceful path. Embarking from Marxism in its essence, the socialist China has turned from strategic rivalry to peaceful co-existence and harmony in diversity. China will never want to be the "cradle" of the world revolution again and say things like saving two thirds of the world population from miseries.

It is understandable that some people tend to relate China's peaceful development with Chinese traditional philosophies. It is true that Chinese people are born with love for peace and have been following such doctrines as "Nothing is more precious than peace (yǐ hé wéi guì)" and "Inner Sage and Outer King (wài shèng nèi wáng)" which are closely related to the spirit of the Chinese path. But the traditional philosophies are just a presupposition. There have to be certain historical conditions which may turn the possibility into reality. In other words, China's peaceful development did not originate from its culture, but from history. Therefore, it is the social situation of

97 Xi *Jinping's keynote speech at the opening ceremony of the Boao Forum for Asia (BFA) Annual Conference 2013*, Wenweipo, April 8th, 2013.

China that chooses the peaceful way of development. Wu Xiaoming once profoundly pointed out:

> Pacifism is the nature of the Chinese path. Although closely related with Chinese traditions, it has actually been directed by the modern history of China.... Since this path cannot follow the example of modern capitalism to obtain any established provisions, it is able to provide a possibility for the resurrection and reconstruction of the Chinese pacifist tradition when critically clarifying the main causes of modern conflicts and wars.[98]

Pacifism in today's China is determined by the unique socialist path with Chinese characteristics, a path which is completely different from that of Western modernization and is intrinsically related to pacifism. The key point is that the Chinese path becomes possible because of the impossibility to adopt the Western model. "For Chinese modernization, when it is unable to achieve success through copying the Western capitalist and imperialist process of modernization, it becomes possible. This path is to some extent limited by Chinese traditional cultures which is also a prerequisite for the peaceful development."[99] Different from Western countries, China's social structure is not based on atomic individualism but collectivism, in which greed and expansion are very unlikely. China is not capital-oriented. Although capital is necessary for developing economy, it is also restricted and transcended. People will be the master instead of slave of capital. In this sense, China is not developing to conquer, to control or to hegemonize. In a word, the Chinese path will not follow the modern capitalist way. It is unique with its specific socialist values and directions. It is exactly the socialist values and directions having transcended the modern capitalism that determines China's peaceful development will be peaceful.

Without doubt, the Chinese path is different from the Soviet

---

98 Wu Xiaoming, *On the peaceful Chinese path and its global significance*, Social Science in China, 2009 (5).

99 Ibid.

socialist model. The vitality of the Soviet model was fully displayed in the age of war and revolution, and after the revolution it also played a significant part in setting a role model of ideal society. However, leaders of the Soviet Union did not make any timely adaptation to new historical conditions and guide it onto a path of peaceful development. Even worse, people at that time still "optimistically took war as the only solution to imperialist conflicts, and regarded world revolution as a direct strategic task". Considering that "the capitalism is always in crisis and is doomed to perish in the near future"[100], the Soviet socialism put its focus on conflicts, revolutions and wars. The Chinese socialism is different from the Soviet socialism in its correct judgment of the features of time. That is, it holds peace and development rather than war and revolution as the theme of the present world. Without a rational understanding of the world war and revolutions and without recognizing that the failure of capitalism and the success of socialism will both take a long time, we cannot construct the socialism with Chinese characteristics. The Chinese socialism has corrected the misunderstandings held by the Soviet socialists. It takes "peaceful co-existence with capitalism" as a "long-term strategy" instead of "short-term expediency and tactics". It also considers "abolishing capitalism" as "long-term strategy" instead of a "near-term goal". In the 21st century, hegemonism and power politics still exist and even have more new developments. Although international terrorism is becoming increasingly rampant and Western anti-China forces have been plotting to westernize and divide China, the Chinese people still believe that the theme of our age is peace and development and are unswervingly pursuing the socialist path of peaceful development with Chinese characteristics.

"Peaceful development" and "harmonious world" are the two key words of the Chinese path. They have explicitly pinpointed the essence of the Chinese socialism as sticking to the peaceful way of

100 Sun Daiyao, *Contemporary development path of China in the global historical view*, Journal of Wuhan University (Social Science), 2002(5).

development and establishing a harmonious world, which will make great contribution to the world peace, stability and development.

"Peaceful development" indicates that China's development relies on its long-term and peaceful bootstrapping instead of aggression and plunder. China will never seek for any kind of "shortcut", but gradual self-development. "The Chinese path of peaceful development is a way for China's peaceful and friendly co-existence and common development with other countries, and a way to revitalize the Chinese nation on the basis of common interests of all people. Drawing upon other nations' experiences, the Chinese path is adapted to the features of the times. It is in the fundamental interests of all people in China, Asia or even the world, and is in accordance with Chinese historical experience and cultural traditions; therefore, it is only choice for China."[101] To be specific, a peaceful path means to make the most of the peaceful global environment on one hand, and on the other hand to make its own contribution to the world peace with self-development. In other words, China gains everything needed for modernization through active participation in economic globalization and exchanges in fair competition, and meanwhile relies on its own strength and efforts in dealing with difficulties.

The keyword "harmonious world" suggests that the Chinese socialism is in pursuit of world harmony and common development. The achievement of socialist modernization and the great renewal of the Chinese nation is the dream of the Chinese path, which means not only the prosperity of China but also the peace, stability and development of the whole world. Firstly, the proposition of "harmonious world" plays a vital role in opposing hegemonism and power politics and maintaining world peace. "After realizing socialist modernization and the great renewal, China will definitely become an important force in opposing hegemonism and safeguarding world peace. Meanwhile, the idea of building a harmonious world will

101 Guo Wanchao, *A scientific understanding of the theoretical framework of the Chinese socialism*, New Horizon, 2009(1).

surely become a consensus of all peace-loving people, and will further become a force for promoting world peace."

Secondly, the idea of "harmonious world" will play a positive part in promoting the global economic and historical development. "As a developing country with a population of over 1.3 billion, China's goal of socialist modernization will contribute to the world historical development and common prosperity. Also, the idea of establishing a harmonious world has very positive significance in carrying forward the spirits of democracy, harmony, cooperation and win-win."[102]

So, the core concepts of "peaceful development" and "harmonious world" fully demonstrate the noble spirit of the Chinese path which has closely linked China's development with the maintenance and promotion of the world peace, combined Chinese people's interests with interests of the people of the world, and integrated self-development with the progress of human civilization. This is exactly China's pursuit of a great country.

In September and October of 2013, President Xi Jinping raised the initiative of jointly building the Silk Road Economic Belt and the 21st Century Maritime Silk Road, intending to establish a community of shared interests and a community of a shared destiny. The Belt and Road Initiative is a Chinese proposal whose aim is to promote peaceful cooperation and common development around the world. Cooperation under the Belt and Road framework is something in which all countries, big or small, rich or poor, can participate on an equal footing. This cooperation is public, transparent, and open, and brings positive energy to world peace and development. It aims to promote regional development, prosperity and stability, and expand dialogue and mutual learning between civilizations. The Belt and Road Initiative reflects that the Chinese government is actively practicing "peaceful development" and constructing a "harmonious world".

The significance of the Chinese path has been recognized by more

102 Zhang Aiwu, *On the global significance of the Chinese socialist theoretical framework*, Marxism and Reality, 2009(3).

and more people. Toynbee, a renowned historian referred to the dead end of Western civilization as "suicide from which civilizations die" and put his hope for restoring peace on China. He said: "Perhaps it is China's destiny now to give political unity and peace not just to half but to all the world."[103] His hope has been realized in today's China. Just as professor Wu Xiaoming stated: "As a great historian, Toynbee's judgment is sound and insightful." Of course, the path of China's peaceful development is "yet to be finished. It is under construction and during this process it has fully demonstrated its necessity"[104]. We believe that China's peaceful development path is gradually "generated in the historical way", which means it has become more and more mature and tends to be perfect, thus presenting more and more convincingly to the world China's contribution to human civilization.

103 Toynbee and Ikeda, *Forecast 21st Century*, Chin.ed. (Translated by Xun Chunsheng et al.), Beijing: International Culture Publishing House, 1985, pp.282-296.

104 Wu Xiaoming, *On the peaceful Chinese path and its global significance*, Social Science in China, 2009 (5).

CHAPTER FOUR
Giving Rise to a New Form of Human Civilization

I. Making Historical Contributions to Human Civilization

Various forms of civilization have brought great progress for mankind. Capitalism, in particular, has pushed this progress to an unparalleled degree. While at the same time, these forms of civilization have also wracked mankind, especially capitalism, which has brought about unprecedented challenges. The reality ruthlessly shows that human civilization is now at an inflection point in its own history, and it is not unlikely that humanity itself will fall with the decay of civilization. Now we are facing the challenges which are mainly manifested in the aggravation of "three major contradictions". The first contradiction is growing human inequality. Capitalist civilization is based on exploitation and pillage which, in the era of globalization, have become more and more severe, thus increasing the inequality among people. Nowadays, the tensions between individuals and society are extremely high, and decadent values characterized by self-centeredness and hedonism have become predominant. The second contradiction is the intensified conflict between man and nature, and nature's ecological capacity for mankind is close to saturation. Industrialization and modernization are achieved at the cost of destroying ecological environment. With the inharmonious human-nature relationship and destroyed ecological balance, we are facing the harsh revenge from nature and are in the danger of losing our homes. Thirdly, unbalanced needs of human beings have gradually made people "one-dimensional" consuming machines. Blindly taking property possession as the objective of life, people are obsessed with satisfying false needs and are gradually getting far away from true human nature.

Therefore, the development of human civilization obviously depends on the resolution of the three contradictions, and the contribution of the Chinese path to the world history and human civilization hinges on whether it could deal with these contradictions. As a matter of fact, the construction of socialism with Chinese characteristics was exactly meant for this problem. Although it cannot be said that China has completely solved the contradictions, it is now leading the way toward success. The Chinese path has demonstrated a significant positive effect on how to solve the problems for different countries and regions, which is its unique contribution to the world.

In the speeches during the Southern Tour, Deng Xiaoping made some famous statements on the essence of socialism, based on which he further stipulated the goal of Chinese socialism, that is, the achievement of prosperity for all. Leaders of China are well aware that the present China is unable to completely eliminate exploitation and polarization and achieve common prosperity. Therefore, we have to face up to the reality. The socialist market economic system is designed to properly handle the relationship between efficiency and equality, in order to keep them in balance and to avoid polarization during the process of economic development, so that we can achieve common prosperity while developing economy. The combination of socialist values with market which is an effective means of allocating resources is a great invention of CPC and the Chinese people. The concept of "socialist market economy" is a major adjustment and breakthrough of the previous planned economy and market economy. When Deng Xiaoping suggested transforming from planned economy to market economy, he proposed to restrict it with a modifier "socialist", hence creating "socialist market economy" which was intended to benefit every person with the wealth they have produced. Practice has proven that the socialist market economy is the best economic system that takes into accounts both efficiency and equality. It is an effective way for avoiding polarization in the process of developing productive powers and enhancing the material base.

The 17th National Congress of CPC held high the great banner of socialism with Chinese characteristics while putting the ecological progress in a strategic position. The 18th National Congress of CPC attached more emphases on the ecological progress by stating that we must "give high priority to making ecological progress and incorporate it into all aspects and the whole process of advancing economic, political, cultural, and social progress", "work hard to build a beautiful country, and achieve lasting and sustainable development of the Chinese nation" and "strive to usher in a new era of socialist ecological progress". Socialism with Chinese characteristics adheres to the basic principles of scientific socialism, and its nature determines that its construction must be carried out in accord with the standard of ecological progress. If the essence and core value of socialism are to create a way of life that is different from the capitalist way, that is, to achieve the comprehensive development of human beings and to truly meet people's demands, and if the socialism with Chinese characteristics sticks to this essence and core value, the Chinese people will naturally take the ecological progress as an important strategy in the great cause of socialism with Chinese characteristics. The reason is very simple: an important precondition for the formation of a new lifestyle is the harmony between man and nature, viz., the promotion of ecological progress. When considering building a harmonious socialist society as the primary task of Chinese socialism, leaders of the country have already put the harmony between man and nature, and ecological progress on the agenda. Harmonious development means ecological progress. Without the harmony between man and nature, there will be no harmonious socialist society, so to say interpersonal and intrapersonal harmony is embraced in the human-nature harmony.

The Scientific Outlook on Development was put forward when China was in desperate need for a transformation in development model, which implies that China has finally found its unique way for development. The Chinese socialism takes the Outlook as a strategy, meaning China's development and rise are "green" not "black". "Green development" is the comprehensive, coordinated and sustainable development suggested in the Outlook. A "green path" refers to the ecological progress. The socialist modernization under the guidance of the Scientific Outlook on Development is entirely different from the Western civilization. It is an ecology-oriented path. In the modern world, no countries or regions have more profound recognition of the severity of ecological crisis and the importance of ecological progress, and no countries or regions have better conditions for solving ecological crisis and promoting ecological progress. There are many causes for the ecological crisis, among which the capitalist way of development is the most prominent one. Its pursuit for efficiency and profit has brought huge damage to the ecology. Now China is also making use of and even developing capital, but in essence, it is not centering on capital. We are now giving full play to the advantages of socialism and trying to find a balance between utilizing and restricting capital, with which we can realize the goals of increasing material wealth and protecting ecological environment, which is unlikely to happen in rest parts of the world. To be more specific, we have made an overall plan for the ecological progress, which includes, as the 18th National Congress of CPC has summarized, improving development of China's geographical space, promoting all-around resource conservation, intensifying protection of the ecosystem and the environment, and enhancing system building to promote ecological progress. This plan gives a clear answer to how to resolve conflicts between man and nature.

II. Signifying the Birth of a New Form of Human Civilization

China is supporting the affluent life of 20 percent of the world population with only 7.2 percent of the land on earth. That is to say, it has nourished four times of the American population with almost the same territory size. The Chinese path has helped people realize the Chinese dream of happiness and prosperity, which is its significant contribution to the world civilization. But this is just a minor part of its contribution. The greatest part lies in that a new form of human civilization has been created in this country with such a long history. Xi Jinping pledged: "We will bring benefit to both the Chinese people and people of the world". People of the world may be benefited in many respects, among which the most prominent is to have a better new world.

As long as we take a look at the goal and content of the Chinese dream, we can easily understand why the Chinese path and the Chinese dream signify the birth of a new form of human civilization.

The Chinese people are striving to realize the great renewal of the Chinese nation, but how is "renewal" defined and what is the criterion for its success? If the renewal is only judged with GDP, it has nothing to do with the new civilization. Looking back to the world history, no matter in the agricultural age or the industrial age, accumulation of material wealth and development of productive powers are only necessary but not sufficient conditions for the birth of a new civilization. The formation of a new civilization is related to new cultural spirit and corresponding mode of production and lifestyle. Only after the cultural spirit prepares mankind for a new state of being, a new civilization will be established. The great renewal is the main goal and essential meaning of the Chinese dream. Only when the renewal is composed of more than material gains such as the doubling of GDP, and also includes the development of Chinese benevolent governance and real Marxism, can we say that the

Chinese dream and China's renewal has created a new form of human civilization.

Xi Jinping proposes the Chinese dream for very clear purposes: prosperity of the country, renewal of the nation and happiness of the people. The key factor is to build a moderately prosperous society in all respects. Obviously, Xi does not propose to build the society only from the economic perspective. "The moderately prosperous society" in his words contains social, cultural, spiritual, and ecological indicators alongside with economy. "Moderately prosperous society" is a very meaningful and Chinese-style expression for the Chinese dream. This concept originated from ancient China, and is now endowed with new meanings. In centuries, expressions such as "moderately prosperous", "moderately prosperous households" and "moderately prosperous society" have been very popular among the people, to whom they are the synonyms for "happy life". So, happiness of people is the criterion to judge whether the society has achieved moderately prosperity or not. Since wealth does not necessarily bring happiness, people do not necessarily feel happy and content in a wealthy society. But in a moderately prosperous China, people will live with affluence and happiness, which is a new state of being. So the goal of the Chinese dream is a moderately prosperous society in which people live with happiness and contentedness. A moderately prosperous China is a country with strength, democracy, harmony, happiness, and beauty. Isn't it a vivid example of a new civilization? The Chinese dream is not only a dream for wealth, but also a dream for democracy, harmony and happiness. Isn't it a dream for a new civilization?

The Chinese dream is the spirit of contemporary China, and has become a major policy of the central government led by Xi Jinping since the 18th CPC National Congress. The pursuit of a new form of civilization through the Chinese path and the Chinese dream is detailed in Xi's report to the 18th National Congress, in which an overall approach was proposed to promote economic, political, cultural, social and ecological progress. In fact, the Chinese dream and the Chinese path are different expressions for a same goal. In explaining the Chinese dream, the central government has been repeatedly stressing the five aspects of the overall approach, which means that the new Chinese civilization includes not only material wealth, but also political, spiritual, social and ecological strength. From the political perspective, it means order and democracy. The government is incorrupt and people are the masters of the country. From the spiritual perspective, it means great improvement in people's literacy and morality. People are sincere to each other, and are living with dignity. The culture industry is getting more and more people-friendly. From the social perspective, social organizations are more orderly developed and functionally optimized, especially with the social service system and social security system getting perfect and public services being equalized. From the ecological perspective, the man-nature relationship has become harmonious. With the sky getting bluer, grass greener, water cleaner and air fresher, the country has become resource-conserving and environmentally friendly. In short, the overall approach has brought progress in all the above-mentioned five aspects, which has greatly surpassed the Western industrial civilization which is now dominating the world. No doubt, China is still in the middle stage of industrialization, that is, it has just finished the transition from agricultural to industrial civilization. As long as we follow the overall approach and make progress in all the five aspects, the future of China will not be an industrial civilization, but a completely new civilization surpassing both agricultural and industrial civilization.

Aggravation of the three contradictions we mentioned earlier is a challenge for mankind. Any development in today's civilization depends on the resolution of the contradictions, which is impossible in the framework of industrial civilization. It has been proven that the Chinese dream explores a new way to face up to and solve the problem, so the process of realizing the Chinese dream is the process of creating a new civilization. The philosophy of "harmony" has a long history in China and advances with the times, and the pursuit of intrapersonal, interpersonal, and man-nature harmony will add a traditional touch to the Chinese dream.

We have discussed the significance of the Chinese path and the Chinese dream for the birth of a new civilization from different angles. Now we need to answer the following question: Is the Chinese Dream necessarily connected with a new civilization? To put it in another way, will the realization of the Chinese dream necessarily lead to the creation of a new civilization? Our answer is YES, because it is what the Chinese dream is meant for.

The key point is that the Chinese path and the Chinese dream are intended for the renewal of the nation. In order to achieve this goal, we should not blindly follow the examples in Western countries or some Eastern countries like Japan. That is, we have to explore a unique way for modernization and renewal, viz., the socialist path with Chinese characteristics. The possibility of choosing this path comes out of the unsuitability of the Western model in China. Since the Chinese path is different from the capitalist way, the prospect of the Chinese dream will be different from the future of Western modernization which has brought about industrial civilization. Therefore, the new Chinese civilization is definitely different from the Western industrial civilization. In the process of realizing the Chinese dream, we are facing with two choices. The first choice is to imitate Western countries, which is unlikely to help us realize the dream. Even if it is partially realized, China will still be led to a westernized industrialization. The second choice is to develop a new path for the Chinese dream and China's renewal, which will lead to the creation of a new form of civilization.

In this sense, since the pathway to Chinese dream is different from that to the Western modernization, the realization of Chinese dream will definitely create a new form of civilization. But why is it improper and impossible for us to follow the Western way? The reason is that China has a totally different cultural background. Features of the

Chinese culture and social reality determine that China will follow a unique pathway to its renewal, which will further lead to a future that is distinct from the Western modernization. In fact, the positive energy and effect of the Chinese dream, and any other factors which are crucial for the birth of a new form of human civilization are closely related to the uniqueness of the Chinese path, Chinese culture and social situation.

China's unique cultural tradition and basic national conditions determine that China shall follow a path different from the Western countries. Xi Jinping explained this point very profoundly in his speech in the National Conference on Publicity and Ideological Work of 2013. He said: "With unique cultural tradition, historical destiny and national conditions, we are bound to follow a path of development which is adapted to China's characteristics." Our path, theory, social system and culture have distinct features and significant advantages, so we are doomed to failure if blindly copying the Western way. Xi added that our present task is to "guide people to a more comprehensive and objective understanding of the contemporary China and the world", in which the most critical step is to explain and elucidate the Chinese characteristics from four aspects: historical tradition, culture, national condition, and specific development path. We have to make clear that the Chinese culture embraces the deepest spiritual pursuit of China and is the rich nourishment for the growth and blossoming of the nation. We have to make clear that China's excellent traditional culture is its outstanding advantage and most profound soft power. We have to make clear that socialism with Chinese characteristics is rooted in the fertile soil of Chinese culture. It reflects the will of the Chinese people, meets the requirements for China's development, complies with the progress of the times, and has a deep historical origin and broad realistic basis. Through making clear the four aspects, it is shown that China should follow a unique development path because of its specific cultural tradition and basic national conditions, and that the Chinese people do have reason to be fully confident of their bright future because of the outstanding path, theory and social system.

In *The China Wave*, Zhang Weiwei states that China is now rising with a model that is not endorsed by the West, creating a great stir all over the world. China's rise is not the rise of an ordinary country, but the renewal of a great civilization with a history of five thousand years, and therefore is the rise of a civilizational state. According to him, China is a unique civilizational state whose ancient civilization completely overlaps with the present state form. He describes the features of China in the following way:

> This type of civilizational state is of long history and ancient culture, and will never blindly follow the others or copy the Western model or whatever. It will only stick to its own specific route and logic for development. Although with hardships and difficulties, the trend of China's rise cannot be halted or reversed. This civilizational state is able to draw upon the others' advantages without losing itself, and therefore making its own contribution to the world civilization because it is an endogenous host civilization which keeps producing new coordinates.[1]

He asserts that, since China rises as a civilizational state with such rich contents, "China will probably bring to the world a 'once-in-a-millennium historical transition'"[2]. Firstly, he pointes out that China is a civilizational state with long history and ancient culture; secondly, he conceives that China will not duplicate the Western way or any other models, and "only follow its own route and logic for evolution and development"; lastly, he declares that China is capable of making use of all advantages of other civilizations without losing itself, and making original contributions to the world's civilization. Actually, Zhang Weiwei has revealed that a corollary of realizing the Chinese dream and the rise of Chinese nation is the creation of a new form

1 Zhang Weiwei, *The China Wave — the Rise of a Civilizational State*, Shanghai: Shanghai People's Publishing House, 2011, p.2.

2 Ibid., p.3.

of civilization, which is constantly generating new coordinates and making new contributions. Isn't it the new kind of civilization that is unprecedented in human history? Isn't it the new kind of civilization that human beings are looking forward to?

Part Two

Chinese Path and Developing Countries

Chapter One

The Acknowledgement of International Community on the Demonstration Effects of Chinese Path on Developing Countries

In the contemporary world, some people strongly deny that the Chinese path has demonstration effects, such as Francis Fukuyama, the author of *The End of History and the Last of Man*, the internationally renowned right-wing thinker and the professor working in Stanford University. While appreciating the Chinese path to a certain degree, he emphasized that the it is not sustainable, and not worth following. "For many countries, China's development model is not easy to follow", he said, "Because this model seems impossible to be universal". [1] "This model is limited to East Asia and not becoming a serious replacement." [2] From now, Fukuyama's view is not accepted by most people. In international community, experts, scholars and media are overwhelmingly in favor of the Chinese path. In fact, its demonstration effects for developing countries has been recognized by international community. It is the tendency that the developing countries learn from the East, trying to find experience in the Chinese path.

The Chinese path is usually internationally expressed by the "Beijing Consensus" which was firstly proposed by an English scholar Joshua Cooper Ramo. In May, 2005, the Foreign Policy Centre, a famous think tank in Britain, published his thesis about Beijing Consensus. This concept has emphasized the enlightenment of the

1 Chen Jiagang: *Francis Fukuyama's Speeches in China*. Central Compilation & Translation Press, 2012, p. 15.

2 http://www.iceo.com.cn/column/32/2012/0523/248788.shtml.

Chinese path for developing countries. After Ramo has analyzed the path that China had taken in the last two decades, he concludes that China's economic development model is not only suitable for China, but also for developing countries that are inclined to growing their economy and improving people's livelihood. The Chinese path has set an example for developing countries.[3] Roma's point has attracted attention in international communities where the "Beijing Consensus", the "Chinese model" and the "Chinese path" become a hit discussed by mainstream media in that month. On May 20th, 2004, the International Herald Tribune Global Edition published an essay entitled "China Transform in its own Way" which appreciated China's gradual way to reform setting an example for international communities especially for the developing countries. On May 24th, in Mexico, *La Jornada* published an essay entitled "China: Asia's Horizon", in which China's miracle is considered to be the result of its social and economic policies based on its conditions, and it has exerted international influences especially the developing countries. On May 27th, "China's Experience in Solving Million's Subsistence" released by the *Guardian* stated that the Chinese path was another powerful choice for developing countries besides the western development model.[4]

As "Beijing Consensus" is internationally acknowledged, the demonstration effect of Chinese path to the world, especially the Third World, is widely accepted by people. Some comments followed:

The former Secretary-General of the United Nations Kofi Annan said in a press conference: "It is worth for other countries, especially the developing countries to learn the beneficial experience that China has gained through its unique model to achieve development."[5]

The former Secretary of States of the United States of America

---

3 http://fpc.org.uk/fsblob/244.

4 Zhou Jianjun: *The Meaning of China's Transformation: From Washington Consensus to Beijing Consensus*, Forum of World Economy and Politics, 2005 (1) .

5 Sun Zhongliang: *The Meaning of Chinese Model in Post-crisis Era*, Scientific Socialism, 2012 (1) .

Henry Kissinger said: "China's development model is of significance for China and the rest of the world."[6]

The former Pakistani Prime Minister Yousuf Raza Gillani stated: "As the largest and most successful developing country in the world, China is a hope for developing countries towards prosperity because China has demonstrated its development model with its brilliant achievements and set an example for developing countries."[7]

Abdullah II Bin Hussein, the King of Jordan, pointed out during his visit to China: "China's development model is an example for many countries in the Middle East. As an important country in the world, China's voice has attracted wide attention."[8]

Mikhail Titarenko, a member of the Russian Academy of Sciences said: "China's experience not only sets an example and provides modernization model for developing countries, but also offers a broad platform for their development and cooperation with China. China's experience has set an example to narrow the north-south gap and break the monopoly of the 'multi-empire' on the world." The great achievements made in China's reform and opening up are of far-reaching significance to the whole world. China's reform experience mercilessly rejected and overthrew such wrong conclusions made by some western politicians and scholars as "Europe should be the world's center, and only the development mode of Europe is the most prospective one". It gives hope for world's civilization and the developing world.

Du Jinsen, director of the Institute of Chinese Studies at the Vietnam Academy of Social Sciences: "If China is right, we are right." "Ho Chi Minh said, China's revolution has enlightened Vietnam. Today, this sentence can be adapted into China's reform has enlightened Vietnam", "China's per capita GDP has reached

---

6 Chen Jinhua: *The China Model & System*, People's Daily, July 5th, 2017.

7 *Chinese Model is the Hope for the Developing Countries—Interview with Pakistani Prime Minister Yousuf Raza Gillani, Guangming Daily*, May 11th , 2009.

8 Su Xiaobo: *King of Jordan: Middle East Learn From China*, Cankaoxiaoxi, Nov. 11th, 2007.

US$3,000 while Vietnam has just reached US$1,000. It is a golden time for a country to rise its per capita GDP from US$1,000 to US$3,000. China has made such progress and Vietnam should learn from it."[9]

An American scholar Joseph Nye who has proposed the concept of soft power said: "China's economic growth is not only a huge benefit for developing countries, its special development model including the special way of democracy is also worth following by west countries. More importantly, in future China's advocacy of democratic values, social development pattern, and foreign policy will exert more influences on the public."[10]

The famous Nigerian scholar Fermi Akomolev stated that "in 1970s and 1980s, China and most of the African countries were in backward economy. Therefore, China's economic take-off offers experience for African people", "Africa can benefit a lot from the big economy-China. Foremost and most importantly, we have to believe everything is possible. The progress made in China's economy is a miracle in any perspective. It demonstrated that what achievement a nation could make with confidence, resolution and vision", "we can also learn that to develop our economy, we can only rely on our own efforts and determination. No country in history has developed its economy by relying on foreigners."[11]

The Former President of Namibia Pohamba said: "African countries should learn from developed countries like Japan and also developing countries like China and India. In this stage, as China's experience is more valuable, we have to learn more from China."[12]

People who highly affirm the demonstration effect of the Chinese path on developing nations are wide spread across the world. Not

---

9 Sun Zhongliang: *The Meaning of Chinese Model in Post-crisis Era*. Scientific Socialism, 2012 (1) .

10 Wu Jiang: *"Chinese Model" is Confronted with Challenges*, Beijing Daily, Feb. 9th, 2009.

11 Xu Chongwen: *The World Significance of Socialism with Chinese Characteristics*, Studies on the Socialism with Chinese Characteristics, 2009 (4) .

12 Tao Wenzhao: *The African Effect of Chinese Model*, International Studies, 2009 (1) .

only that developing countries give high praise to the leading role of the Chinese path, but also that developed countries start to face up to the Chinese path and its demonstration effects on developing nations in particular. Those who praise the Chinese path include politicians, experts and scholars.

That the Chinese path has exerted demonstration effects on developing countries, and that many developing nations take it as an example are the objective results in the world's historical process since 1980s. The demonstration effect of the "Beijing Consensus" and the "Chinese Model" have come into being under the backdrop of fading the "Washington Consensus" and the "Washington Model". The rise of the Chinese path comes with the decline of the "Washington Model", and the two have formed an inverse relationship. Just as irresistible as the recessive influences of the "Washington Model", the expanding impact of the Chinese path has its objective necessity although it occurs inadvertently.

Two great social experiments have been carried out in 20th century. One is the Socialist Experiment sweeping across the earth starting in 1920s, the other is the Transitional Experiment starting in 1980s.[13] The latter one emerged after the former one suffered a major setback, which is to say it emerged when the Soviet Model of Socialism was widely spitted. The Soviet Union and East European countries that were desperate for transformation as well as Third World countries that were eager to develop all looked at the "Washington Consensus" which refers to the reform policies western neoclassical economists made for transitional nations. It is actually a path of neoliberalism, with democratic government and market economy as its main content. "Shock Therapy"[14], which is adopted by the Soviet Union and Eastern Europe, was designed in accordance with the "Washington

13 Zhou Jianjun: *The Meaning of China's Transformation: From Washington Consensus to Beijing Consensus*, Forum of World Economy and Politics, Chin. ed., 2005 (1) .

14 "Shock Therapy", as an economic transformation strategy, is regarded as a trilogy under a certain special economic policy, including liberalization of prices, dependency on fiscal policy and monetary policy to ensure economic stability, and privatization of state-owned enterprises.

Consensus". They correlate economic transition with political system reform closely, emphasizing that the core of the transition is the massive changes in the constitutional system with economic transition as only one part. In concrete implementation of the reform, such three strategies have been promoted simultaneously as price trade liberalization, macro stabilization and privatization of property right, which has resulted in a big social and economic recession in these countries. Besides, the big economic reform movement starting form the end of 20th century in Latin-American countries is actually a neoliberalism movement prompted by "Washington Consensus". Some Latin-American countries which were involved in this reform movement took bold and drastic measures to open their market in accordance with liberalism, and they thoroughly privatized enterprises and public institutions, just like some has said of "selling the whole country". Thereupon, these countries have lost control and management of economic arteries and the entire society, which leads to an all-round crisis in politics, economy and society.

There are three failures of the "Washington Consensus". First, the radical reform and "shock therapy" that have been taken by the Soviet Union and Eastern European countries have brought social and economic setbacks. Second, Latin-American countries have been severely afflicted in economy. Third, financial crisis have taken place in Asia. The three failures have led to the declining influences of the "Washington Consensus". Given that it has failed in Third World countries, international experts and scholars start to reflect on the transformation that the Soviet Union, East European and Latin-American Countries have taken in accordance with it, upon which they have formulated "Beyond the Washington Consensus" and "Post-Washington Consensus". The proposition of the new consensuses has proven that the "Washington Consensus" has become history with no authority.

While some countries are taking radical reforms in accordance with the "Washington Consensus", China does not follow the consensus blindly. China is also carrying out reform, but it is gradual reform through which China has opened up its own development path. Chinese people do not adopt an either/or attitude towards choosing its development path, which is to say that China is trying to open up its own development mode after bidding farewell to the Soviet Model instead of embracing the "Washington Consensus". China is in stark contrast to those countries who acts totally in accordance with the "Washington Consensus", and has achieved great success without following the consensus blindly. Instead of completely accepting Western development mode, China has found a development path suitable to itself through active and creative digestion and absorption. Arif Dirlik, a noted left-wing scholar, believes that a Substitute Model for the "Washington Model" has formed in China while it is exploring its own path. He says the Chinese path is a solution pursuing modernity and future under local conditions, which detours the past and heads for optional future, instead of going back to the past. Its mission is to assist people who have been oppressed or abandoned under capitalist modernity, and point out different opportunities for future.[15]

Practice has proved that the success of a development model cannot only promote continuous and rapid development of domestic economy, it can also generate demonstration effect for other countries through "spillover effect". It is when the "spillover effect" and demonstration effect become increasingly explicit that the "Beijing Consensus" and the "Chinese path" spread like wildfire. To many Third World countries, the significance of Chinese path is that it has provided a Substitute Model different from both the "Soviet Model" and the "Washington Model". After the Soviet Model has been abandoned, those countries who have adopted the "Washington Model" have not obtained social and economic development. Under this backdrop, they can truly feel that compared with "Washington

15 Li Bailing: *Dirlik's Reflections on Global Modernity and Socialism with Chinese Characteristics*, Studies on The Socialism With Chinese Characteristics, Chin. ed., 2008 (6).

Model", Chinese Model is more stable, more harmonious with less pain. Some regard the demonstration effect of the Chinese path on Third World countries as a "soft power", which becomes public property shared by the world. Its attraction is irresistible and cannot be transferred with the subjective will of the state.[16]

The reason why "Beijing Consensus" and "Chinese path" have become successful with enormous demonstration effect is that the consensus and path represent the process a developing country explores a most suitable way for development.

Developing countries have many things in common because they are faced with the same international environment and similar domestic problems. Although Chinese people call their path the socialist path with Chinese characteristics, emphasizing the Chinese features of this path, the path undoubtedly provides inspiration for the whole world, especially for the Third World. "Chinese characteristics" cannot be simplified as "China-exclusive". We do have something unique to ourselves, but much more are in common with other nations, Third World countries in particular. The Chinese path hides its particularity in universality, a universality from the world level, Third World countries in particular. That Chinese path exerts demonstration effect on Third World countries is not accidental. The reason is that China, like all of these Third World countries, is in the process of development. Compared with "Washington Model", the Chinese path is more worth emulating for Third World countries, because the former one cannot adapt itself to these countries while the latter one spreads smoothly into these countries.

It can be said that it is after a series of painful experiences that developing countries have chosen to take the Chinese path as their example. In the past, influenced by the unfriendly remarks of some western politicians about China as well as a series of wrong conclusions made by right-wing thinkers about China, many Third

16 Tang Guanghong: *The International Significance of Socialism with Chinese Characteristics-Also on the So-called Ideological Threat of Chinese Development Model,* Journal of Yangzhou University, 2008 (1) .

World countries keep alert to China. Some worry that China would export socialist ideology while exporting goods and services. Others worry that China's rapid economic development would lead to depredation of resources. Now their worry has been greatly weakened, if not totally eliminated. In general, many Third World countries have turned their alertness into learning from China.[17] Now let us have a look at how the Third World countries learn from China.

East European countries have dedicated themselves to studying Chinese development model while reflecting on the original radical reform model with political democracy and economic privatization as its core. Russian leaders have explicitly pointed out that political democracy is not the only factor either for domestic capital or for foreign capital, and social and political environment is a more important factor. Actually these countries are already learning from China.

In Asia, specific measures of many countries show that they have learned from China's experience. In Indians' eyes, no other countries in the world resembles India as much as China does, but China has left India far behind. They delve into the Chinese path so as to find out a way of developing with Indian characteristics. Socialist countries such as Vietnam and Laos follow China's example too. In the Middle East, many countries make it clear that the Chinese path set them an example to learn from. Even conservative leaders from Iran welcome the Chinese Model[18], let alone countries like Jordan, who attaches much importance to it.

In Africa, the charm of the Chinese path is self-evident. While introducing capital and technique from China, many African countries pay more attention to learning from China's developing mode. They are quite aware that China's development is more of a

17 Qin Zhen: *International Perspective of the China Model - Also on the Socialism with Chinese Characteristics and its International Influences,* Journal of Renmin University of China, Chin. ed., 2008 (4) .

18 Qin Xuan: *International Perspective of the Chinese Model - Also on the Socialism with Chinese Characteristics and its International Influences,* Journal of Renmin University of China, 2008 (4) .

chance than a challenge, with its good side overwhelming the bad.

Attention to the Chinese path is found everywhere in Latin America. From the perspective of those countries, the Washington Consensus is a poison instead of a panacea, which cost ten years' development of the twentieth century. Now, China not only means their biggest trade customer, but also a provider of better experience of development which differs from those of Europe and America.

CHAPTER TWO

The Demonstrative Effects of the Chinese Path on Politics

To avoid the political part of the Chinese path and take the Chinese Model only as an economic one, someone from the international academia proposed that China's reform lied in economics rather than politics. That is to say, from their perspective, the Chinese path only enjoys the success in economics, so that for developing countries, only the economic field is worth learning. But more scholars disagree[1]. They emphasized that if there was no political reform in China, the economic reform was hard to imagine; if China made no successful political reform, such great success in economics was hard to achieve. They held that the Chinese path was an integral concept which included both the economic part and the political part, and not understanding the latter would lead to difficulties in comprehension of other factors including the economic part. Correspondingly, for Third World countries, if the Chinese path is only followed economically, not politically, the demonstrative effect of the Chinese path will not be comprehensive enough for them. As China's economic activities are carried out under a certain sociopolitical order, how can they learn these economic activities without understanding China's sociopolitical order? Honestly, every stage of China's reform has its highlight, such as economics, society, and culture. But political reform underlies all these highlights and is implemented through all of them.

Economic development requires the lowest standard of sociopolitical order. During these years, the whole world, especially

1 Wu Bo, *Research summary of these years on Chinese Model*, Shan Dong Social Science, 2011 (1) .

Third World countries, have envied China for its stable sociopolitical order, under which economy is developed efficiently and in order. Since the early 1990s, China has been a leading power in attracting foreign capital. Just imagine, will the foreign capital flow into China unremittingly if the Chinese sociopolitical environment is not stable? China's stable sociopolitical environment and its incremental reform are inseparable, in other words, the former is the result of the latter. Chinese people know that it is unrealistic to carry out a radical political reform in China, a big developing country, for it brings nothing but turmoil, which can even lead to the disintegration of the country.

From the beginning, China's reform and opening up has targeted at an extensive economic reform, along with incremental, small-scale political reform, which doesn't halt but progresses little by little. China never discards the present political system, but only does some necessary reforms to its unreasonable and improper part. China's incremental political reform stands in contrast to the radical reform which aims at political plurality, and is built on the premise of ensuring stable political order and relatively concentrated political system.[2] It was because of the incremental way of political reform that China's political order could stay stable while China was adjusting the superstructure to the new productive relationship. Scholar He Zengke depicted the progress and result of the incremental political reform in depth and detail:

> First of all, its initiators have been able to lead the reform through to the end, and designed the scheme calmly and rationally; next, initiators chose a way that faced less difficulty, aiming to transform the big reform to some smaller ones, so as to reduce its cost as much as possible, so it is easier than radical political reform to achieve an organic unity between political reform and political stability; third, incremental political reform was carried out on a minor scale and was tested in practice, and the

2 Zhang Weiwei, *The China Wave: Rise of a Civilizational State*, Shanghai People's Publishing House, 2011, p. 27.

> reform scheme was modified and adjusted according to the outcome of the test, so that the innovation of system and the uncertainties of dealing with the outcomes of the reform were formed as an organic whole to avoid the inextricable trap; last, the achievement of incremental political transformation was more solid. The reform scheme was decided upon the experience of the test, so the possibility of success was greater. The progression of reform matched the progression of social structure and political culture, which underlay the transformation of political system, so the system became more solid.[3]

During these years, China has faced upon unimaginably complicated and tough difficulties, but its leaders handled then in an easy way and solved them one by one. China the mighty ship, bypassing submerged reefs and riding on the giant tide, has always been marching with great success. Evidently, it is owed to the powerful and able Chinese government. China's mighty government won much compliment from other developing countries for its decision-making power and execution power. The government was not bound by any vested interests, nor were its leaders talking empty talks incessantly. An article of the *United Morning Post* from Singapore reported that: "If China's political system is viewed globally, you will find that the real distinctive feature of China is the efficient leadership of a party."[4] People all hoped that their country was ruled under an authoritative and mighty government instead of a weak government without prestige. Of course authority came with legality, but where did the legality of the Chinese government come from? That is a question that dignitaries and scholars who have delved into the Chinese path mainly research into and think about. Thomas Heberer, the institute director of the political institute of the University of Duisburg-Essen, held the view that the CPC had entered the "adaption stage" after going through the stages of "transformation" and "consolidation". In

3 He Zengke: *Incremental Political Reform and the Transformation of Democracy*, Journal of Beijing Administrative College, 2004 (3) .

4 Zhai Huixia, etc: *The New Research Perspective of the West to Chinese Model*, International Communications, 2012 (1) .

this stage, the legality of the party came mainly from the promise of "modernization", enhancing the nation power and building socialist democracy.[5] To some extent, the view of Thomas Heberer is right. The legality of Chinese politics does not come mainly from the legality of procedure, which means the legality from defined procedure. Rather it pays more attention to the legality of its demonstration, and that is to say, the legality gained from the practical welfare provided to its people.[6]

In China, people recognized the Communist Party's leadership and considered it as rightful and proper, not mainly because that the leading party was selected through the right procedure, but mainly because that this leading party did represent their interests. During these years, China paid special attention to people's livelihood, and put forward the conception of "people's livelihood is the first priority". The Chinese government took improving people's livelihood as priority among priorities, and it did make historic miracles in that field. For the achievements in people's livelihood, we may hear Samir Armin's pertinent comment, who relied much on theories: "social inequality, unemployment, rural workers coming into cities, these much talked-about questions were much severer in capitalist countries, including those who were honored to create miracles". Chinese people may underestimate themselves for they didn't know the outside situation, but those who know about Third World countries are quite aware that compared with other peripheral countries, the situation in China was much better than that of them.[7] The legality of Chinese government came from the democracy of a "better situation" and the practical welfare gained by the people under a "better situation". Chinese leaders believed in the old saying "those who win people's

5 Xu Juezai: *View of Foreign Scholars on Socialism with Chinese Characteristics*, Studies on the socialism with Chinese characteristics, 2008 (3) .

6 Yao Yang: *The Global Significance of Chinese Path*, International Economic Review, 2010 (1) .

7 Chunyan Fan: *The Controversies among Western Left-wing Scholars on the Socialism with Chinese Characteristics and its Enlightment*, Foreign Theoretical Trends, 2011 (7) .

heart win the world". China's ruling party inherited honestly the cultural tradition that represented the overall interest of people. The conceptions of "people's support" and "people's will" took deep root in China's leaders' heart. Chinese government, through fighting for people's interests, has gained legality from practical welfare it gave to its people, and built its prestige, and the transformation from people's "attention on procedure" into "attention on result" is indeed exemplary to extensive developing countries, and more and more of them are gaining interests from it.

Although both procedural legitimacy and performance legitimacy are of great importance, Chinese government has resolutely chosen the latter when they can only achieve one of them, which means to win public support and trust by making achievements. Similarly, if it is impossible to ensure both the purity and effectiveness of institutions, the priority always goes to the effectiveness despite the fact that both of the two are highly necessary. During the institutional transformation and development in the past three decades, Chinese government, which has realized the importance of institutional construction, emphasized institutional effectiveness rather than purity. This realistic attitude is highly inspiring for developing countries to launch their institutional constructions, especially in political area.[8] Different from Western people who see the government as a necessary evil, Chinese people believe the government is a necessary kind, which has been interpreted in recent years as all the virtues of officials and the efficiency as well as effectiveness of government. Not only does Chinese government pursue clear governance, it also pursues good governance, which means to rule the country in a way that suits national conditions the best. Just as Zhang Weiwei, a famous Chinese politician, once said, it is not that autocracy is more effective than democracy, but good governance can do a better job than bad governance. The success of

8 Yao Yang: *The Global and Historical Significance of the Chinese Path*, International Economic Review, Chin. ed., 2010 (1) .

China's model shows that a good political system, no matter what it is, shall ensure good governance and observe the principles of people oriented and to rule with diligence.[9] According to some scholars, focusing on institutional effectiveness and good governance is by no means a political expediency but an innovation. And the focus on effectiveness creates a new tendency of innovation that might lead to a discovery of new system that is unknown to the West.[10] During the way of institutional reconstructing, some developing countries blindly copied foreign and especially western institutions. But China's focus on institutional effectiveness overturns the blind attitude, hence making China's focus increasingly inspiring to those developing countries.

China's focus on institutional effectiveness is strongly proven by the fact the CPC emphasizes to work for the interests of the entire nation rather than a certain class or group. When it comes to the studies on modern political changes of China, Thomas Heberer requires special attention to the fact that the CPC has changed from a party that works for certain classes to one that works only for its people. The change, said Heberer, can also be proven by the important thought of Three Represents proposed by Jiang Zemin, President of China from 1993-2003. The important thought of Three Represents demonstrates rapid changes in Chinese society as the CPC represents not only the interests of workers and farmers, but also the interests of the entire nation.[11] Although Thomas Heberer wrongly believed in the change of the CPC in its class attribute, he was right to recognize its effort to stay clear from any social groups and to avoid discriminative policies against certain social groups for its own good. Chinese government

9 Zhang Wei: *Chinese Shock-the Rise of a 'Civilisational State'*, Shanghai People's Publishing House, Chin. ed., Shanghai, 2011, pp. 134-135.

10 Yao Yang: *The Global and Historical Significance of the Chinese Path*, International Economic Review, Chin. ed., 2010 (1) .

11 Xu Juezai: *View of Foreign Scholars on Socialism with Chinese Characteristics*. Studies on the Socialism with Chinese Characteristics, Chin. ed., 2008 (3) .

is now working on the great enterprise of Chinese Dream to achieve the great rejuvenation of the Chinese nation, the key of which is to motivate its people and make sure that they are positively encouraged. China's success in recent years should attribute to the neutral impression[12] left by government. It gathers everyone into what the government is doing and is naturally praised and copied by many developing countries.

Following today's trend of democracy, China has attached great importance to democratic politic construction during its political reconstructing. China's democratic politics with distinct characteristics has won the world's recognition. An article on India Information Network in 2007 pointed out that democracy doesn't exist only in the west as it can be achieved as long as its nature—people being the master of the country, be upheld. Instead of emphasizing competition and participation as western democracy does, Chinese democracy value people's rights to run the country, which turns out to be more effective. Thereforc, China is developing a new model for the global democratic systems.[13] Stephen C. Angle, a professor of philosophy in Wesleyan University of America, also gives nod to Chinese democracy by saying that unlike many countries who see representative democracy as the final goal in their transformation, China believes that simply copying a competitive democracy will lead to great unfairness. China nowadays practices a reformed democratic centralism, which can boost political participation of the general public, rather than the competitive multiparty democracy. According to Angle, at least nowadays, the reformed democratic centralism might be the right goal for Chinese people to pursue.[14] A French

12 Yao Yang: *The Global and Historical Significance of the Chinese Path*, International Economic Review, Chin. ed., 2010 (1) .

13 Xu Juezai: *View of Foreign Scholars on Socialism with Chinese Characteristics*, Studies on the Socialism with Chinese Characteristics, Chin. ed., 2008 (3) .

14 Xu Juezai: *View of Foreign Scholars on Socialism with Chinese Characteristics*, Studies on the Socialism with Chinese Characteristics, Chin. ed., 2008 (3) .

scholar Tony Andreani comments that it is foolish to want China to copy western democracy as it is hopelessly decaying. China, actually, is building socialist democracy despite great challenges in waiting.[15] The secret of China's successful democratic-political construction is creating consociational democracy and deliberative democracy with distinct Chinese characteristics on the basis of national conditions rather than introducing the competitive democracy that is highly recommended by the west. Ancient society of China has a traditional worship of the rule of man and hierarchical politics. Traditional Chinese culture values highly the pursuit of harmony, cooperation and balance. These are the reasons why only by consociational democracy and deliberative democracy can lower political cost of democracy and to encourage participants to cooperate and exchange ideas. Practice shows that the above-mentioned two democracies are the only way to improve political legitimacy and public governance without causing social conflicts and chaos. John Thornton, Chairman of the Board of the US Brookings Institution, points out that Chinese has realized the importance of elections but they insist on deliberative democracy as a better choice than multiparty competition. China's choice is understandable, said Thornton, they don't like broad freedom of speech, press and assembly as the West does but prefer to expand these freedom step by step so as to maintain social harmony. Chinese believe that practicing deliberative democracy to ensure citizens and organizations have their own say in decision-making is what democracy is all about.[16] China's democracy is indeed becoming a new member of the world's democracies.

For all the developing countries in today's world, it doesn't matter whether or not to exercise democracy but to exercise it in an appropriate manner as not all experience about doing democracy

15 Li Qiqing: *Contradictions against Two Denials on Socialism with Chinese Characteristics*, The Modern World and Modern Socialism, Chin. ed., 2005 (4).

16 Xu Juezai: *View of Foreign Scholars on Socialism with Chinese Characteristics*, Studies on the Socialism with Chinese Characteristics, Chin. ed., 2008 (3).

is trustworthy. China's democratic system, which emerges at a time when the Third World countries are in urgent need of a new democratic model, is imposing increasingly strong influences on the world, especially the Third World countries.

CHAPTER THREE

The Demonstration Effects of Chinese Path on Economy

For the world, especially the Third World countries, the strongest impact of the Chinese path undoubtedly comes from the economic area. After decades of hard work, China has become the world's second largest economy by GDP. What's more, as is predicted by an increasing number of global mainstream economists, China will be the largest in about ten to twenty years. A British scholar Angus Maddison did the largest and the longest-running comparative study on the global economy by Purchasing Power Parity. He came to a conclusion that in 1992, the size of China economy has surpassed that of Japan and in 2009 that of twelve old developed countries in Western Europe in total (Britain, Switzerland, Sweden, Norway, Finland, Italy, Germany, France, Denmark, Belgium, Austria).

By the end of 2015, China's economy will have exceeded American economy; by the end of 2030, China's economic scale will have become 1.13 times the scale of American economy.[1] Through these analysis and statistics, Zhang Weiwei tries to prove that China's economy is striding towards to excel the US. While the rise of China had been recognized by other countries in the world and China's economy had achieved amazing development then, some people at home should raise doubts about China's progress, which confused Zhang a lot. He responded to such doubts: "Chinese people are long-sighted, cool-minded, modest and prudent. Though we do

1 Zhang Weiwei, *The China Wave: Rise of a Civilizational State*, Chin. ed., Shanghai People's Publishing House, 2011, p. 27.

not show off our achievements, the rise of China still shocked the world, whether it was expected or not."[2] The remarkable progress China has made in economy does influence the economy of the world, and we can describe such influences from three perspectives: China exports substantial low-priced yet high-quality goods to other countries; China enjoys the biggest market in the world, and is a perfect investment target for commodity traders and multi-national companies; China is a large economy, and provides huge momentum for the development of global economy. In addition, the economic progress of China provides a development model for other countries, especially those Third World countries on how to get rid of poverty and develop towards prosperity.

The rise of China gave the Third World countries an inspiration: the modernization is a necessary and achievable goal for their development. These countries all draw critical lessons from the process that China creates economic miracle.

"A consensus on development" is a prerequisite for this miracle. From the late 1970s to the early 1980s, the chief architect of the reform and opening up, Deng Xiaoping, decided to transfer the work focus to economic building and repeatedly emphasized the focus. The change triggered successive reforms, and was also a significant turning point. From then on, Chinese people cultivated a consensus on development, especially on economic development, and China entered a new period. A primary imprint of the period was that the whole country, whole nation worked together to achieve economic development. It was also during this period that the concepts like "development is the top priority" and "poverty should not occur in socialism" were instilled into everyone's mind. During the past three decades, the speeches delivered by whichever leader of China in whichever conferences, all stressed that we should "unswervingly center on economic construction" and take development as the top

2 Ibid., p. 14.

priority. Looking back on the history, every time China was faced with new challenges, the golden means that Chinese governments adopted to react to new conditions or solve new problems was persisting in development, especially economic development to resolve conflicts. We all can see that our leaders have been attaching great importance on the stability of society. “Stability matters the most”, which is the legacy from Deng Xiaoping. Deng Xiaoping once said in a speech delivered during the Southern Tour: “The most important issue of China is maintaining stability. Without stability, there will be no achievements or further development”. Chinese governments and the people all bear the truth in mind. However, how can we realize our goal? The answer is to balance reform, development and stability. In other words, Chinese governments should be aware of centering on putting primary efforts into economic development and creating more social wealth.

The stability of China’s society is based on the rapid economic development, but we have to clarify that “the shared sense on development” among the people is not an impulsive decision, it is a sense based on insightful analysis of China’s development in different ages. What we talk as the development of an age, or the changes that shape an age, is indeed a reflection of the world’s development trend. As early as in the 1970s, according to the international situation then, China’s leaders decided on the development direction, and firmly believed that the theme of the future generations should be peace and development, instead of war and revolution.

Based on such an awareness, they began to transfer the work focus to economic building, and cultivate a consensus. By contrast, a critical reason for the retarded development of some other developing countries was their failing to develop a consensus on development, which caused that even they had the wish to drive development, yet their wish lacked the support of rational judgments about the changes of a time, so they could not overcome obstacles to achieve long-term sustainable development. In such a condition and in an attempt to realize economic development, some developing countries began to draw lessons from China, learnt to develop global horizon and started to cultivate consensus on development in their countries.

However, with cultivated consensus on development and transferred focus on economic development, we were faced with a practical question: how to drive economic development? The way Chinese governments adopted was to open up to the world, and proactively learn everything that was advanced and potentially useful to economic development from other countries, to promote the economic communications at home and abroad. The change from a once closed self-sufficient country to a country opening to the world was another great strategic tuning point after transferring the work focus to economic development, and also a success in realizing leapfrog development on economy. As such, the key what other developing countries tried to learn from China was how to open up to the world. We know that Deng Xiaoping attributed China's impeded development in modern history to the policy of cutting the ties between China and other countries. That was also why he decided to break the self-closed or half-closed dilemma during Cold War, promoted engagement in international market and competition, and proposed to improve and develop China through international competition. China's opening up began with opening coastal cities, then cities along the Yangtze River, and finally all mainland cities. Three decades have passed, and China has finished the systematic and coordinated opening up. This was a process of continuous economic development, during which the opening up was positively linked with economic development. The development history revealed to people the truth that: only proactive engagement with globalization can make further development possible. Opening up in economy and engagement in international labor division mean that a country can give play to their advantages, and develop scale economy of production through international market. The lessons that China draws from past experiences prove that for developing countries with adequate labor force but relatively less capital, opening up is particularly significant.

The justification is that, these countries can improve income through international trade to accumulate capital so that they can upgrade and improve the industrial structure, and give more play to their advantages, to gradually gain a higher position in the areas they are skilled at in the international labor force division. For developing countries, opening up "can be seen from the increase of international transactions in commodity market, and also the capacity to absorb capital from other countries".[3] Obviously, the opening up policy did bring China tangible benefits, and China's success of implementing the policy provides an example for other developing countries seeking further development.

However, if people simply take "opening" as everything of the opening up policy, they are absolutely wrong. Actually, China was not the only country that tried to implement the opening up policy, but other countries failed while China succeeded. Why? To answer the question, Detlef Kotte, the Economic Affairs Officer at the United Nations Conference on Trade and Development, compared the situation of China and some Latin American countries during the opening up:

> People's living standard in some Latin American countries like Mexico, Brazil and Argentina were pretty higher than that of Chinese people about 20 to 25 years ago, but later, their national economy became troubled by severe debt crisis. The reason was these countries borrowed too much from international capital market, and adopted a policy of stimulating input and development with reliance on capital from other countries to. With interest rate abruptly surging and the loan pressure increasing, finally these countries were no longer able to pay the debt, which gave rise to debt crisis and economic downturn. In contrast, though substantial private capital flew into China's market, this was not what China relied on. Besides, China has managed to maintain the stability of interest rate and currency rate, so as to keep the competitive advantages of products made in China. In this

3 Lu Ming: *Scientific Policy, Economic Increase and Development-the Chinese Path and its Meaning to the World,* Academic Monthly, Chin. ed., 2008 (6) .

> way, the high exports supported the increase of imports. Now, many Latin American countries began to improved based on their reflection on the success of China and their past experiences.[4]

Detlef Kotte pointed out a significant difference between China's opening up and the Latin American countries: China ensured that the implementation of opening up policy was under control of Chinese government. This is a key to China's success. At the very beginning when implementing the opening-up strategy, China was aware that opening to other countries was "proactively" adapting to international community, and "selectively" learning from the outside; it was not following others like sheep, but customized to the conditions of our country. Simply put, China ensured everything under control. Deng Xiaoping once proposed three points in the dialogue with Kadar, the Communist leader of Hungary then, now recognized as three principles clarifying China's opening up: no blind learning from Western countries, no blind imitation of other socialist countries, and no giving up our own advantages. It was these three principles that helped China keep its own advantages while learning from others. When the financial crisis swept through the globe, China was not hindered by the crisis, and took the lead to recover from it instead. To a great extent, this was benefited from the opening-up policy that was under control of Chinese government. Many developing countries have already been aware of the key, and learnt to ensure the implementation of opening up under control.

Immediately after the shifting from closing to opening to the outside world, the next critical issue China confronted was what to be learnt first from abroad especially from Western countries? What advanced knowledge or technology should be introduced into China first from abroad especially from the West? Considering the situation, the government of China specified in time that the market economic model was the first to be learnt and the market economic mechanism

4 Xu Chongwen: *The Global Significance of Chinese Path*, Red Flag Manuscript, Chin. ed. , 2009 (15).

was the first to be introduced from the West. Deng Xiaoping emphasized that not only capitalism but also socialism could take advantage of market, which neutralized the market that had been considered as a privilege of capitalism, laying a theoretical foundation for China to establish market economic system. Then the great transformation from planned economic system to market economic system was realized in ancient land of China. It was another great social transformation following the accomplishment of China opening to the outside world from being closed. Practices have proven that this transformation had decisive influences on the development of Chinese economy because it has successfully solved problems of information and incentives. Many developing countries give the credit of Chinese economy success for the introduction of market economic system, which is reasonable because it could be said that the productive forces of China can be improved to an unprecedented level just thanks to the magic of market economic system.

The success of China cannot be simply ascribed to the opening-up policy, likewise, it can't be simply attributed to the introduction of market economic system from the West. As learning the opening-up policy from China doesn't mean opening to the outside world is enough, learning how to develop market economy doesn't mean copying the market economic system of the West is enough. Such learning won't get any "key" of Chinese success. Some far-sighted foreign scholars have realized clearly that the experience of China's market economy has strong Chinese characteristics, the key of learning how to construct market economy from China is to grasp the "Chinese characteristics". Detlef Kotte pointed out the differences in opening-up policy between China and other countries and the feature of market economic system constructed in China. In his view, the feature lies in the fact that "It's a successful strategy to attach great importance to organic integration of policy measures and market forces rather than merely relying on market forces to develop economy"[5]. Professor Peter Nolan from University of Cambridge named the market economy road of China as "The Third Way", which was, as he said, a way where the relationship between state and market is mutual, symbiotic and creative. The Third Way of China is "a complete philosophy that combines the specific methods encouraging and controlling market with the profound thoughts of the moral system originating from rulers, officers and common people. When the moral system runs well, the non-ideological action of the government that solves the practical issues which cannot be settled by the market improves the foundation of the philosophy"[6]. The Associate Professor Leo AO from Griffith University of Australia considers that the economic reform in China has created "a market economy which completely departs from the neo-liberal market economic model". In China, the zest that happened in East Europe for "replacing the central planning with market and the privatization of enterprise does not exist. On the contrary, the market and private enterprises are merely supplements to the plan and state ownership. As the different reserved systems are receiving more and more rewards, Chinese market reform is bound to have path dependence that the decision-maker is still subject to available theories and ideology[7]". Western left-winger Nate Winst says that the reason why China can wall itself off from the economic crisis in capitalist world owes to "the more direct and effective regulation and control of the state. And China can apply such direct regulation and control because the state-owned economy and planned regulation haven't been replaced but balanced and adjusted by private ownership and marketization"[8].

5 Qin Xuan: *International Perspective of the China Model & Also on the Socialism with Chinese Characteristics and its International Influences*. Journal of Renmin University of China, 2008 (4) .

6 Xu Juezai: *Views of Foreign Scholars on Socialism with Chinese Characteristics*. Studies on The Socialism With Chinese Characteristics, 2008 (3) .

7 Xu Juezai: *Views of Foreign Scholars on Socialism with Chinese Characteristics*. Studies on The Socialism With Chinese Characteristics, 2008 (3) .

8 Fan Chunyan: *Disputes and Enlightment on Socialism with Chinese Characteristics of Western Left-wingers in Recent Years*. Foreign Theoretical Trends, 2011 (7) .

These scholars explain the feature of Chinese market economy in different languages and ways. Like what they have said, when Chinese government emphasizes the function of market, it never slides to the idea of omnipotent market or neo-liberalism of market worship, that is to say, market fundamentalism has some influences in China but never takes up the dominant place. China has developed the Chinese reform on marketization under the lead of the CPC, combining the market economy which is regarded as a kind of resources allocation with the value target of socialism and calling its market economy system "socialist market economy". Integrating market with plan, China insists on the macroscopic readjustment and control of the government on market. These characteristics have ensured that China can escape both "government failure" and "market failure" in the development of economy. As some foreign scholars have pointed out, whether Third World countries can really learn experience of how to develop market economy from China all depends on whether they can understand and apply these characteristics formed in the process of China developing market economy.

While implementing marketization, another reform that matches it is developing intensely, which is privatization, viz. private economy. Private economy, opening-up policy and market mechanism are three factors for the rapid economic growth of China. But if the Third World countries who wholeheartedly want to learn from China regard China's developing private economy as just privatizing state-operated economy, they are turning down their head and are bound to fail to realize their expected effect. The Chinese government has had the experience that the previous state-owned sector was so huge that it led to the low economic efficiency and benefits, thus a reform on state-owned economy was of great need. However, the government didn't negate state-owned economy completely, neither did they carry out a wild economic reform focusing on privatization. Instead, the government only changed the rigid model of the previous state-owned economy to make it adapt to the new environment all the time.

Public ownership remains dominant in China and is protected by the constitution and laws. With public ownership playing the dominant role, China introduces and encourages diverse forms of ownership including privately-owned, joint-venture and foreign-funded ownership, etc..

After the middle of 1990s, the economic reform of "retaining the large, releasing the small", a reform program with great strategic significance, was carried out on previous state-owned enterprises in China. By "retaining the large", China had reorganized large state-owned enterprises. Meanwhile, by "releasing the small" China had provided incentive mechanism through privatization for small and medium-sized ones. The most successful policy of China is the one implemented on land ownership. With the establishment of market economic system, calls for complete marketization of land elements and the state' waiving the control of land grow rapidly. However, Chinese government didn't blindly follow those calls. Since China is one of the countries with smallest per capita arable land in the world, what is most likely to happen if privatizing land ownership is that land will be collected by the minority in a moment and most farmers will fall into poverty when losing their land. The policy on separation of land ownership and land-use right implemented properly by Chinese governments not only ensures that the state are able to control the land ownership but also protects the farmers for possessing land-use right.[9] Many people all over the world admire the realization of the world's largest urbanization, the world's biggest real estate market, the accomplishment of the homeownership rates even higher than those of the developed countries, the world's biggest high-speed rail network and the world's second biggest expressway network of China, but what they must know is that all those achievements are closely related to the right policy on the issue of land ownership carried out by Chinese governments. Currently, China has built a Mixed or

9 Zhang Wei. *Chinese Shock-the Rise of a 'Civilisational State'*. Chin. ed., Shanghai People's Publishing House, 2011, p. 109.

Compound Ownership Structure, in which the public ownership plays a dominant role with other diverse forms of ownerships co-existing and developing forward. This kind of structure survives the financial crisis and reveals its advantages, therefore, as the structure grows sophisticated, it will have greater influences on developing countries.

CHAPTER FOUR

The Demonstration Effects of the Chinese Path on Ideology and Culture

Recently, more and more foreigners, especially dignitaries and scholars from Third World countries, try to figure out secrets of China's high-speed development from its politics and economics but mainly from ideology and culture, so which in accordance becomes a possible access for them who also endeavor to learn and master experiences of China. Besides demonstrative effects on politics and economics, the Chinese path also exerts increasingly significant influences on ideology and culture. On that very year Joshua Cooper Ramo summarized characteristics of the Chinese path from the same perspective in the famous article about the "Beijing Consensus". He defined it as "to carry out innovation and experiment arduously and proactively; to defend country's territory and interests firmly; and to gather strength as a resort thoroughly and deliberately".[1] Indeed, the essence of the Chinese path is a kind of ideological and cultural mode in the first place. It is clearly known to Chinese government and people that achievements made by China in politics and economics in those years are all based on the foundation of ideological and cultural changes and there will be no radical renovation in both fields without a shift in ideology and culture or thinking mode. As the Modernization Drive in Western societies is also first stimulated by ideological enlightenment, same situation recurs in China. Try to imagine whether China can still make such achievements today if it

1 Zhou Jianjun, etc: "*The meaning of China's Transformation: From Washington Consensus to Beijing Consensus*", Forum of World Economy and Politics, 2005 (1) .

has not reached a consensus on the debate over Criterion of Truth, if it has not rehabilitated ideological line of seeking truth from facts, if it has not introspected profoundly the question that "what is socialism and how to build socialism" and made clear that it is still at primary stage of socialism, and if it has not reassessed the international situation and recognized the fact that peace and development are the themes of our times. Today, there is a fashionable and integrated system of expressions in China, which apparently doesn't belong to those "Western Discourses". Unlike in some Third World countries "Western Discourses" can be seen or heard everywhere which makes people feel like having arrived in some western countries, streams of words and expressions with Chinese characteristics are more usual in China, because China creates its own words without conceding western words system as the top.[2] These words with Chinese characteristics, which belong to language expressions only, reveal China's unique ideology and culture. China's unparalleled expressions and its foundation, China's distinct ideology and culture, both exert their roles as integral parts of the Chinese path and Chinese experience.

What impresses the world most is China's attitude toward its traditional culture in its achievements on ideology and culture, therefore demonstrative effects of this field should also symbolize how to treat this matter properly at first. There is no doubt that China's rise essentially is a development from pre-modern time to modern time, and from agricultural civilization to industrial civilization, which belongs to one part of whole human modernization process. As human's modernization process originates from western societies, it's reasonable for some scholars to regard the restructuring process of modern society as the process of Westernization and Europeanization. People define China's modernization as "later" and "outside" modernization which reveals the fact that it's stimulated by influences from western countries and consider western modernization as a

2 Zhang Weiwei: *The China Wave: Rise of a Civilizational State*, Chin. Ed., Shanghai People's Publishing House, 2011, p. 125.

reference. Given these conditions, China is definitely confronted with such a problem: Does modernization refers to separation from China's tradition? Does traditional civilization has completely been turned to a burden for modern Chinese who aims to enter a society with modern civilization? Chinese government replies that exceedingly long history and significantly profound cultural accumulation of China will not become a burden to Chinese people but vital ideological and cultural resources in the process toward modernization. They successfully combine national tradition and modernization together, and turn splendid part of conventional heritage into motivation and spiritual stimulation in modernization drive. In world history, there are about over twenty ancient civilizations but nearly all of them are interrupted except Chinese culture. As the only country who maintains history and cultural continuation, languages and cultural traditions, the symbol of China, has never been observed discontinuity in 5000 years.[3] Chinese government believes that continuity and uniqueness of China's culture demonstrates its ability of self-creation and self-renovation and that incredible traditional civilization has unified Chinese nation's self-driven pursuits of spirits and their durable legacy. This is the most valuable and unparalleled historical legacy of our nation and is urgently needed by China in modern times who endeavors to achieve its modernization. On the basis of preliminary assessment of China's traditional culture, the government works hard to protect basic parts of national civilization and to improve exploration and explication of values behind outstanding traditional culture and ideologies, aiming to help many factors in traditional culture achieve transformation, revive and play a positive role in the process toward modernization. Therefore, while those traditional cultures encourage Chinese people to move forward as spiritual forces, Chinese path is also attached tightly to previous traditions of China in carrying on cultural legacy of ancestors. With the rapid rising of China, Chinese

3 Guo Wanchao: "*Science Positioning of Socialism with Chinese Characteristics*", New Horizon College English, 2009 (1) .

traditional culture has also achieved unprecedented rejuvenation. Gennady Zyuganov, the General Secretary of Communist Party of Russia, summarizes Chinese path with such equation: China's success = socialism + Chinese tradition + state - controlled market + modernized technologies and management.[4] In this equation, the inheritance of national convention takes an extra significance in Chinese Path. Zhang Weiwei draws a conclusion on the rise of China: Unlike a common country, China's rise reflects the great rejuvenation of a continuous culture with 5000 years, and the rise of a "civilized country". He even said that "China's ruling party today is still the group with 'Mandate of Heaven' who is committed to the mission of renewal of Chinese nation" and that "the party still inherits political traditions of Confucianism in ancient China which represents the whole interests of people".[5] Absolutely, the strategy adopted to the inheritance of traditional culture does not only follow "Plagiarism", with which traditional conventions will not exert such significant influences on the process of China's rise. So Chinese government makes a correct baseline, "take the essence and discard the dregs, and make the past serve the present and weed through the old to bring forth the new", and endeavors to transform traditional culture to modernized part.

One more point must be noticed is that the inheritance to tradition emphasized by the government also includes to tradition of China's ruling party. China's leaders recently put forward meaningful rejection to fallacy covering the period of reform and opening up, which means denying behaviors after that period under the principles of previous times, and vice versa. At the beginning of the times of new development, some countries deny their past completely as if they will not make new history and prove today's correctness without

4 Chang Zongyao: *"About the World Significance of Socialism with Chinese Characteristics"*, Theoretical Exploration, 2008 (4) .

5 Zhang Weiwei: *Chinese Shock-the Rise of a "Civilisational State"*, Shanghai People's Publishing House, 2011, p. 137.

choosing this way, in a stark contrast to China. Some western scholars, especially some left-wing scholars, see Chinese government's inheritance to tradition and continuity of its history as resources and dynamics to help China move forward steadily and rapidly. The representative personage of World System School Amin said that "achievements made by China in the past decades, including economic balanced growth, large-scale urbanization, and extraordinary learning ability on technologies, are all described as miracles, which will never happen without basis built by renovations".[6] Other figures of the School, like Giovanni Arrighi, also discuss interrelationships between reforms and revolutionary legacies from different perspectives. They believe that Chinese ruling party's awareness of it and they carrying it out contribute to the great achievements of China today.

Aside from correct attitude toward its traditional ideology and culture, a country needs to handle foreign cultures properly for its rapid development, and China's relevant experience is worthy of imitation by other Third World countries. There is no doubt that China's opening up will lead to the inundation of foreign civilizations, including not only foreign capitals and technologies, but also ideologies and cultures from overseas, especially from western societies. In face of different cultures, Chinese government handles them positively, instead of forbidding and banning them as threats. There is an old Chinese saying that "where there are three men walking together, one of them must be qualified to be my teacher". As a nation with positive attitude toward knowledge, Chinese government leads people to be motivated to learn western ideologies and cultures. In this process, Chinese people show their powerful ability to learn and absorb civilizations with open attitude and positive spirits. So we can say that China's rise is closely related to the process of learning and absorbing ideologies and cultures from foreign land, especially from

6 Fan Chunyan: "*Disputes and Enlightment on Socialism with Chinese Characteristics of Western Left-wingers in Recent Years*", Foreign Theoretical Trends, 2011 (7) .

the west. These outstanding spiritual achievements applied in China's modernization drive is conducive to developing ideological resources, and Chinese path will therefore better indicate the history of zeitgeist and world cultural development. Deng Xiaoping formulated the concept that "To perform strongly ,compared with capitalism, socialism must assimilate and refer to various cultural achievements of human society, as well as advanced operation mode and management which reflect modernized productive disciplines of other countries including developed capitalist states."[7] Ideas that "various cultural achievements of human society" emphasized by Deng absolutely also cover the fruition of ideology and culture made in western world.

It can be argued that simply attributing China's success in dealing with Western ideology and culture these years to a modest learning attitude is far from enough. It is worth noting that China does not lose itself in the process of learning from others. Therefore, it is reasonable that nowadays some scholars in the Third World countries focus on analyzing why some countries completely lose themselves in the process of learning from the West but China does not. The famous philosopher Russell once wrote in his book "The Problem of China": "I believe that glorious achievement featured by the blend of positive Chinese and Western civilization can be produced if Chinese people can freely absorb the advantages and abandon the shortcomings of the western civilization." What Russell predicted at that time is now realized in today's China. We succeed in absorbing advantages and abandoning shortcomings in dealing with Western ideology and culture. The Chinese government is soberly aware that there is good stuff but also a lot of dross in Western ideology and culture. Therefore, we should actively learn the good and firmly refuse the bad. While emphasizing the need to boldly absorb and learn from classic Western ideology and culture, Chinese leaders have repeatedly opposed that some leading powers interfere with other countries' internal affairs

7 *Selected Works of Deng Xiaoping*, Chin. ed., People's Publishing House, Beijing, 1995, p. 373.

under the guise of "democracy", "freedom" and "human rights". The Chinese government often warns itself by living examples: some countries blindly introduced Western ideology and culture, and suffered from serious social and political consequences. The Chinese government leads Chinese people, the intelligentsia in particular, to judge Western ideology and culture with their own eyes and selectively accept some of them. In China, it is good to see that we accept and absorb excellent stuff in Western ideology and culture; in the meantime, we criticize and resist decadent stuff without hesitation. This approach is indeed enlightening to the Third World countries.

China today has formed its own unique ideology and culture through correctly facing both traditional and foreign ideologies and cultures. What really has a strong impact on the Third World countries is the unique ideology and culture itself as well as the thinking pattern formed on its basis. As some foreign scholars put it, if we cannot understand and grasp China's currently popular thinking pattern based on certain ideology and culture, we cannot fundamentally learn from China's experience. Learning from China should begin with studying these thinking patterns. Here we list a number of thinking patterns that foreign scholars, especially scholars in the Third World countries, are concerned about:

First, being pragmatic. China enjoys a tradition of "seeking truth from facts" which is not confined to the advocacy of honesty in doing research. Generally, it also demands a pragmatic attitude in deeds to explore their nature. With the unprecedented promotion of such a tradition in the last three decades since the reform and opening up, being pragmatic has become a common mode of thinking among Chinese. Zhang Weiwei while summarizing the eight characteristics of the Chinese path, listed "practical reason" as the top one and while summarizing the eight ideas that China "might influences the world", he listed "seeking truth from facts" as the top idea. His choice is reasonable. China didn't initiate the reform and opening up until it was fully convinced that "Practice is the sole criterion for testing truth". This idea sounds empty and philosophical, but in fact it's a very extensive and effective principle that has helped China shun away from numerous political and economic traps. Under its guidance, China has drawn on the experience and advantages of the development models of all times both at home and abroad without being shackled by any established theories and ideologies. Some foreign scholars use the word "pragmatism" to sum up the ideological and cultural characteristic of the Chinese Path. The Japanese scholar Watanabe Toshio thinks that the most remarkable feature of the reform launched by Deng Xiaoping is "experimental pragmatism". The German scholar Thomas Heberer considers "ideologies being gradually replaced by pragmatism" the most important part in China's social transformation.[8] These scholars emphasize that in order to create a better life for hundreds of millions of Chinese people, China follows the saying "It doesn't matter whether a cat is black or white as long as it catches mice". According to them, the saying is just another expression of "The end justifies the means" and "It bears no difference with the pragmatism prevalent in Europe and America".[9] Although it's a misconception for foreign scholars to equate the Chinese mode of thinking of being pragmatic with pragmatism popular in the West, but they unveil the truth that China has broken away from political romanticism. The Chinese scholar Lu Ming holds the opinion that "the tests of the system" embody the Chinese mode of thinking of being pragmatic. He puts forward that the most valuable experience drawn from China's economic transformation and development is to test the system like "crossing the river by feeling the stones" and such tests can be found in the various fields and stages of the reform and opening up. "Compared with Commonwealth of Independent States and eastern European countries, the core feature of China's

8 Xu Juezai: *Foreign Scholars' Views on Socialism with Chinese Characteristics*, Studies on Socialism with Chinese Characteristics, 2008 (3) .

9 Xu Juezai: *Foreign Scholars' Views on Socialism with Chinese Characteristics*, Studies on Socialism with Chinese Characteristics, 2008 (3) .

gradual economic transformation is the tests of the system." He thinks that China's success is attributed to "the consensus on development + necessary governmental execution + political competitiveness + effective stimulus + the tests of the system"[10], among which "the tests of the system" plays an important role.

Second, balance seeking. Zhang Weiwei ever commented: "The most distinctive feature of China's development in the past 30 years is moderateness. By learning the lesson from the past and stepping onto the path of steady and solid reform, China is rising rapidly. Indeed, the rising has brought new problems. However, even if the problems are many, for most Chinese, it is better to solve these problems under the golden doctrine of "Mean" and "harmony without uniformity". This is also the principle practiced by Chinese in governing the large and complex society in Chinese history."[11] Just like what Zhang Weiwei said, China in these years has put the doctrine of Mean to the full play. The so called "Mean" attaches great importance to balancing, combination, coexistence, harmony and coordination. Scholars like Xie Yongkuan holds that the doctrine employed by the Chinese is fundamentally different from the popular doctrine in Western countries. Such difference has brought changes to China in at least three aspects: first, compared with the economic system in capitalist countries, which overemphasizes individual interests and free flow of capital, China's economic system, characterized by "combination" and realized by balancing, has provided institutional support for the benign interaction between the whole society and the individual; second, compared with political system in capitalist countries, which overemphasizes confrontation, check and balance and competition, China's political system, characterized by unification, concerted effort and coordination, has inherited and upgraded the great power

10 Lu Ming: *Appropriate Institution, Economic Growth and Balanced Development - Development Path of China as a Big Country and Its Implication for the World*, Academic Monthly, 2008 (6) .

11 Zhang Weiwei: *China Shock - the Rise of a "Civilized Nation"*, Shanghai: Shanghai People's Publishing House, 2011, p. 141.

of social cohesion, balancing and regeneration embodied in our traditional national system; third, compared with logic "survival of the fittest" in capitalist countries, China's system featuring harmonious coexistence, has nurtured the bases of psychological identification, basic principle of behavior and core values, all of them have inherited Chinese traditional wisdom of survival, conformed the law of development and met the requirement of the times.[12] As one of the key guiding ideologies of socialism with Chinese characteristics, the Scientific Outlook on Development was put forward to formulate the basic strategies for comprehensive, coordinated and sustainable development. Obviously, this has indicated the employment of "balancing". Chinese leaders have defined "harmonious society" as the essential attribute of socialism with Chinese characteristics and profoundly expounded the internal relationship between socialism with Chinese characteristics and the construction of a harmonious society. Obviously, without balance-seeking thinking patterns, there would be no concept of "harmonious society". Admittedly, China is still on its way to modernization and it will unavoidably be confronted with dilemma in this stage. However, the reason why Chinese government has not been bogged down in the dilemma, to some extent, is that Chinese leaders have followed the doctrine of "balancing", being good at keeping the opposite sides tense and keeping balance in confrontation. Take their attitude to capital for example. In order to promote productivity, Chinese government will make use of it and develop it. However, in order to protect the ecosystem, the capital will be restricted and regulated. In this way, China has thus been able to maintain tension between the use of capital and the limitation of capital and find a balance between economic development and environmental protection.

Third, pursuit of innovation. "Innovation" can be regarded as the

12 Xie Yongkuan: *A Multidimensional Perspective on the Advantages of the Socialism System with Chinese Characteristics under the Background of International Economic Crisis*, Theoretical Exploration, 2012 (2).

most commonly-seen word in today's China. "Pursuit of innovation" is the most prominent thinking pattern of Chinese people. Ramo brought up with "Beijing Consensus", namely "three theorems about how to organize the place of a developing country in the world". "The first theorem" he mentioned is "repositioning the value of innovation, that is, using innovation to reduce the friction losses of reform". This shows that from Ramo's point of view, the core content of the so-called "Chinese model" and "Chinese experience" is active innovation. The Chinese government and Chinese people understand that China's national conditions are unique. China's development is faced with unique internal and external environment. Neither the traditional Soviet model adopted by socialist countries nor the American model, Rhineland model and Japanese model advocated by capitalist countries is suitable for China's development due to its national conditions. China must boldly innovate in practice, combining its national conditions with the reality of socialist development, the features of globalization and informatization in our age and useful experience of developed countries' development mode. Only in this way can we find a development mode suitable for our own features.[13] Jiang Zemin said: "Innovation is the soul of a nation's progress, inexhaustible force for a country's prosperity, and source for a political party's vitality."[14]

Over the past few decades, China has been carrying forward the spirit of exploration and trials, and vigorously promoting innovation. Looking at China's politics, economy, ideology and culture, all of them are products of Chinese people's continuous innovation in practice. Chinese people's courage in innovation and practice presents to the whole world, especially the Third World countries the truth: only an innovative ruling party and an innovative country can mobilize

13 Chang Zongyao: *The World Significance of the Road to Socialism with Chinese Characteristics*, Theoretical Exploration, 2008 (4) .

14 *Selected Works of Jiang Zemin*, Eng. ed., People's Publishing House, Beijing, Vol. III, 2006, p. 537.

the enthusiasm of its people, handle all kinds of complex situations, and constantly break new ground, thus constantly broadening its modernization road and vitalizing the modernization course featured by its characteristics.

Part Three

The Chinese Path and the World Socialist Movement

To study the significance of the Chinese path to the world, it is essential to explore its impact on the world socialist movement. The Chinese path, namely, socialism with Chinese characteristics, is deeply rooted in the soil of contemporary China and at the same time sticks to the basic principles of scientific socialism. Socialism itself is a worldwide historical process. Socialism with Chinese characteristics, as an important part of the historical process of world socialism, inevitably influences the world socialist movement. An important aspect of the historical value of the Chinese path is that it opens up a new realm of scientific socialism and represents a new threshold of the development of the international socialist movement. Socialism with Chinese characteristics has not only developed but also saved the world socialist movement. It is exactly the socialism of Chinese characteristics that revived the world socialist movement, opens up a new world for the development of contemporary world socialism, and speeds up the world socialist development. Socialism with Chinese characteristics has in fact become the pillar of contemporary world socialist movement. The theory of socialism with Chinese characteristics is not only the lighthouse to guide the advancement of Chinese socialism, but also the most brilliant chapter in the theory of contemporary world scientific socialism. If Marx and Engels transformed socialism from utopia to science, Lenin developed socialism from theory to practice, then the socialism with Chinese characteristics realized the developing process of socialism from establishment to construction. The value of socialism with Chinese characteristics to the world socialist movement can never be overestimated too much.

CHAPTER ONE
Leading the World Socialist Movement out of the Trough

When the Chinese people had just been on the path of socialism with Chinese characteristics, Deng Xiaoping predicted that the opening up of this path would have profound significance on the international socialist movement. According to Deng, this path "is more important in showing mankind that socialism is the inevitable course and is better than capitalism", "We will make use of the last score of this century and the first half of the next, which is seventy years in total, to prove to the world that socialism is better than capitalism. With the practice of developing productive force and science and technology, as well as the achievements in the construction of spiritual and material civilization, we will prove that socialist system is superior to capitalist system, and let the people in developed capitalist countries realize that socialism is indeed better than capitalism." The practice of the Chinese path over the past few decade has fully verified the prediction made by Deng Xiaoping. Although Deng Xiaoping has repeatedly stressed that China should "keep a low profile" and should not take the lead and carry the flag, China's low profile can not conceal its growing achievements made by Chinese people under the banner of socialism with Chinese characteristics. At the same time, the growing significance of the path of socialism with Chinese characteristics chosen by Chinese people to the world socialist movement also can not be concealed.

People of China chose the path of socialism with Chinese characteristics when the world socialist movement was in times of distress. In the late 1980s and early 1990s, the Radical Social Changes in Soviet Union and Eastern Europe had brought unprecedented setbacks to the world socialist movement. First of all, the communist regimes which originally belonged to the Soviet Union and Eastern Europe camps had been overturned, thus the world socialist domain had been significantly reduced; secondly, the world's communist parties, even some socialist parties, had suffered a lot, many forced to dissolve or change their nature, while the rest left in a difficult situation. There was no doubt that the world socialist movement was at a low ebb. "Socialism has failed", "the history of socialism has ended", "the socialist regime has been buried in the grave of history" and other words spread far and wide and caused a great clamour. The declaration of the death of socialism in *The End of History* written by the American right-wing scholar Fukuyama is familiar to us, while the presumptuous assertion of former US President Nixon are still ringing in the ears. Nixon declared in Beyond Peace: "As history has abandoned communism, it has also abandoned communists." "The twenty-first century can be a century in which the majority of people of the world enjoy economic freedom. The twentieth century provides us with four major experiences from the economic aspect:

Communism is not working; socialism is not working; state control is not working; only free market can fully liberate individuals' creativity and lead to progress." In the face of the major setbacks of the world socialist movement and the great clamor of international capitalism, many people began to doubt that China may follow the footsteps of countries like the Soviet Union and embrace Western capitalism. However, the Chinese Communist Party maintained sober mind and led the Chinese people to withstand the severe challenges posed by the domestic political turmoil and the Radical Changes in Soviet Union and Eastern Europe.

Rejecting both the old and rigid closed-door policy and any attempt to abandon socialism, the Chinese Communist Party led people to break a new path of socialism with Chinese characteristics. The banner of socialism still stands firm in China, and will be held high in the future.

While the world socialist movement is still in a slump, China has demonstrated a thriving situation of socialism. Besides sticking to socialism at home, China has also revitalized socialism of the whole world. China's achievements are made under the banner of socialism and the leadership of the Chinese Communist Party, so they are definitely linked to socialism and are recorded in the history of world socialist movement. The path of socialism with Chinese characteristics has "reversed the slumping trend of world socialist movement in the second half of the twentieth century", "maintained the prestige of socialism in the whole world" and saved "the socialist ship on the brink of distress". The path of socialism with Chinese characteristics has led the world socialist movement out of the trough by avoiding the retrogression caused by the collapse of some socialist countries, thus breaking new ground for the development of the contemporary world socialist movement. The path of socialism with Chinese characteristics has been a "shot in the arm" for the contemporary world socialist movement in distress, so that it is gradually revitalized and strengthened. Socialism with Chinese characteristics has greatly boosted confidence of socialism worldwide and enabled people of the world to see the hope of socialism during its hard times. Due to the rise of the path of socialism with Chinese characteristics, people of the world has come to realize that the Radical Changes in Soviet Union and Eastern Europe don't mean the end of the evolution from capitalism to socialism. The Chinese path has reshaped people's understanding of socialism. The path of socialism with Chinese characteristics has in fact become the starting point of a new force for the world socialist movement, providing it with a way out. The success of socialism with Chinese characteristic is in sharp contrast to the failure of the socialist theory and practice in the Soviet Union and Eastern Europe. In a certain sense, it is the "rebirth of socialism" in China. It is exactly the "rebirth" that has boosted the vitality, attractiveness and development of socialism in the whole world. Just as Deng Xiaoping said: "As long as China stands still, there will be one fifth of the world population adhering to socialism", "As long as Chinese socialism stands firm, socialism will always stand still in the world".

With twists and turns, the world socialist movement of twentieth century has experienced a high tide, a low tide, another high tide, another low tide, and then a high tide again. The first high tide was marked by the October Revolution, which transformed socialism from ideal into reality, from theory to social system. The October Revolution shook the whole world. Under its influence, the proletarian revolution was set off across Europe, and the Communist Party emerged one after another in other continents. The socialist movement extended from Europe to the world, becoming a worldwide movement. In the mid-1920s, the failure of the armed uprising conducted by some Central and Western European proletariat who followed the October Revolution, as well as the failure of the Chinese Revolution in 1927, caused the world socialist movement at the first high tide to hit the rock bottom.

The second peak of the twentieth century world socialist movement was marked by the success of the Chinese Revolution and the formation of the world socialist system. After World WarII, thanks to the victory if the anti-fascist war, fifteen countries which accounted for one third of world's population and one fourth of world's territory took the path of socialism, thus forming a powerful world socialist system.

The success of the Chinese Revolution, in particular, fundamentally changed the balance between the power of world socialism and capitalism, pushing the second upsurge of the world socialist movement to its peak. Under the influence of this new upsurge, the national liberation movement in Asia, Africa and Latin America was irresistible, and some third world countries which had gained national independence claimed to take the path of socialism. The second upsurge of the world socialist movement actually began to turn to its low ebb in the 1960s, and plunged to the trough between 1980s and 1990s.

It is the socialism with Chinese characteristics that has led the world socialist movement out of the second trough. The beginning of the path of socialism with Chinese characteristics marks a new starting point of the revival of the world socialist movement, and is to some extent a sign of its another upsurge. Besides rejuvenating the Chinese nation, the path of socialism with Chinese characteristics has also revitalized the world socialist movement. The path of socialism with Chinese characteristics and the rejuvenation of the Chinese nation have, to a large extent, contributed to the revival of the world socialist movement.

Socialism with Chinese characteristics is based on China's national condition, but it is also an important achievement of the socialist practice worldwide. It has an important place in the history of world socialist movement because it reflects pattern of socialist development. Socialism with Chinese characteristics is deeply rooted in the soil of contemporary China, and in the meantime sticks to the universal value of socialism. As a result, it is not simply socialism with Chinese characteristics, but also scientific socialism, which definitely diversifies the world socialism. Socialism with Chinese characteristics has an inseparable inherent connection with the world socialist movement. The theory of socialism with Chinese characteristics is the product of not only the development of socialism with Chinese characteristics, but also the development of contemporary world socialism. The problems settled by socialism with Chinese characteristics belong to not only China, but also socialist movement in the whole world. The theory of socialism with Chinese characteristics not only reveals the law of socialist construction under China's special circumstances, but also reflects some essential and universal law of contemporary socialist development.

Therefore, the theoretical and practical significance of the path of socialism with Chinese characteristics will go beyond border and extend to the whole world. Socialism with Chinese characteristics has in fact become a banner of the advancement of the world socialist movement.

It has been universally acknowledged that socialism with Chinese characteristics leads the world socialist movement out of the trough. In April 25th, 2003, the German magazine *Our Times* published an article entitled "China 2003 - Towards the Path of Socialism", which pointed out: "China's development has shown people a way out of the world dominated by capitalism, and has given people hope for socialism. "Titarenko, a member of the Russian Academy of Sciences, said, "When socialism was in the face of serious crisis and strategic retreat, the Chinese Communist Party shouldered the responsibility to reserve and develop socialism in accordance with the requirements of the times and the new historical opportunities. The theory of building socialism with Chinese characteristics proposed by Deng Xiaoping prevented socialism from disappearing on the stage of history." Another Russian scholar Yakovlev believed that socialism with Chinese characteristics not only reversed the plunging trend of world socialism in the late 20th century, but would also exert immeasurable impact on the development of socialism in the 21st century. Ni·Popov, a Bulgarian theorist, said, "The model which is currently chosen and practiced in China, is the only one to save and build socialism, and the only one which is correct and promising." The Communist Party of Vietnam made the following statement on socialism with Chinese characteristics:

> Internationally, the success of reform and opening up has saved and developed socialism, which is a significant contribution in the history of the development of world socialist revolution. Since the socialist system in the Soviet Union and Eastern Europe has already collapsed, if the system in China also collapses, then socialism will disappear from the world, and the world socialist movement will plunge into centuries of darkness. The success of building socialism in China proves the superiority of socialism to the whole world, refutes all kinds of distorting and slandering arguments

from hostile forces, and restores people's confidence in socialism.

First, let us take a look at how the other socialist countries draw upon the experience of Chinese path. These countries follow China's example, endeavor to explore suitable socialist system for their national condition, and clearly put forward to take the path with their own national characteristics. For instance, during the meeting with former Chinese President Jiang Zemin, the leader of Cuban Communist Party Fidel Castro said:

"Cuba is practicing reform and opening up steadily, building socialism with Cuban characteristics." These countries follow Chinese society's ownership and distribution structure, namely, the basic economic system of keeping public ownership as the mainstay and allowing diverse forms of ownership to develop side by side, and the diversified structure in which distribution according to work is leading factor and many distribution methods coexist. Over the years, the non-public economy in Vietnam, Cuba and other socialist countries has been developing at a fast pace. China's national development strategy, that is, focusing on economic construction and fulfilling national modernization through reform and opening up, has also exerted significant impact on these countries, as Laos and Vietnam have proposed the focus transfer of the Party and the state. China's approach to establish a socialist market economy and boost socialism with the help of market has been generally accepted by these countries. Vietnam has declared that it will transfer from a planned economy to a market economy.

Secondly, let us take a look at how the developing countries which have not yet taken the path of socialism follow China's example and speed up their process of replacing capitalism with socialism. The path of socialism with Chinese characteristics has powerful demonstration effect on these developing countries. Deeply attracted by Chinese experience, these countries began to follow "Beijing model" instead of "Washington model", which means they chose socialism instead of capitalism. Socialism with Chinese characteristics shows them the essence of socialism -- liberating and expanding the productive forces, eliminating exploitation and polarization, and ultimately realizing common prosperity. This kind of social system is obviously superior to the capitalist system, thus provoking these countries' pursuit of socialism. By drawing upon China's successful experience, they develop national economy and pay attention to people's livelihood. By following China's example in the field of politics, economy, ideology and culture, some fundamental elements of socialism were emerged in these countries.

Finally, let us take a look at how the people in today's developed capitalist countries, especially the leftists, are inspired by the Chinese path. Many people in these countries, especially the leftists, have changed their skepticism towards the Chinese path into high appraisal of socialism with Chinese characteristics. They place more and more hope of realizing communism on China, which still adheres to socialism. The success of the path of socialism with Chinese characteristics encourages their faith in the goal of communism and provides them with practical basis for their adherence to communism. Under the influence of the success of the Chinese path, they reexamine the question whether socialism is superior to capitalism, and lead anti-capitalist movements whose fever keeps rising. These movements against capitalism are an important part of socialist movement in developed capitalist countries. The socialist movement in those countries has always been closely related to the success of socialist countries, for the smooth development of socialist countries will exert positive impact on the socialist movement in the developed capitalist countries. Therefore, the Chinese path has played a vital role in the revival of the Communist Party in the developed capitalist countries.

It must be pointed out that the third peak of the world socialist movement which is marked by the emergence of the path of socialism with Chinese characteristics is different from the previous two peaks.

If we only look at the extension of the movement, then it extends less obviously than the previous ones. In other words, at the climax of the world socialist movement, there were not so many countries that joined the socialist camp at once like the previous two movements. If simply judging from this point, we can not say the world socialist movement has escaped from the trough and is moving toward the peak. However, considering that the key to understand it is that the peak of this world socialist movement is not mainly manifested by its extension, but its intension, the movement of socialism is now at its third peak. The path of socialism with Chinese characteristics has not only improved the world socialist movement in quantity, but also in quality. The path of socialism with Chinese characteristics gives the world socialism a new intension, enabling it to extend and develop in a new form, which to a large extent changes the tradition and process of the world socialist movement. Instead of simply copying traditional socialism, socialism with Chinese characteristics thrives the innovation of traditional socialism theoretically and practically. Therefore, socialism with Chinese characteristics sticks to and promotes the world socialist movement through innovation.

The reason why socialism with Chinese characteristics keeps moving forward in such a difficult situation is not sticking to the old way, but continuously finding new direction through practice. It is exactly this new direction that exerts a huge positive impact on the world socialist movement. The successful practice and theoretical innovation of the path of socialism with Chinese characteristics shows that there is a path towards revival for socialism. Just imagine, if China is still confined to the socialist framework of the Soviet model, with the dogmatic understanding and utopian illusion for socialism, without seeking for new theoretical exploration and practical innovation for the development of the path of socialism with Chinese characteristics, how can China form its unique path for socialist development and exert such a huge influence on the world socialist movement? Though the third upsurge of the world socialist movement seems not so largescale as the previous two ones, its socialist vitality, attractiveness and competitiveness, which come from the success of socialism with Chinese characteristics, are not inferior to any previous ones'. Due to the success of socialism with Chinese characteristics, the vitality of socialism has been presented to the world in an unprecedented degree. China has made itself the second largest economy in the world in such a short period, and has demonstrated its "unique competitiveness, efficiency and adaptability" when coping with the US financial crisis and European debt crisis. Therefore, many foreign politicians and scholars come to realize the superiority of socialism with Chinese characteristics and of the socialist system. The path of socialism with Chinese characteristics is a modern social choice, which is different from the development path of capitalism. The path of socialism with Chinese characteristics has successfully created the "national form" of socialist construction and development, which to some extent is a new form of contemporary socialism. This new form undoubtedly indicates that the world socialist movement has come to a new historical stage.

CHAPTER TWO
Settling the Problems of the World Socialist Movement

Unlike the prediction made by the founders of Marxism, the world socialist movement of the 20th century did not first succeed in the developed capitalist countries with high productivity and advanced civilization. Instead, it was those less advanced and civilized countries that first took the path of socialism. However, after seizing power and establishing socialist system, how these countries with backward economy and culture built, consolidated and developed socialism remained a problem of the world socialist movement in that era. Lenin once said, "Our revolution is easy to start but hard to continue, while that of the Western Europe is just the opposite." Here "to start" meant to seize the political power and establish socialist system, and "to continue" obviously meant to consolidate and develop socialism. This showed that the founder of the world's first socialist country had already realized that in a backward country, it was difficult to consolidate and develop the socialist system after the establishment. The Radical Changes in Soviet Union and Eastern Europe in the late 1980s and early 1990s had not only confirmed the existence of this worldwide problem, but also presented it more acutely in front of those who supported and upheld socialism.

Zhang Shujun regarded "what is socialism and how to build socialism" as "the question for the world" which "was closely related to human destiny and was a great concern to the world, especially to the Communists". He believed that socialism with Chinese characteristics was the most scientific and influential answer to "the question for the world" at our time.. The value of socialism with Chinese characteristics to the world lied in ending some Western forces' prediction about the collapse of socialism, demonstrating the significant truth value of the basic principles of scientific socialism, and indicating the general trend of the development of human society. Just as he said, the world value of socialism with Chinese characteristics lied in scientifically answering the "the question for the world" about "what is socialism and how to build socialism". The beginning of the Chinese path helped the backward countries to consolidate and develop socialism after they had established the socialist system in the world socialist movement. The theoretical system of socialism with Chinese characteristics was constructed during the process of finding ways to build socialism for backward countries. The process of forming and perfecting the theory of socialism with Chinese characteristics was also the process of settling the backward countries' problem about building socialism. As the largest developing country in the world, China's exploration about building socialism under the context of economic ad cultural backwardness is universally and typically significant to the construction of socialism for the developing countries in the whole world.

Some people attribute the Radical Changes in Soviet Union and Eastern Europe in the late 1980s and early 1990s and the ensuing difficult situation of the world socialist movement to those backward countries' violating Marx's intention while building socialism. In other words, their way of building socialism is unreasonable and has original sin, which is a mistaken understanding. If we do not change people's wrong impression, we will not be able to understand the root cause of the collapse of socialist system in the Soviet Union and Eastern Europe, and we will also fail to fully understand the pioneering significance of the path of socialism with Chinese characteristics.

In fact, Lenin didn't violate Marxism either broadly or narrowly when he carried out the October Revolution and socialist revolution in the backward Eastern countries.

As it's known to all, in Marx's old age, he proposed that Russia and backward Eastern countries could cross the capitalist "Caudine Forks" and adopt socialism directly on the basis of his "new speciality" in the Russian land system, that is, the Asian production mode. Apparently, Marx's argument about the necessity and possibility of socialism did not come from the acuteness of the basic contradictions of capitalism. What Marx followed was another idea, revealing the law of social development: although Russia was a backward country with Asian production mode of the rural commune, as long as it was in the capitalist era, it could make use of the "best opportunity" provided by history to carry out socialist revolution, cross capitalist "Caudine Forks" and build socialism. The process the October Revolution was the process of crossing the capitalist "Caudine Forks", whose success partly proved Marx's assumption of building socialism in backward Eastern countries. The October Revolution provided China with Marxism-Leninism, which was in fact the successful example of crossing the capitalist "Caudine Forks" and embracing socialism in backward Eastern countries. The Chinese Communists, represented by Mao Zedong, eventually found the correct path to rejuvenate China by crossing the capitalist "Caudine Forks" and establishing socialism. Like the October Revolution, the success of the Chinese revolution also partly proved Marx's assumption of carrying out proletarian revolution in the backward Eastern countries.

Hence, the backward Eastern countries did not violate but follow the Marxist "dogma" when they crossed the capitalist "Caudine Forks" and established socialism directly. They were neither "unreasonable" nor "having original sin". So why did the socialism established by these backward countries later suffer serious setbacks or even collapses? The problem was that after establishing the socialist system, the leaders of these backward countries chose wrong paths and policies. Although Marx did not elaborate on the main features of socialism established after crossing the capitalist "Caudine Forks", it was certain that he held a strict distinction between socialism caused by the acuteness of the basic capitalist contradictions and socialism established after crossing the capitalist "Caudine Forks". He pointed out in particular that the latter could "skip all the terrible obstacles of capitalist production", but "draw on the achievements of capitalist production". That is to say, the main difference between the two kinds of socialism was that the former was "post-capitalist", which was established on the basis of "all the capitalist achievements", while the latter was "pre-capitalist", which was going to "draw on all the capitalist achievements" and was on the same level of capitalist production. However, the leaders of these countries, including Stalin in the Soviet Union and Mao Zedong in China, ignored the difference emphasized by Marx between the two kinds of socialism, confusing socialism established after crossing the capitalist "Caudine Forks", which was going to "draw on all the capitalist achievements", with socialism caused by the acuteness of the basic capitalist contradictions, which was built on the basis of "all the capitalist achievements". As the former was developed according to the model of the latter, socialism failed in the Soviet Union and Eastern Europe and was seriously frustrated in China. On the one hand, this showed that the setbacks and failures of socialism in the backward Eastern countries were not because of the lack of suitable condition for socialism or crossing "Caudine Forks", but should be attributed to the confusion of the two kinds of socialism, guiding the one which was going to "draw on all the capitalist achievements" according to the socialist model which was established on the basis of "all the capitalist achievements". On the other hand, this showed that in the world socialist movement, although the problem about how the backward countries could establish socialist system through revolution had been resolved, how they build socialism after establishing socialist system remained a problem.

With the beginning of the path of socialism with Chinese characteristics, that remaining problem was finally settled. The key of solving the problem was that the path of socialism with Chinese characteristics had a clear distinction between the two kinds of socialism. Deng Xiaoping emphasized that our current socialism had Chinese characteristics and was on the initial stage, because he wanted to distinguish it from the socialism in Marx's *Capital* and other works. The essence of the theory of socialism with Chinese characteristics is to guide the construction of Chinese socialism according to the socialist model established after crossing the capitalist "Caudine Forks", instead of the model formed due to the acuteness of the basic capitalist contradictions. At Marx's old age, he proposed to realize socialism in backward Eastern countries. Lenin and Mao Zedong has only achieved half of it, which is establishing socialist systems in the Soviet Union and China after crossing the capitalist "Caudine Forks". The other half of Marx's proposition, maybe a more important part, is to draw a distinction between the two kinds of socialism, thus guiding the construction of socialism according to the model established after crossing the capitalist "Caudine Forks", and realizing socialism and communism depicted in Marx's *Capital* and other works. Therefore, the Chinese path can also be taken. The theory of socialism with Chinese characteristics with the aim to draw a distinction between the two kinds of socialism has comprehensively carried out Marx's proposition of realizing socialism in backward Eastern countries, and has thus explored and found answers to the new challenging issue faced by Marxism currently.

Starting from drawing a distinction between the two kinds of socialism, the theory of socialism with Chinese characteristics determines the historical position of China's current developing stage. China's current socialism is the one established after crossing the capitalist "Caudine Forks" according to Marx.

Although it is called socialism, it is the same as the capitalist production mode in terms of the economic tasks, for they will both end in the socialism (called "classic socialism" by some) depicted in Marx's *Capital* and other works. In other words, they are both the means to realize industrialization, and will ultimately be replaced by classic socialism and communism. According to Marx's proposition at his old age about realizing socialism in backward Eastern countries, the main differences between the socialism established after crossing the capitalist "Caudine Forks" and the one caused by the acuteness of basic capitalist contradictions are as follows: the former is pre-capitalist, while the latter is post-capitalist; the former is going to "draw on all the capitalist achievements", while the latter is established on the basis of "all the capitalist achievements". The theory of socialism with Chinese characteristics is centered on how to "draw on all the capitalist achievements", no matter in terms of its discussion about the path of development, the stage of development, the fundamental task, the force of development for socialism or its illustration about the external condition, the strategy, the leadership and the reliance for socialism. Why did China carry out reform? Because China wanted to change its overly undiversified ownership structure and planned economic system which were not compatible with the "pre-capitalist" socialism, and the related political system of excessive concentration of power, and build the economic and political system which were suitable for the "pre-capitalist" socialism and could "draw on all the capitalist achievement" effectively. Why did China open up? Why does China treat it as a long-term, basic national policy? Because China wanted to change its inward-looking state, learn and introduce the advanced experience and technology overseas, and make most use of all the outstanding achievements of civilization in the world, especially all the capitalist achievements. Judging from all the discussions about the necessity of reform and opening up in the theory of socialism with Chinese characteristics, it is clear that this theory is based on the inherent requirement of the development of Chinese socialism, which means that the socialism established after crossing the capitalist "Cauding Forks" must "draw on all the capitalist achievements" in order to develop.

In today's China, the world problem about how to build socialism after establishing socialist system in the backward Eastern countries has been solved through successful practice and has developed into a relatively comprehensive theoretical framework. The key points of the theory are as follows: to build socialism, the backward countries must consider their own national conditions, take account of the reality and take their own paths, instead of copying the Marxist books or other countries' models; they must base themselves upon the initial stage of socialism, and understand that the material and technological foundation required by socialism can only be gained after a long historical period; they must center on the economic construction, regard the development of production as the fundamental task, and focus on realizing modernization; they must carry out reform as the driving force of development, emancipate and develop the productive forces through reform, and understand that there will be no way out without reform, and they will go astray if the reform is not carried out in the socialist direction; they must regard the opening up as the necessity of modernization, by which they can draw on and make use of all the achievements made by other countries, including the developed capitalist countries, thus striving for favorable international environment and creating a good external condition; they must adhere to the " Four Cardinal Principles", regarding it as the political guarantee of reform and opening up and modernization, and ensure that reform, opening up and economic construction are carried out in a stable and solid political condition and in the socialist direction; they must formulate correct strategy for development, carry out scientific strategy for development, try to avoid major mistakes which may affect development, and guarantee the high efficiency and speed of development; under the correct leadership of the Marxist political party, they must continue to improve the ruling party's understanding of Marxism and the art of leadership, strengthen and upgrade the party's leadership, enable the ruling party to lead and support people to build socialism. Hu Jintao pointed out in the report of the 18th CPC National Congress that "the path of socialism with Chinese characteristics means basing on the basic national condition, centering on economic construction, sticking to the Four Cardinal Principles, adhering to reform and opening up, emancipating and developing the productive forces, constructing socialist market economy, socialist democratic politics, advanced socialist culture, harmonious socialist society and socialist ecological civilization, promoting people's comprehensive development, gradually realizing common prosperity, and building a modern socialist country of prosperity, democracy, civilization and harmony under the leadership of the Chinese Communist Party." This is the basic content of the path of socialism with Chinese characteristics, and also the concentrated generalization of the basic experience of building socialism in the backward countries.

The model created in the Chinese path for backward countries to build socialism, is not only the "national form" with Chinese characteristics in line with China's national condition, but also the "world model" which universally significant to all the backward countries. This model of building socialism can be summed up as the socialism which is based on national condition, continues to develop the productive forces, carries out reform and opening up, practices market economy, emphasizes independence and peace, follows the scientific outlook of development, combines the ideals of realizing national rejuvenation and communism. Looking at the international socialist movement, there is indeed no other socialist country like China that can solve the problems related to the future of socialism both theoretically and practically, and create such a comprehensive model to build socialism in backward countries. The solution of the problem and the creation of the path have overcome various drawbacks of traditional socialism, given vitality to socialism, bettered capitalism and demonstrated the superiority and bright prospect of socialist system to the whole world. Since the direction of path usually determines future and destiny, the formation of the path of socialism with Chinese characteristics has not only brought prosperity to China, but also brought hope to the world socialist movement.

The path of socialism with Chinese characteristics is the path of building socialism in backward countries. The development of the path is by no means smooth, for it has endured the rapid changes of international situation, fought against the influence of the Radical Changes in Soviet Union and Eastern Europe, and developed itself in the process of facing and settling contradictions. To sum up, it has faced and settled four major contradictions when building socialism in backward countries. The first contradiction was between socialist system and backward productive forces. In socialist countries established in a economically and culturally backward condition, the contradiction between socialist system and the incompatible backward productive forces truly existed. Socialism with Chinese characteristics settled this problem through its theory of the initial stage of socialism. The second contradiction was between planning and market. Socialism with Chinese characteristics settled this problem by combining the means of resource allocation in market and the goal of socialism to build a sound socialist market economic system. The third contradiction was between reform and the adherence to socialist direction. Socialism with Chinese characteristics didn't change the nature and fundamental system of socialism in the reform, but regarded the reform as the self-improvement of socialist system, thus realizing the integration of reform and the adherence to socialist direction. The fourth contradiction was between the development of socialist market economy and the adherence to communist ideology. Socialism with Chinese characteristics put forward the "grasping both hands" strategy. On the one hand, attention was paid to material construction; on the other hand, importance was attached to spiritual construction. On the one hand, attention was paid to reform and opening up; on the other hand, importance was attached to combating corruption and economic crimes. This has in principle demonstrated the relationship between the development of socialist market economy and the adherence to communist ideology. In the process of solving this series of contradictions, the path of socialism with Chinese characteristics has been formed, and the world problem about how to build socialism after establishing socialist system in backward countries has also been resolved.

CHAPTER THREE

Reshaping the Relationship Between Socialism and Capitalism

For socialists in the 19th century, capitalism was their deadly enemy, so it was perfectly justified to eradicate capitalism. Sometimes they would also make compromise on capitalism, but the compromise was tolerated only when it was strategically reasonable. In the 20th century, the socialist camp led by the Soviet Union emerged. Generally speaking, the world pattern of the 20th century was the rivalry between the socialist camp and the capitalist camp. Stalin once described the rivalry between socialism and capitalism like this: internally, socialist factors can not be generated inside capitalism, and they must create new form of economy in the "open space"; externally, the contradictions between socialism and capitalism are irreconcilable, which will lead to "the collapse of the united and inclusive world market" and the emergence of "two parallel and mutually opposing world markets". Based on the theory of two parallel and opposing world markets, the socialist of the 20th century believed that there was no coexistence but serious opposition between socialism and capitalism. At that time in the socialist camp, some people still called for coexistence with capitalism, but their voice was always submerged in the stronger urges for the opposition against capitalism, which made the former seem unreasonable due to its lack of persuasive theoretical basis and corresponding social environment. If socialism is always opposed to capitalism, it is hard for it to exist, let alone develop. The "socialist camp" will have no future if it is "uniform" internally and confronts with developed capitalist countries externally.

The path of socialism with Chinese characteristics has formed relatively complete theory and practice of handling the relationship between socialism and capitalism, thus providing the international socialist movement with successful example of handling the relationship between the two. The Chinese path has been reconstructing the traditional relationship between socialism and capitalism, which will exert profound influence on the future of the world socialist movement. This is one of the reasons that the Chinese path is significant to the world socialist movement.

Based on the correct judgment of the international situation, the designers of the Chinese path changed the long upheld "opposition" thinking on the relationship between socialism and capitalism, and began to rethink and shape their relationship. They have realized that they are no longer living in an era of war and revolution, but an era of peace and development, which is marked by economic strength, technological strength and comprehensive national strength. Although the world situation is still complicated and changeable, the world stability, peace and development have always been the pursuit of people all over the world. Based on this judgment, the designers the Chinese path realize that to adhere to and develop socialism, it is necessary to learn to coexist with capitalism, to make good use of the world peace to boost self-development, to make positive interrelation between self-development and peaceful international environment, and to actively engage in economic globalization, draw on the advantages and avoid disadvantages. Deng Xiaoping said, "One of the important reason that China has long been in a backward and stagnant state is the closed-door policy. Our experience has proved that China's development is inseparable from the world, and will never succeed under the closed-door policy." Based on the current "two systems of the world" and the reality that capitalism is dominant in the two "two systems", the designers of the Chinese path has reconsidered the relationship between socialism and capitalism. The reality of the world clearly shows that the problem related to socialism and capitalism is not only about their coexistence, but about their existing inside each other. The hot and cold wars between socialism and capitalism don't change the fact that they will coexist in the long term. Although the ideological differences between the two systems can not be evaded, these differences don't mean isolation as in the past. Instead, the two systems can continue common development in the premise of recognizing the diversity of the world. It is obvious that capitalism can not be eliminated in a short time. Although it has suffered from many crises, and some were quite devastating. they will never put an end to capitalism or affect it fundamentally. Although socialism has plunged to the trough after the Radical Changes in the Soviet Union and Eastern Europe, it has survived and begun to demonstrate its vitality and superiority with the rise of socialism with Chinese characteristics. In this case, the two social systems must be interdependent, while peaceful coexistence, cooperation and exchange, and peaceful competition must become the best situation of the relationship between the two systems.

In the face of such a situation, the Chinese leaders have adjusted their relationship with capitalism in time, and regarded the common development and peaceful coexistence as the fundamental strategy. This is not a short-term expedient, but a long-term strategy. The path of socialism with Chinese characteristics faces current challenges proactively with an "open" and "win-win" strategy rather than a "closed" and "exclusive" one. Deng Xiaoping said:

"To win comparative advantage over capitalism, socialism must boldly absorb all the civilization achievements made by the human beings, and draw on all the advanced business modes and management methods in the whole world, including developed capitalist countries, as long as they reflect the modern social production law." Deng Xiaoping not only elaborated the basic principles for socialism with Chinese characteristics to coexist with capitalism, but also justified those principles.

It is under the background of globalization that the path of socialism with Chinese characteristics reshapes its relationship with capitalism. In connection with the whole world, including capitalist countries, China established socialism. In the meantime, China can only build socialism in a globalized world. Regarding the historical position and current features of socialism with Chinese characteristics in a global vision, it is necessary for China to try to coexist with capitalism. In today's world, with the political multipolarization, cultural diversity and the scientific and technological informatization, economic globalization is deepening the theme of peace and development all-roundly and promoting modern civilization in the human society profoundly. Globalization is not only the product of the interdependence and mutual influence of different countries, but also a long-term process which requires all countries' cooperation and joint effort. In the process of globalization, the diversity of different countries is not isolated, but coexistent in the world system, which can promote cooperation in many ways. The continuous advancement of globalization enables the earth become the common home of human beings. In a globalized world, the concept that capitalism and socialism are absolutely opposing each other, no matter in the field of economic development strategy, politics, culture or social construction, will be abandoned. No country and nation in the world can be separated from globalization. All of them must face challenges in globalization, and then determine their own historical direction. The socialist country is no exception. The history people talk about in today is the world history, which means socialism itself is a product of world history. Socialism can only manage to survive with its connection with the world, including the capitalist countries. Socialism should not undermine the general development of productive forces and world exchanges, but consciously control and develop the global relationship of comprehensive production and comprehensive dependence. The designers of the Chinese path have scientifically understood the relationship between China's development and the world, especially the capitalist countries in the era of economic globalization. Considering the overall connection of the world, they have put forward the basic strategy of opening to the world. The so-called "opening to the world" means adjusting to and integrating into the world historical process proactively, and obtaining interests when tackling with the challenges brought by economic globalization. Obviously, the gist of this strategy is to establish interactive and mutually beneficial relationship with the capitalist countries.

In any case, these developed capitalist countries have many achievements of human civilization. To be isolated from these countries, to some extent, is to be isolated from the achievements of human civilization. To confront with these countries, to some extent, is to confront with achievements of human civilization. If the continuance and coexistence of capitalism and socialism are studied dialectically in the long history, it is clear that the two oppose each other but also influence each other, confront with each other but also coexist with each other. The experience of the Chinese path shows that on the one hand, it is important to be aware of the consistency of the pursuit of socialist value and the pursuit of the human civilization value; on the other hand, it is vital to understand that the developed capitalist countries have many achievements of human civilization. Only then can the relationship between socialism and capitalism be reconstructed. In the meantime, the experience of the Chinese path also shows that the socialist countries can achieve their pursuit of socialist value only when they establish new cooperative and coexistent relationship with the capitalist countries. Indeed, socialism has its own pursuit of value, such as the goal of comprehensive development to adhere to freedom, the harmonious development between man and nature, man and society and among people, etc. However, all these goals can by no means be achieved by an isolated country in today's world. As a result, these pursuits should be integrated into the entire system of civilization and can have greater possibility for their realizations through international exchanges and cooperation. Lenin once said, "whether socialism can be realized depends on whether the Soviet regime and the Soviet management organization are well combined with the latest advances of capitalism." Lenin's "whether socialism can be realized" first refers to the realization of the goal of socialist value.

It is undeniable that today's globalization is dominated by developed capitalist countries. The path of socialism with Chinese characteristics has built a new relationship between socialism and capitalism, which can promote today's globalization to be more just and more reasonable. The essence of globalization is the historical process in which capitalist production relation and social system expand to the world, indicating the bourgeoisie pursues profits all over the world. Thus, globalization has its downside because of capitalism. Its economic structure is clearly unjust and unreasonable, which put the majority of the third world countries in a passive position. In such a state, it seems that those third world countries only have two choices: either to close the "door" to reject globalization or to be harmed in the globalization of economic system. The facts have proved that these two options can not work. So, is there a third option? Yes, that is the Chinese path. The path of socialism with Chinese characteristics has built a new relationship with capitalism. With this new relationship, China can take the initiative in globalization. That is to say, the Chinese path chooses to participate in globalization proactively. In the face of the "double-edged sword" of globalization, China endeavors to maintain a clear mind to draw on the civilization achievements of capitalism, and to realize the transfer of socialist system and the great-leap-forward development of economic society. It is gratifying to see that today's globalization, led by developed capitalist countries, is transforming to be more just and reasonable. This transformation is apparently closely related to China's strategy of opening to the world and the rebuilding of relationship between the path of socialism with Chinese characteristics and capitalism. The path of socialism with Chinese characteristics has contributed to the transformation of globalization led by developed capitalist countries. Since the bourgeoisie began to open up markets everywhere, the just, reasonable globalization which benefits the majority will ultimately replace the one dominated by the western powers and only benefits the minority, and the globalization dominated by socialist countries will ultimately replace the one dominated by developed capitalist countries. We can see that as the path of socialism with Chinese characteristics has built new relationship with capitalism, it is possible for the goal to come into reality. The new relationship between socialism and capitalism is beneficial to both of them, but in the long run, it will be far more beneficial to socialism.

The path of socialism with Chinese characteristics is committed to rebuilding the relationship between socialism and capitalism, indicating that it is a path of peaceful development. Rebuilding the relationship and taking the path of peaceful development can be mutually causal: to take the path of peaceful development, the relationship between socialism and capitalism must be rebuilt; to rebuild the relationship, it is necessary to adhere to the path of peaceful development. Taking the path of peaceful development is the inherent requirement of socialism with Chinese characteristics. Deng Xiaoping once described socialism with Chinese characteristics as "the socialism which develops the social productive forces and advocates peace". The Chinese path creatively connects "development" and "peace", emphasizing that the smooth development can only be realized in a peaceful environment. Deng Xiaoping said, "The stronger China becomes, the more reliable the global peace can be." The Chinese path considers its own peaceful development from a world perspective and is committed to maintaining the peaceful development of the whole world. In the report of the 17th National Congress of the Communist Party of China, Hu Jintao pointed out, "no matter how the international situation changes, the Chinese government and people will hold high the banner of peace, development and cooperation, pursue the independent peaceful foreign policy, defend state sovereignty, security and development interests, and adhere to the purpose of the foreign policy to maintain world peace and promote common development." The core content of "holding high the banner of peace, development and cooperation" and "adhering to the purpose of foreign policy to maintain world peace and promote common development" is to improve China's relationship with the capitalist countries, pursue common development instead of mutual opposition, and rebuild a new relationship with capitalism. The concept of "peaceful development" of the Chinese path is associated with the concept of "harmonious world". To judge whether a world is harmonious, one has to see whether the relationship between the countries of this world is harmonious, and whether the relationship between the capitalist countries and socialist countries is harmonious. China is sincere to build a "harmonious world of lasting peace and common prosperity", and to improve its relationship with capitalist countries and rebuild the relationship between socialism and capitalism. The Chinese path's concept of building a harmonious world will surely promote world peace, stability and development. The Chinese path is committed to creating a new path of peaceful development for human civilization, and building a harmonious world, which is also the process of rebuilding the relationship between socialism and capitalism.

CHAPTER FOUR

The Chinese path has innovated and developed the theory of scientific socialism

The theory of socialism with Chinese characteristics established its spatial location based on "Chinese characteristics". Specifically, the practice with the connotation of "Chinese characteristics" is different from the abstract principle, and the unique meaning with the connotation of "Chinese characteristics" is different from other countries' theory and practice. However, this doesn't mean socialism with Chinese characteristics is related to petty nationalism. On the contrary, its universal significance for scientific socialism becomes more and more conspicuous. To some extent, the theoretical system of socialism with Chinese characteristics is the great development of scientific socialism in the contemporary era, and is the theory of scientific socialism in the new era. The Chinese path has innovated and developed the theory of scientific socialism, which guarantees the irreversible value of the basic principles of scientific socialism, shows the general trend of human society, and guides people toward that direction.

The path of socialism with Chinese characteristics doesn't come out from nowhere, instead it has its historical root and realistic basis. Therefore, to understand how the path of socialism with Chinese characteristics innovated and developed the theory of scientific socialism, it is important to know how it came into being. It is particularly important to study its relationship with the Chinese new democratic society and with the traditional socialist society represented by the Soviet model. Only by scientifically understanding the relationship of the path of socialism with Chinese characteristics with the path of Chinese new democratic revolution, and with the path of traditional socialist development can we correctly comprehend the innovation of the path of socialism with Chinese characteristics.

The path of socialism with Chinese characteristics has inherited and improved the features of Chinese new democratic society. The members of the Communist Party of China, represent by Mao Zedong, has put forward the "the theory of new democratic revolution " according to the basic principles of Marxism, the social nature, historical status and specific national conditions of the old China, and the characteristics of the world history after the October Revolution. They believe that Chinese revolution must take two steps: first, the new democratic revolution; second, the socialist revolution. They emphasize that the Chinese new democratic revolution is different from the western bourgeois democratic revolution and the Russian socialist revolution, instead it is a path of revolution with Chinese characteristics which develops from new democracy to socialism. The success of the Chinese new democratic revolution has provided a fundamental guarantee for China to take the path of socialism. The new democratic society built in China has laid foundation for socialism in the fields of economy, politics, ideology, culture and society, etc. In fact, the Chinese socialism has inherited the features of new democracy, and those historical features will play an important role in the Chinese socialist society, thus becoming the characteristics of Chinese socialist society. The Chinese new democracy has an inseparable relationship with socialism. The Chinese new democratic revolution is a unique path of revolution, the Chinese new democratic society is a unique form of society, and the Chinese socialism based on it is also unique. In view of this, the Chinese construction is unique because its pioneer--the Chinese new democratic revolution is unique.

After the reform and opening up, the Chinese Communist Party has summed up the experience of the traditional socialist development represented by the Soviet model, thus developing the path of socialism with Chinese characteristics. It is undeniable that the traditional socialist development has a profound influence on the path of socialism with Chinese characteristics. The exploration of the path of socialism with Chinese characteristics is based on the path of traditional socialism, so forming a correct view of the traditional socialism is the starting point to explore the path of socialism with Chinese characteristics. Deng Xiaoping has always been adhering to and respecting the most fundamental things left by traditional socialism. He said, "we adhere to the principles of public ownership and distribution according to work. We insist on the policy of socialist economic construction by keeping self-reliance as mainstay and foreign aid as supplement, learning and introducing foreign advanced technology. We strive to act in accordance with the objective economic laws. That is to say, we adhere to the scientific socialism. " Deng Xiaoping has made it clear that the path of socialism with Chinese characteristics must follow some basic principles of scientific socialism reflected in traditional socialist society. To adhere to these basic principles is to insist on scientific socialism. However, on the basis of recognizing the significance of the path of traditional socialism for the path of socialism with Chinese characteristics, we should also keep in mind that the two have marked differences--the path of socialism with Chinese characteristics has surpassed and innovated the path of traditional socialist development.

The path of socialism with Chinese characteristics has abandoned the shortcomings of traditional socialism, making the socialist construction more realistic and practical, which is a great change of traditional socialism. The Chinese people took the path of socialism with Chinese characteristics under the banner of "reform", and the so-called "reform" is actually abandoning the downside of traditional socialism. That is to say, if we do not get rid of the disadvantages of traditional socialism, it is impossible to have the path of socialism with Chinese characteristics. Although the path of socialism with Chinese characteristics developed from traditional socialism, they are quite different in the fields of politics, economy, culture, society and foreign relations, etc. All these differences represent not only the breakthrough the path of socialism with Chinese characteristics has achieved out of traditional socialism, but also the innovation of the entire theory of scientific socialism.

On the one hand, the Chinese people has accepted the legacy of new democratic society; on the other hand, they have been consistently making breakthroughs and reform based on traditional socialism. Thus, the path of socialism with Chinese characteristics have come into being. So how to make breakthroughs and reform? The key is to adhere to the basic principles of scientific socialism, and in the meantime demonstrate distinctive Chinese characteristics according to the reality of China and the feature of the era. The path of socialism with Chinese characteristics is the result of combining the basic principles of scientific socialism with the national condition and the world situation.

The Chinese path's breakthrough and reform of traditional socialism are based on the full understanding of the national condition and the world situation, which helps to realize the theoretical innovation and development of scientific socialism. Therefore, to fully understand how and why the Chinese path can innovate and develop the theory of scientific socialism, we have to further explore the methods that how the Chinese people combine socialism with the national condition and the world situation.

The Chinese path has successfully combined the basic principles of scientific socialism with the Chinese condition. This experience shows that if a Marxist political party can not combine the basic Marxist theory with its own national condition, only using the Marxist conclusions instead of trying to relate theory to reality and working creatively, on the one hand the socialist cause will be trapped in serious crisis or even destructive danger, and on the other hand Marxism will be in a rigid state without any vitality, let alone innovation and development.

To combine scientific socialism with the world situation, is to fully understand the general trend of world development, so as to synchronize the Chinese socialist construction with the times. The path of socialism with Chinese characteristics is the scientific reflection of the theme of the times. When the designers of the Chinese path consider how to build socialism with Chinese characteristics, they analyze the national condition and the world situation together. The world situation is not discussed without talking about national condition, and the national condition is not analyzed without considering the world situation. In this way, the path of socialism with Chinese characteristics not only has distinctive Chinese characteristics, but also has the features of the times. The path of socialism with Chinese characteristics follows the tide of the times, committing itself to solving thc major problems appeared due to the development of the times. The theoretical system of socialism with Chinese characteristics puts great emphasis on problems. Its main aim is not to establish a universal system of "eternal truth", but to solve the problems of the times, so it is full of the spirit of the times. In the report of the 16th National Congress of the Communist Party of China, Jiang Zemin emphasized, "the entire party should always maintain the spirit of keeping up with the times, consistently developing the Marxist theory... Keeping up with the times means that all the theories and work of the party should reflect the spirit of the times, conform to laws and stay innovative. Whether or not we can do this determines the future of our party and our country. " The top leaders of the Communist Party of China has put the features, patterns, themes, internal laws and the requirements of the times into the theoretical system of socialism with Chinese characteristics. The theme of the times recognized by the path of socialism with Chinese characteristics is to replace wars and revolutions with peace and development. The path of peaceful development taken by China is first determined by the socialist system in China. Deng Xiaoping said, "China is a socialist country. The nature of our social system determines that we pursue a peaceful foreign policy." It is undeniable that the path of peaceful development taken by China is determined by the world situation in which peace and development have become the theme of the times. As early as in the 1980s, Deng Xiaoping has stressed that China should take the two international strategic issues of peace and development seriously, regard them as the international background for China build its own socialism and understand its significance.

After exploring the reason and basis of the Chinese path's innovation and development of the theory of scientific socialism, we can specifically analyze what innovation and development the Chinese path has made to the theory of scientific socialism. Since Deng Xiaoping Theory, the important thought of Three Represents and the scientific outlook on development are the three main components of the theoretical system of socialism with Chinese characteristics, we will briefly discuss how they contribute to the innovation and development of the theory of scientific socialism.

Deng Xiaoping Theory has resolved the problem of how to build socialist system in a economically and culturally backward country. It has established the theory of the primary stage of socialism, the theory of socialist essence, the theory of socialist reform and opening up and the theory of socialist market economy. All these theories are the result of the deepening of Deng Xiaoping's socialist ideology. They are the Chinese Communist Party's comprehensive and scientific elaboration of the question of "what is socialism", and the significant development of the theory of scientific socialism. Under the new historical condition, Deng Xiaoping, through drawing on experience of the development of socialism in China and in the world, has not only answered the question of "what is socialism", but also solved the problem of "how to build socialism", which marks that the theory of scientific socialism has developed into a new phase. Many socialist theories of Deng Xiaoping have enriched the socialist theory of Marx and Engels.

The important thought of Three Represents has solved the problem of how to build the Marxist political party after it transformed from a revolutionary party to a ruling one. Looking at the history of the international socialist movement, this problem has long been a fundamental problem that the Marxist political party, ruling party in particular, wanted to solve but failed. As a result, the important thought of Three Represents is not only important to the development of Marxist political party, but also a prominent contribution to the theory of scientific socialism. Under the new historical condition and on the basis of the new practice, it has expanded the path of socialism with Chinese characteristics. In the meantime, it has put forward a series of new idealism new perspectives and new theories to build socialism, deepened the understanding of the laws of socialist construction, and further developed scientific socialism.

The scientific outlook on development has answered the question of how to realize scientific development under the background of the deepening of socialist modernization. In order to solve the problems in modernization, how to realize scientific development has become the new issue of the times. At this moment, the scientific outlook on development takes the overall situation of building and developing a socialist China into consideration, draws on the experience of other countries' development, points out that development should be comprehensive, coordinated and sustainable, scientifically answers the questions of "what kind of development should be pursued", "how to develop" and son on. The scientific outlook on development has enhanced the understanding of development of socialism with Chinese characteristics. In the meantime, it has also given a new connotation to the theory of scientific socialism. The scientific outlook on development is a significant development of the guiding principles of socialist modernization, and is interlinked with scientific socialism. It gives human beings a new perspective to understand the future and seek development, which will surely have profound influence on the development of scientific socialism.

Scientific socialism is a complete theoretical system, composed of a series of theoretical point of view. The following focuses on the innovation and development the path of socialism with Chinese characteristics has made on each component of the theoretical system of scientific socialism.

(1)The theory of the primary stage of socialism has made significant contribution to the theory of the developing stage of socialism of scientific socialism. The developing stage of socialism is one of the issues discussed by revolutionary mentors. Through more than half a century of practice, the Communist Party of China has established the theory of the primary stage of socialism, which is the first time in the history of scientific socialism. Deng Xiaoping said, "socialism itself is the primary stage of communism. China is at the primary stage of socialism, that is, the underdeveloped stage. We should be realistic, and make plans according to the reality." According to Deng Xiaoping's scientific judgment, the Chinese socialism at today's stage is not yet the first stage of communism envisioned by Marx and Engels, instead it is the immature socialism which has developed from the semi-feudal and semi-colonial society. Deng Xiaoping's judgment has pointed out the historical position of socialism with Chinese characteristics, and laid theoretical foundation for it. The theory of the primary stage of socialism not only has a groundbreaking significance for correctly understanding the major contradictions, fundamental tasks and strategic steps of Chinese society, but also plays a general guiding role for economically and culturally backward countries to build socialism.

(2)In the history of scientific socialism, the theory of the essence of socialism has made the most brilliant and comprehensive answer to a most fundamental question "what is socialism". The revolutionary mentors have discussed the essence of socialism in different times, on different occasions and under different conditions. Due to various reasons, however, they have all failed to make a brilliant and comprehensive generalization of the essence of socialism. After a long developing process with ups and downs, the Communist Party of China has revealed the essence of socialism under the premise of upholding the basic socialist system. The following words of Deng Xiaoping can be regarded as the latest understanding of the Communist Party of China on the essence of socialism: "emancipating and developing the productive forces, eliminating exploitation and polarization, and finally achieving common prosperity." These words constitute an organic whole. Emancipating and developing the productive forces are from the perspective of the composition of the productive forces, eliminating exploitation and polarization is from the perspective of the composition of the production relation, and achieving common prosperity is the ultimate goal of socialism which differs it from capitalism fundamentally. The generalization of the Communist Party of China on the essence of socialism reflects the party's deep understanding of socialism. It has revealed the essence of socialism in the deepest and most complete sense. To some extent, it enables people understanding of socialism to transform into a more realistic one.

(3)The theory of the driving force of socialism has further developed the concept of driving force of scientific socialism. According to the theory of scientific socialism, the fundamental contradiction in a socialist society is still the one between the relations of production and the productive forces, between the superstructure and the economic foundation. Resolving this contradiction can promote the development of the socialist society. So how to resolve this contradiction? For a long time, class struggle, line struggle and "further revolution under the dictatorship of the proletariat" have been regarded as the fundamental way to resolve the contradiction, and thus the fundamental driving force for the development of socialist society. The path of socialism with Chinese characteristics has broken through the concept of "taking class struggle as the key link", and confirmed that reform is the driving force for the development of socialist society. That is to say, China will resolve the fundamental contradictions in socialist society through reform. Deng Xiaoping pointed out, "after the establishment of the basic socialist system, we have to fundamentally change the economic system which hinders the development of the productive forces, build a vibrant and dynamic socialist economic system, and promote the development of the productive forces. This is reform. Reform also means to emancipate the productive forces." Deng Xiaoping regards reform as the driving force for the development of socialist society, which is a theoretical innovation on the issue of the driving force for socialist development. It is this theoretical innovation that opens the way for the development of Chinese productive forces and Chinese socialist society. It has been proved by practice that reform and opening up is the way for socialist China to strengthen itself, and is the historic decision which determines China's fate. The theory of the driving force of socialism put forward by the Communist Party of China is one of the most valuable theories among all the supplements made by the path of socialism with Chinese characteristics for the theory of scientific socialism.

(4)The theory of socialist market economy has opened a new chapter for scientific socialism.

Marx's and Engels' conception of socialism is planned economy without market. As a result, the traditional socialism believes that market economy is exclusive to capitalism, and planned economy is the basic characteristics of socialism. Deng Xiaoping has corrected the misunderstanding that market is exclusive to capitalism, pointed out that socialism can also have market economy, and put forward the blueprint and basic framework for establishing socialist market economy. Deng Xiaoping pointed out, "Do not think that planned economy is definitely socialist, and market economy is certainly capitalist. It's not the case at all. The two are both means. Market can also benefit socialism." The theory of socialist market economy has promoted China's reform and opening up, and made the whole social society more vibrant and dynamic. The theory of socialist market economy has resolved the problem of combining socialist public ownership and market economy in the history of international socialist movement, which is the greatest theoretical innovation in this history. The theoretical innovation on other aspects of scientific socialism made by the path of socialism with Chinese characteristics might be based on scientific socialism, and might be the revision, supplement and development of the original theories of scientific socialism. The theoretical innovation on the theory of socialist market economy is a "refutation" of the original theory, which is formed only after the original one is overturned. Therefore, the theory of socialist market economy is particularly valuable. It has opened a new chapter for scientific socialism.

(5)The theory of "emancipating the mind and seeking truth from facts" has corrected the ideology of scientific socialism. "Emancipating the mind and seeking truth from facts" is the generalization of the ideology of Marxism and scientific socialism made by Deng Xiaoping in the Third Plenary Session of the 11th CPC Central Committee. Deng Xiaoping and other leaders have made profound elaboration on "emancipating the mind and seeking truth from facts" theoretically. "Emancipating the mind and seeking truth from facts" is not only the Marxist ideology advocated by the Communist Party of China, but also the foundation of the theoretical system of socialism with Chinese characteristics. It is with this ideology and foundation that China has found a way to develop socialism which is suitable for national condition and world situation. We can say that the resolving of every major problem, the establishing of every important theory and the developing of every new field in the theoretical system of socialism with Chinese characteristics are inseparable from the influence of "emancipating the mind and seeking truth from facts". Looking at the history of international socialist movement, it is not difficult to see that "emancipating the mind and seeking truth from facts" is theoretically innovative. It not only helps the Chinese people to understand what socialism is and how to develop socialism, but also exerts positive influence on correcting the ideology of world socialist movement. The ideology of "emancipating the mind and seeking truth from facts" established by the Communist Party of China has opened a new chapter for the world socialist movement.

The list of examples about how the path of socialism with Chinese characteristics innovated and develops the theory of scientific socialism goes on and on, but from the above examples we can see that with the development of the path of socialism with Chinese characteristics, the theory of scientific socialism has been enriched. It is the path of socialism with Chinese characteristics that has upgraded and developed a series of theories and conclusions of scientific socialism of Marxism, and has begun a new historical period in the history of the development of the theory of scientific socialism.

Part Four

Chinese Path and Marxism

The correlation study on Chinese path and Marxism usually looks at how Chinese path exploits thought resources from Marxism, or how Marxism leads China to open up its road. However, as we are going to expound the worldwide significance of the opening up of Chinese Path, we need to explain the interrelationship between Chinese path and Marxism, and that is to mainly discuss what has Chinese path brought to Marxism indeed.

Marxism remains the most influential ideology in present world. In a sense, human's destiny depends on that of Marxism's. Accordingly, to understand the worldwide significance of Chinese path, we must research into the significance of Chinese path to Marxism. Other perspectives of the worldwide significance of Chinese path forms an organic integration with the path's significance to Marxism.

The significance of Chinese path to Marxism is: First, the path, by its own practice, proves that the series of basic theories of Marxism is not outdated, so that it shows to the world that Marxism remains the banner leading the course; next, it, by its own practice, overthrows some untimely conclusions of the original Marxism, to make it purer; last, it, in the same way, carries forward Marxism, to make it more adjust to the need of the era and stay revolutionarily young. The "verification", "falsification" and "development" which Chinese Path has brought to Marxism constitute the whole significance to Marxism.

Chapter One
The "Verification" of the Chinese Path to Marxism

Opening up Chinese path needs various resources of thoughts, and Marxism is the most important one without doubt. The process of opening the Chinese Path is also the process of Chinese Communist Party localizing Marxism in China and executing Marxism to China's reality. The Chinese path proves by its own practice that the series of basic theories of Marxism is not obsolete. The verification of the Chinese path to Marxism is multifaceted, and here we only choose some of its perspectives to elaborate on.

I. The Chinese path proves that the basic contradiction theory of socialist society by Marxism is an incontrovertible truth.

If human can only understand the law of natural movement, variation and development after a lengthy and hard journey, then it would be lengthier and harder to know the law of social activities. The myth of social structure and the law of social movement were not unveiled until Marx and Engels' time, and to be specific, until their work *The Communist Manifesto* came out. The book is a great discovery. After Marx's death, on his funeral speech, Engels mentioned that the significance of this discovery was as much as that of Darwin's theory of organic evolution.

The law of social development discovered by Marx and Engels was: During every historical period, the economic production and its inevitable results of social structure are the base of the spirit and history of that period.[1] Engels pointed out in the preface of *The Communist Manifesto*, German edition of 1883, that this is the basic idea that runs through the whole book.[2] And in the preface of *The Communist Manifesto*, English edition of 1888, he again pointed out that this is the basic idea of the book's core.[3]

The great discovery of the law of social development is actually a "simple truth" covered all the time by "various ideologies": Humans need to eat, drink, be sheltered and dressed before they engage into political, scientific, artistic and religious activities. Therefore, the direct production of material subsistence, and accordingly the material base as a result of the economic development of a nation or an era, the idea of national facilities and law, the idea of art and religion, were developed on that base, rather than the thought of the past, which was the opposite.

The basic idea that runs through the great discovery of Marx and Engels considers the society and its development as a natural process. The so-called natural process means that society, like the nature, goes through a regular developing process, and its law is objective and certain and doesn't change according to men's will. This law is that the production relationship must correspond with the condition of productivity, and the superstructure must correspond with the economic base. The controversy between productivity and production relationship, between economic base and superstructure are the basic controversies of society. The two pairs of basic controversies determine the social development.

The basic contradiction theory of society is the basic content of materialistic conception of history as well as the core principle of Marxism. The essence of Marxism is definite, that is the social

1 *Selected Works of Mark and Engels*, Chin. E. People's Publishing House, Beijing, Vol. X, 1994, p. 9.

2 Ibid., p. 9.

3 Ibid., p. 14.

contradictions from the theory of social dynamics. So long as the theory is not outdated and can stand on its own feet, so does Marxism. Chinese path was the great fruit bred exactly during the process of the CPC and Chinese people localizing materialistic historic ideology based on the social contradictions from the theory of social dynamics. Basic contradiction theory of socialism is an important growing point for the theory system of socialism with Chinese characteristics. Of course, the vice versa is also true. Marxist materialistic historic ideology, with basic contradiction theory of socialism as its core, helped by the success of Chinese path, is again verified under new historical conditions. And it is also because Chinese path has proved the above-mentioned to be bare truth, so that Marxism is proved to fit the times on the whole and in essence.

Chinese path holds on to the focus of economic development, which is actually the focus of developing the productive forces. The focus of economic development is the result of the practical application of Marxist basic contradiction theory of socialism, and the success of its application first forcibly verified the theory. To focus on economic development relies on the theory of materialistic historic ideology, and to be specific, the social contradictions from the theory of social dynamics, which regards productivity as the whole historical base of humans. The basic principle of the theory of materialistic historic ideology is that productive forces determine production relations, and while productive forces still fall behind, of course no qualified socialism exists. Based on this, the only choice is to develop productive forces.

Deng Xiaoping said: "The fundamental principle of Marxism is to develop productive forces. The highest aim of Marxism is to achieve communism, which is based on highly-developed productive forces. Socialism is the first phase of communism, which is a long historical period, and during this period, the primary task is to develop productive forces and improve people's materialistic and cultural life criterion step by step."[4] During the late 1970s and 1980s, China determinedly shifted the focus to economic development. Since then, Chinese people have shared the consensus of development and especially that of economics. The whole nation, whole country operated in the aim of developing economics and developing productive forces. This is a significant turning point for China, which had the decisive implication, and actually also a significant turning point for Marxist materialistic historic ideology. Now people owe the success of about thirty years to the success of the turning point, which means shifting the emphasis to economic development and developing productive forces, and of course, it can naturally be concluded as the success of the practice of Marxist materialistic historic ideology in China.

Chinese path makes it clear that China is still at an early stage of socialism, and the opening up of the path is built on the basic recognition of the present nature of Chinese society. Accepting that productive forces determine production relations is the key to understanding social development in a materialistic way. Marxist materialistic historic ideology emphasizes that productive forces determine production relations, and to grasp the essence of materialistic historic ideology is to understand the law that production relations must coincide with productive forces. The pathfinder of Chinese Path followed faithfully the demand of the development of our present productive forces, and from the practical standpoint, put forward the idea that our country was at the primary stage of socialism, which underlay the courses, guidelines and policies. We can safely say that the primary stage of socialism of our country is the result of deeply understanding the basic rule revealed by the materialistic historic ideology that production relations must correspond with the condition of productive forces. Of course, the scientific recognition of the present social nature of China proved

4 *Selected Works of Deng Xiaoping*, Chin. ed., People's Publishing House, Beijing, 1993, Vol. III, p. 116.

convincingly the absolute correctness and almighty power of the law revealed by the materialistic historic ideology. To confirm that our country is at the early stage of socialism mainly aims to make sure that the form of ownership correspond with the condition of the development of our productive forces, which means that in the basic economic system public ownership plays the dominant role and non-public economic sectors are developed. This economic system has public ownership as the major part and develops various kinds of economic ownership. According to this basic economic system, the initiator of Chinese path and its leaders brought forward two guidelines of "unswervingly", that is, to consolidate and develop public-owned economy unswervingly, to encourage, support and lead the development of non-public economy. Because the basic economy system and the basic guidelines suit the need of the development of productive forces, productive forces are boosted effectively.

The process of opening up Chinese path is also the process of continuously implementing reform according to dialectical relationship between productive forces and production relations. Marxist materialistic historic ideology tells people that productive forces and production relations are two perspectives of production, which together organically form a certain kind of production mode.

The development of social production mode is promoted by the contradictory movement of productive forces and production relations.

The key, on the one hand, is to strive to make production relations, which suit productive forces, play a dynamic anti-role to the development of productive forces, that is, to provide a promising prospect for it; on the other hand, is to transform unremittingly social production relations which change according to the change and development of material instrument of production and productive forces, that is, to actively regulate and change the part of production relations which don't fit in with productive forces. The essence of reform, which was advocated by Deng Xiaoping, is to actively regulate and change the part of production relations which don't fit in with productive forces, in the light of Marxist materialistic historic ideology. He made it crystal clear: "After the establishment of the basic system of socialism, the economic system which encumbers economic development must be transformed radically, and a buoyant and energetic economic system of socialism is to be founded. Boost the development of productive forces is one part of reform, so that reform is also to liberate productive forces."[5] Undoubtedly, reform is a key factor of China's success, and the key of a successful reform lies on the fact that productive forces are liberated and developed because the reform have regulated and changed the part of production relations which don't fit in with productive forces. In that sense, reform is the necessary requirement of the development of the movement of fundamental socialist social contradictions, which is presented by Marxist materialistic historic ideology, and it is also the natural development and continuation of the theory of social basic contradictions. Marxist theory of social basic contradictions is again verified here.

II. The Chinese path prospered the ideological line of Marxist dialectical materialism.

If you read *History and Class Consciousness* by Lukács, the founder of western Marxism, you must be absorbed in the view at the first page that the core of Marxism lies in its "method", and sticking to the "orthodoxy" of Marxism is mainly to hold on to its "method". If Marxist methodology and Marxist outlook are connected with each other, then Lukács' view, in some sense, can be acceptable. Indeed, epistemology and methodology of Marxist dialectical materialism remain at the heart of Marxism. Sticking to Marxism is sticking to the Marxist outlook and Marxist methodology, which is at the bottom sticking to the ideological line of Marxist dialectical materialism, and

5 *Selected Works of Deng Xiaoping*, Chin. ed., Foreign Language Press, Beijing, 1995, Vol. III, p. 370.

that is, sticking to the epistemology and methodology of dialectical materialism.

The epistemology and methodology of Marxist dialectical materialism is the passive materialistic theory of reflection. Marxist active theory of reflection has inherited from the tradition of materialism, which resolutely makes the basic premises that "matter primary and consciousness is secondary and the latter is the reflection of the former" the base of epistemology and methodology. It not only regards people's general consciousness and natural knowledge as the reflection of social existence, but also considers people's social consciousness and social knowledge as the reflection of social existence. The principles of the theory of reflection are implemented all through historical fields of society, and the phenomenon of social consciousness is explained in a materialistic way. At the same time, Marxist active theory of reflection has introduced a scientific view of practice to epistemology, and explained in an inclusive and scientific way the interrelationship between thought and being, subjectivity and objectivity during the cognitive process. The epistemology and methodology of Marxist dialectical materialism, with Marxist active theory of reflection as its major content, is the result of summary of experience of history of cognition and scientific techniques, as well as the guideline of actively leading the development of scientific cognition.[6] Mao Zedong has summarized the epistemology and methodology of Marxist materialism with the connotation "to seek the truth from facts": "facts" means specific reality and practice, and "to seek the truth" means to gain the understanding of objective laws through specific reality and practice. Mao Zedong has put forward the idea that where men's right thoughts came from, and he thought that they came only from practice, and could be enriched, developed during this process, and men again practice, again recognize things… and so on and so forth.

---

6 *Dialectical Materialism Principle*. People's Publishing House, Beijing, 1981, pp. 306-310.

Unquestionably, the opening up of China's socialist path can't be done without the ideological line of Marxist dialectical materialism, which runs all the way through Chinese path. Had it not been for the initiators of Chinese path, who brought order out of chaos, which means to back to the ideological line of "to seek the truth from facts" of dialectical materialism, China couldn't have the achievement of thirty years or so. On the path of reform and opening up, Marxist ideological line of dialectical materialism has showed its mighty power. We can say that Marxist philosophy, even its quintessence, is again forcibly proved by the help of Chinese path.

On December 13, 1978, Deng Xiaoping gave a speech entitled as "Emancipate the mind, seek truth from facts, and unite to look forward" on the losing ceremony of the working conference held by the CPC. The speech is regarded as 'the declaration of opening up a new road in a new era, and established the new theory of socialism with Chinese characteristics. This working conference of the Central Committee made a full preparation for the following the Third Plenary Session of the 11th Central Committee of the Chinese Communist Party, and Deng Xiaoping's talk was actually the keynote speech of the Third Plenary Session of the 11th Central Committee of the Chinese Communist Party.[7] If we read the document today, we will see that its most important contribution is to resume the party's ideological line of "to seek the truth from facts", to emancipate people's minds and promote the party and even the whole country to advance in the light of the ideological line of Marxist dialectical materialism.

Deng Xiaoping made it clear in this speech that "A party, a country, a nation, if holds on to book worship, rigid thinking, and superstition, then it can never advance and will lose its vigor to the point of death", "Only by liberating thoughts, seeking the truth from facts and integrating theory with practice can our socialist modernization go

7 *Selected Works of Deng Xiaoping*, Chin. ed., People's Publishing House, Beijing, 1994, Vol. II, p. 140.

smoothly, and the theories of Marxism-Leninism and Mao Zedong thought develop successfully".[8] And in that speech, Deng Xiaoping stressed in particular that holding on to the ideological line of seeking the truth from facts is holding on to Marxism, because "Seeking the truth from facts is the basis of the world outlook of proletariat and the basis of Marxist thoughts. In the past, we relied on it to gain the success of revolution; today, we still depend on it to achieve the four modernizations".[9]

On the occasion of Deng Xiaoping's speech, a discussion of the criterion of truth spread to all over the country. Even the simplest problem of Marxist philosophy could arouse a wild debate. The fact showed it crystal clear that nothing could be done if rigid thinking couldn't be got rid of and if the ideological line of dialectical materialism was not established. It was not by coincidence that China opened its new development road by discussing the criterion of truth. Deng Xiaoping made a summary about the heated debate, and he pointed out that: "The present discussion about whether practice is the sole criterion for testing truth is in fact the discussion about whether to free the mind. People think that the discussion is both necessary and of great significance, and judging from the condition of discussion, it is all the more important". "The debate over the criterion of question is indeed a question of ideological line and politics and has everything to do with the prospect and destiny of our party and our country."[10] He highly affirmed the great significance of the debate, and regarded regulating the ideological line as a political question, and understood it as something important to the point of having to do with the prospect and destiny of the party and the nation.

At that time, China was a devastated country which needed to

8 *Selected Works of Deng Xiaoping*, Chin. ed., People's Publishing House, Beijing, 1994, Vol. II, p. 143.

9 *Selected Works of Deng Xiaoping*, Chin. ed., People's Publishing House, Beijing, 1994, Vol. II, p. 143.

10 *Selected Works of Deng Xiaoping*, Chin. ed., People's Publishing House, Beijing, 1994, Vol. II, p. 143.

be rebuilt, and Deng Xiaoping created a historic turning point by facilitating the party's ideological line back to dialectical materialism.

Since the Third Plenary Session of the 11th Central Committee of the Chinese Communist Party, a series of new policies of reform and opening up has been implemented, which achieved the shift of focus of the party's work, and China has officially stepped on the road of socialism. Evidently, the road was initially paved by setting thoughts right from wrong.

We have seen that during the thirty years or so, the progression of the path of socialism with Chinese characteristic is also the process of the party's sticking to the Marxist ideological line of seeking the truth from facts. The main line that runs through the path of socialism with Chinese characteristic is the ideological line of dialectical materialism. Every time when it is the key point to the advance on the path, the Chinese leaders always at first bring forward the question that what ideological line we should adhere to. As is known to all, Deng Xiaoping's South Talk brought the path of socialism with Chinese characteristics to a new stage. In this speech, Deng Xiaoping gave direct answers to the problems which haunted China's reform and opening up, and when he answered it he always at first told people that sticking to the ideological line of seeking the truth from facts was the prerequisite of correctly understanding and answering these problems. It was in the speech that Deng Xiaoping said, "Recently, I have heard from some foreigners that Marxism is invincible. Invincibility is not because of bookishness but because the truth of Marxism is incontrovertible. Seeking the truth from facts is the essence of Marxism, which, instead of bookishness, should be advocated". "Practice is the only criterion for testing truth. I haven't read many books, but I believe in one thing that told by our Chairman Mao, that is to seek the truth from facts. In the past, we relied on it to win our battles; now, we also depend on it for our construction and reform. We have delved into Marxism for our whole life, but actually Marxism is not a myth. It is a plain thing, a very plain truth". The reality is as Deng Xiaoping said, the success of Chinese path is totally the result of "practice and seeking the truth from facts", which is proved to be successful by the success of Chinese path. Also, because seeking the truth from facts is the essence of Marxism, the success of the ideological line of seeking the truth from facts again proved the success of the Marxist ideological line of dialectical materialism.

III. The Chinese path demonstrates the rightness of the judgement of Marxism that socialism is certain to replace capitalism

In some sense, the Marxist theory can be referred to as the scientific socialist theory. Marx declared in *The Communist Manifesto*, "The collapse of bourgeoisie and the success of proletariats are both certain". The tenet of Marxism is to argue that capitalism is bound to collapse while socialism and communism are bound to succeed. The theory of "two certains" is the most important theoretical basis of the communist faith, and also the most important theoretical basis of the legality and rationality of the existence of the CPC. The most important thing is that the theory of "two certains" by Marx is not groundless, but is established on precise scientific reasoning. To be specific, the theory of "two certains" by Marx and Engels is not the "certain" that is brought by "oughtness", but is the theory demonstrated by the research based on the reality of history and the reality. Marx and Engels not only made the conclusion of "two certains", but also expounded on the basis of it in details and in depth. Correspondingly, it is totally justified to add the word "scientific" to the Marxism scientific socialism theory.

It is because of the tenet of Marxism, which says that capitalism is bound to collapse and socialism and communism are bound to succeed, that as long as the basic judgement can stand on its feet till today, Marxism is realistic on the whole.

On the contrary, if the basic judgement of Marxism loses its timeliness, then overall, Marxism will become outdated. The materialistic conception of history, communism, and the revolutionary idealism are conceptions connected together, and the negation of one is certainly the negation of the other two; correspondingly, the affirmation of one is also the affirmation of the other two. The aim of communism is the prerequisite of revolutionary idealism, and the former is philosophically based on the Marxist historical materialism theory. In turn, the Marxist historical materialism theory contains the aim of communism, and the aim of communism determines the attitude towards life of revolutionary idealism. In that case, if a person judges the Marxism that capitalism is certain to be replaced by socialism, he has already abandoned the revolutionary idealism which fights for communism, and in fact, he has left communism and become a stranger of Marxism.

And what dose Chinese path mean to Marxism? This question is somewhat determined by whether or not can it prove the basic judgement of Marxism. If the success of Chinese path can further prove the basic judgement to be correct, then the practice of Chinese path can perfectly prove Marxism. But if not, it will be a counterexample. Deng Xiaoping made a clear explanation about this point. He emphasized that the path is to show the world that socialism is inevitable and superior to capitalism[11] and that China will take the last two decades of this century and the first five of the next to demonstrate to the world, especially developed countries the superiority of socialism over capitalism by the development in productivity, science and technology, material civilization as well as spiritual civilization.[12] A clear conclusion can be drawn from Deng's words that Chinese path has correctly proved the Marxist judgement about the inevitable replacement of socialism for capitalism.

---

11 *Selected Works of Deng Xiaoping*. Chin. ed., People's Publishing House, Beijing, 1993, Vol. III, p. 225.

12 *Biological Chronology of Deng Xiaoping 1975-97*, Chin. ed., Central Party Literature Publishing House, Beijing, 2004, Vol. I, p. 1255.

Chinese people chose to practice socialism with Chinese characteristics and achieved great success at a time when the global socialist movement was all-time low. China not only helped socialism to settle on its own land, but also encouraged socialist enterprises all over the world. Since China's success is achieved under the guidance of the CPC, it is naturally attributed to the world's socialist enterprises. Deng Xiaoping made a good point by saying that socialism will always be supported by one fifth of the world's population as long as China is there[13] and socialism will always have its place as long as China is there.[14] Socialism with distinct Chinese characteristics not only demonstrates the rules emerged during socialist construction in special circumstances, but also demonstrates one of the universal rules that capitalism is bound to be replaced by socialism.

Deng Xiaoping's comments are highly justified as Chinese path practices socialism with Chinese characteristics rather than capitalism and Chinese path is guided by scientific socialism rather than democratic socialism or something else. Deng Xiaoping strongly believes in the socialist essence of reform and opening up led by the CPC who declares any connection of it with capitalism to be avoided. According to Deng Xiaoping, at the end of this century, Pudong New Area of Shanghai and Shenzhen should answer the first question about the socialist nature rather than capitalist nature of reform and opening up and to prove it with huge achievements.[15] Although as the initiator of the reform and opening up, Deng Xiaoping sees it as only a method to improve socialism, which on the other hand, provides principles, premises and goals for the reform. Reforms and opening up exist for cementing, improving and developing socialism rather than for weakening, shaking or even subverting it. What's more, he sets the socialist tune for the reform by making it clear that

13 *Selected Works of Deng Xiaoping*, Chin. ed., People's Publishing House, 1993, Vol. III, p. 321

14 Ibid, p. 346.

15 *Biological Chronology of Deng Xiaoping 1975-97*, Chin. ed., Central Party Literature Publishing House, Beijing, 2004, Vol. I, p. 1340.

the reform and opening up should be designed to cement socialist system and the leadership of the CPC and to boost productivity.[16] The reforms and opening up serve for socialism and Chinese path which becomes a socialist path with distinct characteristics. This leads to three conclusions. Firstly, China's achievements made along the path have proved socialism rather than capitalism is a right choice for China. Secondly, the reforms and opening up are proved to be socialist in essence. Thirdly, the basic judgement of Marxism about the superiority of socialism over capitalism and the inevitable replacement of socialism for capitalism is correct.

Chinese path is developed by relentlessly exploring an important question of what socialism is and how to carry out socialist construction. Chinese path, on the one hand, upholds strictly the socialist essence and on the other hand, learns from capitalism to better construct socialism on the basis of national and global conditions. The pioneers of Chinese path know that building Chinese socialism by learning from capitalism is a historical must. But it doesn't mean to shift to capitalism in essence nor deny the superiority of socialism over capitalism or the basic judgement of Marxism no longer make sense. Utilizing capitalism and practicing capitalism are different in nature. The former is to learn from capitalism while being highly alert to any possible negative effects and holding tightly the power to constrain and to judge capitalism with socialist values and systems.[17] The latter is to fully put capitalist values and systems into practice without restraint and finally surrender to it. It is the former rather than the latter that is happening in China where socialism is taking the place of capitalism while learning from it.

---

16 *Selected Works of Deng Xiaoping*, Chin. ed., People's Publishing House, Beijing, 1993, Vol. III, p. 241.

17 Chen Xueming. *Why Does China Still Need Marxism—Answers to Ten Questions about Marxism*, Chin. ed., Tianjin People's Publishing House, Tianjin, 2013, p. 262.

IV. The Chinese path confirms the validity of the Marxist conclusions about the leadership of proletarian party being a must for people's liberation

No matter where do scholars from home and abroad begin their studies on Chinese path, they attribute the success of the path to the political system practiced in China nowadays. That is to say, the success of Chinese path is because China strengthens and sticks to the leadership of the Communist Party of China. In the study on the secrets of Chinese path's success, Zhang Weiwei singled out firstly the contribution made by the "tough government" of China. According to him, during the reform and opening up in the past three decades, it was the authority of government and the party accumulated along Chinese history and the long process of revolution and development respectively that were used to implement all the policies and resolve problems. The gigantic size of China determined country governance to be a complex and tough job, which could only be undertaken by China's traditional and effective government system.[18] Francis Fukuyama, a Japanese American scholar, described China's political system as authoritarianism, which is the reason for China's success. According to Fukuyama, the primary characteristic of Chinese model was the CPC being a part of the huge bureaucratic system of authority centralization.

"This system, which is a modern version of the traditional one, governs China in a highly effective way.[19] On the one hand, it has an authoritative and effective government. On the other hand, it remains free from the constraint led by democracy and laws that are born together with market economy and export-oriented growth

18 Zhang Weiwei. *Chinese Shock-the Rise of a 'Civilisational State'*, Chin. ed., Shanghai People's Publishing House, Shanghai, 2011, p. 102.

19 Chen Jiagang. *Francis Fukuyama's Speeches in China*, Chin. ed., Central Compilation & Translation Press, Beijing, 2012, pp. 47-48.

model".[20] Zhang Weiwei recognized the "tough government" to be indispensable for China's success while Fukuyama gave the credit to authoritarianism so as to prove Chinese path to be unworthy of copying. But the two opposite perspectives revealed a truth that the rejuvenation of Chinese nation could not be achieved without the guidance of the CPC, a party that led to national liberation and the great achievements in these thirty years. All in all, China's success should be attributed ultimately to its political system, including the people's democratic dictatorship, the system of National People's Congress and multi-party political consultation under the leadership of the CPC.

Since the credit of success of Chinese path mainly goes to China's political system, it could also prove Marxist theories on state and party to be valid as they provide the theoretical basis of the current political system in China—multiparty political consultation under the leadership of the CPC with the CPC as the only ruling party.

According to Marxist theories on state and party, proletariat dictatorship, which is named as people's democratic dictatorship in China, should be experienced during the transition from class society to a non-class one. As the latest emerged state system, proletarians rule the country by their party—the communist party. Lenin gave a definition on the relations among people, classes, party and its leaders by saying that the people fall in various classes, which are ruled, at least in civilized countries by a certain party. Normally the party is led by a stable group of leaders that possess the highest authority and the richest experience and occupy the most responsible positions through elections.[21] Conclusions can be drawn from Lenin's definition that proletarians are ruled by their communist party in proletariat countries. And the communist party is "operated by a relatively stable group whose members are honored as leaders".

---

20 Ibid., p. 51.

21 *The Collected Works of Lenin*. Chin. ed., People's Publishing House, Beijing, 1958, Vol. XXXI, p. 23.

On the one hand, the two Marxist theories tell us the importance of proletariat parties holding absolute leading power after proletarians getting political power to found countries of their own. Marx and Engels pointed out in *The Communist Manifesto* that founding an independent political party (the communist party) for proletariat revolution is indispensable for proletarians to fulfill their historic responsibility of building a new society after they subvert the capitalist society. They emphasized that the communist party should represent proletarians and lead the proletariat revolution. Their leadership in the right direction provides the foundation of finishing the historic task of proletarians. According to Marx and Engels, workers had been doing continuous damage by inner competition to the process of proletarian organizations forming from a class to a party. The organization, however, could always gain rebirth and grow stronger and more powerful than before.[22] Marx wrote in his draft of *General Rules* for International Workingmen's Association that proletariat can only represent an independent class in its struggle against propertied union by making itself a party that is different from and against any parties founded by propertied class. He also noted the necessity of proletariat organization developing a party so as to finally eliminate classes and make social revolution a real success.[23] Founding a party of its own exist throughout the entire process of proletariat completing its mission. It is so during the revolution when they struggled for the political power and the construction period after that.

On the other hand, Marxist theories on state and party reveal the responsibility on the communist party's shoulder after the founding of proletariat regime. According to the theories, proletarian dictatorship requires its party to not only lead in proletariats and working public's suppression against resistance, destruction and aggression from class

22 *Complete Works of Marx and Engels*, Chin. ed., People's Publishing House, Beijing, 2009, Vol. II, pp. 40-41.

23 *Selected Works of Marx and Engels*. Chin. ed., People's Publishing House, Beijing, 1995, Vol. II, p. 611.

and outside enemies, but also in the socialist construction of economy, politics and culture so as to transform the society in a comprehensive and profound way, realizing the great mission of Communism by eliminating class difference, antagonisms and state.[24] Besides, something of great significance during the process is boosting the development of social productivity, laying solid material foundation for class elimination.

Just as Engels once claimed that rapid development of productivity and abundant resources created to produce social wealth cannot only guarantee increasingly abundant material life for citizens, but can also make sure that their intelligence and energy be fully and freely developed and used.[25] Therefore, it is safe to say that the communist party's leadership over proletariat and making productivity development its focus are what proletarian dictatorship is all about.

Thanks to the deep understanding of Marxist theories on state and political party, pioneers of Chinese path have placed focus on the Four Cardinal Principles, the people's dictatorship and the leadership of the Communist Party of China while proceeding with reform and opening up. Because they know it clearly that Chinese Path can yields no achievements without a strong country adhering to people's dictatorship and the leadership of the CPC. Not long after the CPC shifting its focus on productivity did Deng Xiaoping propose clearly to stick to the Four Cardinal Principles. In his speech representing CPC's central committee during the theory-discussing conference, he said that sticking to the Four Cardinal Principles on spiritual and political basis is the fundamental premise of realizing Four Modernizations in China.[26] Besides, adhering to proletariat dictatorship and the leadership of CPC are two principles of the four.

---

24 Xiao Qian, *Theories on Historical Materialism*. Chin. ed., People's Publishing House, Beijing, 1983, pp. 229-230.

25 *Selected Works of Marx and Engels*, Chin. ed., People's Publishing House, Beijing, 1972, Vol. III, p. 322.

26 *Selected Works of Deng Xiaoping*, Chin. ed., People's Publishing House, Beijing, 1994, Vol. II, p. 164.

Deng Xiaoping also made it clear that every member of the party shall not be forgiven if there are any mistakes on the fundamental stance, let alone the theorists of the party as mistakes on any one principle of the four will do great harm to our socialist enterprise and our modernization.[27] He later put special emphasis on the leadership of the party during the talk with propaganda department officials by saying that "the core of Capitalist Liberalization goes against the leadership of the communist party, without which there will be no room for socialist system. To avoid the situation we can't repeat the past to launch political movements but the weapon for self-criticism can't be lost.[28] Therefore the four Cardinal Principles, together with reform and opening up, form one of the basic aspects of the fundamental path at our new time."

A review over China's growth in the past three decades tells us that Chinese path develops under the guidance of the Four Cardinal Principles. Every time when the path reaches a critical moment, there will come CPC leaders emphasizing its significance, especially the significance of CPC's leadership, which is now an indispensable political guarantee for Chinese path going smoothly ahead. Actually, the political guarantee is rooted deeply in Marxism on state and party, which has been effectively implemented and further proved by theories and practices of the CPC at the end of the 20th century and the beginning of the 21st century.

V. The Chinese path proves Marxism on oriental society to be feasible

In 1970s - 1980s, Marx suspended composing and reviewing volume two and three of *Capital* for a critical shift on theoretical study, which referred to the shift from critical study on Western capitalist society

27 Ibid., p. 173.

28 *Selected Works of Deng Xiaoping*, Chin. ed., People's Publishing House, Beijing, 1994, Vol. II, p. 391.

and its politics and economy to a "new special study" on the Asian production mode in Russia. Then here came the assumption of Russia and other backward countries in the East going beyond the capitalist Caudine Forks and entering directly into socialism. This assumption, together with other thoughts related are later concluded as Marxist theory on oriental society. Instead of demonstrating the necessity and possibility of socialism by the intensification of basic contradictions of capitalism, Marx followed a different way by revealing a rule of social development that undeveloped countries that practices traditional production mode of rural communes as Russia does can seize the "best opportunity" in capitalist time to launch proletarian revolution, overcome Caudine Forks and finally realize socialism. In Marx's eyes, for all the connections of between Asian production mode and backward dictatorship in Eastern societies, it shows a different mode from the West for Eastern countries. Going capitalism is not the only way out for the East as Marx designs for them a brand new possibility.

Marx has proposed to realize socialism in oriental backward countries in his later life.

Lenin and Mao Zedong are all half-way there to achieve this goal, having spanning the "Caudine Canyon" set up by capitalism, and having established the socialist system in Soviet Union and China respectively. The other half-way, which is the more important one, is being gradually realized by the creation of the Chinese path. It has separated the two socialism, directing its construction in accordance with the requirements entailed by the socialism founded after striding over the capitalist "Caudine Canyon", and finally heading for the kind of socialism and communism depicted by Marx in his great works like *Capital*. Aiming at separating the two socialisms, the Chinese path has comprehensively and completely achieved old Marx's idea of realizing socialism in oriental backward countries, which makes Marx's theory of oriental society become a reality.

CHAPTER TWO

The Chinese Path's Falsification of Some Part of Marxism

While the Chinese path has testified a series of basic principles of Marxism, its successful practices have also falsified some original ideas and conclusions of Marxism. The study of falsification is absolutely more difficult than the study of the testification, but it does not mean that the research on the latter is not more important than the research on the former. Here we would like to have a try on exploring how the development of the Chinese path has rendered some of Marx's original ideas and conclusions outdated. It should be noted that by saying the original ideas and conclusions of Marxism rendered falsified by the Chinese path, it refers to not only those proposed by Marx and Engels under their historical conditions, but also those added by the successors of Marx and Engels, which is also included in Marxism. The two kinds of ideas and conclusions are hard to be distinguished under many occasions because people have become accustomed to merging them together, and accepting and disseminating them by calling both Marxist theory.

I. The Chinese path's falsification of "Socialism has no market"

The Classical writers of Marxism have never mentioned explicitly in their works that there are commodity and market existing in the first stage of socialism. They all agree that socialism that substitutes capitalism should adopt planned economy without commodity and market. Marx, the founder of Marxism, has a most classical and representative elaboration in *Critique of the Gotha Programme* in 1875, "In a collective society based on public ownership of means of production, producers do not swap their products, and the labor consumed by the products is not turned into value, neither into the property of the products. The reason is that contrary to capitalist society, individual labor exists as a part of the overall labor, instead of undergoing twists and turns".[1] Here Marx points out explicitly that socialism should adopt planned economy without commodity and market.

Some scholars frequently cite elaborations in Manuscript on Economics from 1857 to 1858, the first manuscript of *Capital*, to illustrate Marx's affirmation of socialist market economy, which is actually a serious mistake. Marx said:

> "People's dependency, which is totally natural in the beginning, is the first social state, under which people' s producing capacity develops within a narrow range in an isolated location. People's independency based on dependency on material is the second social state based on people's independency, under which a system could be formed of all-round relations, diverse demands, comprehensive abilities and general exchange of social material. Free individuality is the third stage based on individual all-round development and their common social productive capacity becoming their social wealth. The second stage creates conditions for the third stage. Therefore, with the development of commerce, luxury, currency and exchange value, patriarchal and feudal state disappears while modern society rises."[2]

What Marx mentions by commerce, luxury, currency and exchange value are the most essential elements of market economy. From the elaboration of Marx above, we can see Marx's affirmation of

1 *Selections from Marx and Engels*, Chin. ed., People's Publishing House, Beijing, 1995, Vol. II, p. 303.

2 *Selections from Marx and Engels*, Chin. ed., People's Publishing House, Beijing, 1979, Vol. XLVI, p. 104.

the historical status of market economy, believing that it is the development of market economy that make patriarchal and feudal state disappear and make modern society rise. However, we cannot see that Marx believes market economy is eternal, which still exists in the third development stage of human society, a society where people's common social productive capacity becomes their social wealth. On the contrary, Marx has stated clearly that market economy is historic only belonging to the second development stage of human society where human independency exists based on their dependency on material. Marx has also stated that market economy could open the way for socialist society to replace capitalist society, but it cannot exist in socialist society.

As is known to all, Lenin has implemented New Economic Policy in his lasting years, based on which some scholars propose that Lenin's action is to eliminate commodity economy, having realized the necessity of combining socialism with market together. But connecting Lenin's action directly with the idea of combining socialism and market together does not conform to the fact. Lenin's action is on account of his awareness that it is beyond the capacity of the Soviet Union to achieve direct transition to pure socialism and socialist distribution.[3] Therefore he asks the Soviet Union to become a smart wholesaler, with every citizen participating in the cooperatives' business and learning how to be a civilized businessman. He also requires the basic products of society to take the form of goods, enterprises to practice economic accounting according to business principles, etc.[4] Lenin proposes merging planned economy with market and carry out Soviet Union's economic work with consideration of the existence and rules of the market, regulating the circulation of market and currency through systematic and thoughtful economic measures which is based on precise evaluation of market

3 *Selections from Lenin*, Chin. ed., People's Publishing House, Beijing, 1995, Vol. 4, p. 720.

4 Nie Yunlin: *Study on the Theoretical System of Socialism with Chinese Characteristics*, Chin. ed., People's Publishing House, Beijing, 2011, p. 109.

process.[5] However, Lenin's words and action are not sufficient to prove that Lenin has the awareness of socialist market economy because in his saying and doing so he repeatedly declare that the changing attitude of the Soviet Union towards market is not to change the unified national planned economy and is not to go beyond the scope of planned economy, but to change the way to realize the planned economy.[6] That is to say though Lenin has realized the importance of market in a socialist system, he is affirming its status under the big framework of socialist planned economy, emphasizing that market is complementary to planned economy. Therefore, Lenin supports the system of socialist planned economy. We cannot forget that it is Lenin who has said that the huge task of socialist revolution is to turn all the national economic institutions into a big whole machine, namely an economic organism that allows tens of millions of people to work under one plan.[7]

All in all, in traditional Marxism, there is no doubt to believe that socialism is opposed to market, that market economy equals capitalism and planned economy equals socialism. Samuelson, a famous contemporary economist, has pointed out several ways used by human society to solve basic economic problems, one is free enterprise economy of capitalism. Socialists express doubts toward the free activity of gaining profit through laissez-faire economy, so they insist on introducing planned system to coordinate different departments.[8] Socialists believe that the planned system is what Marx has advocated. What the western market socialists are trying to do in testifying market socialism is to change Marx's idea that market and capitalism are connected which is further considered as socialism has no market.

5 *The Assembly of the Communist Party of the Soviet Union*, the Congress and the Central Resolution, Chin. Ed., People's Publishing House, Beijing, 1964, Part II, p. 137.

6 Ibid., p. 137.

7 *Selections from Lenin*, Chin. ed., People's Publishing House, Beijing, 1958, Vol. XXVII, p. 78.

8 Paul A. Samuelson. William D. *Nordhaus: Economics* (Translated by Gao Hongye), Chin. ed., The Press of Chinese Development, Beijing, 1992, p. 40.

That is to say in the eyes of market socialists, it is absolute that traditional Marxism puts market and socialism in opposition. Nearly all versions of textbooks of Marxist Political Economy at home and abroad have taken the rule of planned and proportional development as the basic rule of socialist economy. *The Textbook of Political Economy*, compiled by the Institute of Economics of Soviet Union's Academy of Science, has stated that capitalism is not possible without waste of social labor and anarchic production; socialism is not possible without reasonable and economical use of social labor and outcomes through planned development of national economy.[9] The former one is the derogative comment towards market economy given by orthodox Marxists; the latter one is the compliment towards planned economy given by orthodox Marxists. This means that the basic idea of this textbook is that capitalism is unimaginable without market, and socialism is inconceivable without plan. One of the important idea of *Textbook of Political Economy*, compiled by professor Jiang Xuemo after Cultural Revolution with tens of millions of circulation, is testifying the inevitability of the planned and proportional development of socialist production, emphasizing that the transition from anarchic production to planned socialist production is the main feature of socialist economy.[10] The idea that market economy and planned economy are the main symbol to distinguish capitalism and socialism is so inveterate that the United Nations has classified those applying national planned economy as socialist countries, and those applying market economy as capitalist countries.

If we say the core of the Chinese path is to implement socialist market economy and that the success of the Chinese path lies in combining market and socialism together, then we can get the conclusion that Chinese path does falsify Marxist judgment of

9 Economic Research Institute of Soviet Academy of Science. *Textbook of Political Economy*, Chin. ed., The People's Publishing House, Beijing, 1959, p. 465.

10 Jiang Xuemo: *Textbook of Political Economy*, Chin. ed., Shanghai People's Publishing House, Shanghai, 1980, p. 257.

putting market and socialism in opposition, and further prove that this falsification is correct.

Although from 1950s, the Soviet Union and some East European Countries have kept trying to reform the original socialist planned economy, they have not walked out of the mistake of dividing plan and economy. Some western market socialists have already begun their discussion on whether it is possible to merge market and socialism, but their discussion is just empty talks and purely theoretical. And very frequently they express hesitation in terms of theory. The one who explicitly puts forward merging socialism and market and establishes socialist market economy and puts it into practice is undoubtedly Chinese Communists after 1980s. It is also Chinese Communists after 1980s who have made explicit negation of the original Marxist judgment of putting market and socialism in opposition.

In 1979 when meeting with foreign guests, Deng Xiaoping says, "It is not right to say that market only exists in capitalism and there is only capitalist market economy. Why couldn't socialism apply market economy? We are socialist market economy with planned economy dominating and market economy combined."[11]

Deng Xiaoping clearly puts forward the concept of "socialist market economy", which he has always been paying attention to and mentions many times. In his talk with several leading comrades of the Central Committee in 1990, Deng Xiaoping emphasized that, "We must make it clear theoretically that the distinction between capitalism and socialism is economy and plan", "It is nonsense to say it is capitalist road with a little form of market economy mingled in it."[12] During the South Talk in 1992, Deng Xiaoping gives a clearer elaboration on the relation between market and socialism. This talk has been regarded as one of the most important historical documents

11 *Selected Works of Deng Xiaoping*, Chin. ed., The People's Publishing House, Beijing, 1994, Vol. II, p. 236.

12 *Selected Works of Deng Xiaoping*, Chin. ed., The People's Publishing House, Beijing, 1993, Vol. III, p. 364.

in the new historical period for China's Communist Party of China, because it is in this talk when the CPC has officially put forward the theory of socialist market economy, which has decisive influence on finally realizing the transition from planned economy to socialist market economy. Deng Xiaoping said, "It is not the proportion of plan and market that decides the essential difference between capitalism and socialism. Planned economy does not equal socialism as capitalism also has plan; market economy does not equal capitalism as socialism also has market. Plan and market are both economic means."[13] Deng Xiaoping proposes this idea in an atmosphere where socialism and market are generally believed to be in opposition, and to a certain extent, his idea is against the original Marxist judgment that socialism and market are in opposition. After South Talk, socialist market economy has gradually been established and improved in China, which could be regarded as another name for Chinese path. This fact is obviously a significant rectification and breakthrough towards the original Marxist judgment that socialism has no market.

II. The Chinese path makes the "Confrontation Philosophy" of Marxism out of place

Although Lukács, the founder of western Marxism, has a partial understanding of Marxist dialectics, his conclusion of Marxism as dialectics and his belief that adhering to Marxist dialectics is adhering to Marxism are all right. It is true that the understanding of Marxist dialectics is of great significance for understanding the whole Marxism philosophy.

Marxist dialectics is the reflection of materialist dialectics as an objective dialectics, a scientific system composed by a series of philosophical categories patched together based on their relations. Different elements of Marxist dialectics expose the general nature

13 Ibid., p. 373.

of the links and the development of objective things from different aspects.

Such are basic laws of Marxist dialectics as the Law of Interchange of Quality and Quantity, the Law of the Unity of Opposites, the Law of Negation of Negation, which are exposed by such categories as quality and quantity, unity and opposite, affirmation and negation.

Engels said, "The law of dialectics is abstracted from the history of nature and human society and it is the basic laws of the development of history and human thinking pattern. In essence, they can be concluded as including the following three laws, the law of Interchange of Quality and Quantity, the Law of the Unity of Opposites, the law of Negation of Negation."[14]

Among the three basic laws of Marxist dialectics, the Law of the Unity of Opposites is said to be the most important or even the core. Lenin said, "Dialectics could be simplified as the Law of Unity of Opposites, which could help us grasp the core of dialectics, and which also entails elaboration.[15] A unity could be split into two parts, and the understanding of its contradicting part is the core of dialectics."[16]

Marxist dialectics emphasize that in order to understand the Law of Unity of Opposites, one must correctly understand the contradicting categories of Marxist dialectics, which requires to understand the meaning of and the relations between unity and opposite, or between identity and conflict. In the concrete elaboration of this relation, Marxist dialectics stresses conflict. The fundamental viewpoints of Marxist dialectics are that the conflict is unconditional and absolute while the identity is conditional, temporary and relative, and that conflict settles itself in identity and identity contains conflict.[17] About

14 *Selections from Marx and Engels*, Chin. ed., People's Publishing House, Beijing, 1972, Vol. III, p. 484.

15 *Selections from Lenin*, Chin. ed., People's Publishing House, Beijing, 1972, Vol. II, p. 608.

16 Ibid., p. 711.

17 Ai Siqi: *Dialectical Materialism and Historical Materialism*, Chin. ed., The People's Publishing House, Beijing, 1961, p. 91.

this Engels said, "It can be found in every objective thing that identity itself contains diversity. Here the predicate must be different from the subject just as identity must be complemented by everything different from it."[18] Lenin said more clearly, "unity, or identity, or balance, the opposite part of conflict, is conditional, temporary and relative. The confrontation between the two contradicting sides is as absolute as development and movement."[19] Marxist dialectics regard the conflict of contradiction as a broad philosophical category, highlighting the greatest universality and generality of this category.

"Confrontation Philosophy", abstracted from Marxist dialectics' understanding of the relation between contradiction's identity and conflict, which stresses that objective things' development mainly relies on the opposition and conflict of different aspects within its inner contradiction, which reflects itself as the whole development process of the same contradiction. Engels once points out that the evolution of nature mainly relies on confrontation, "The theory of evolution proves how a simple cell evolves through inheritance and adaptation, and turns into the most complicated plant or people."[20] Lenin said, "One must see the development process as identity if he wants to self-movement and self-evolution of all processes on the earth."[21] Mao Zedong has explained the confrontation philosophy more clearly, "Everything' movement has two states, a state of relative stillness and a state of marked change. The two states' movement are triggered by the conflict between the two contradicting parts within an objective thing." Mao even said, "Some has called communist theory as confrontation philosophy, which I think is correct. Confrontation philosophy is first founded by slave owners, feudal lords and capitalist

18 *Selections from Marx and Engels*, Chin. ed., People's Publishing House, Beijing, 1972, Vol. III, pp. 537-538.

19 *Selections from Lenin*, Chin. ed., People's Publishing House, Beijing, 1972, Vol. II, p. 712.

20 *Selections from Marx and Engels*, Chin. ed., People's Publishing House, Beijing, 1972, Vol. III, pp. 534.

21 *Selections from Lenin*, Chin. ed., People's Publishing House, Beijing, 1972, Vol. II, p. 712.

who suppress ordinary people. Marxism, the confrontation philosophy of those being suppressed, has come into being much later with thousands of years' struggle."[22]

The above elaboration proves that confrontation philosophy is logically abstracted from Marxist dialectics. It has been rooted in people's mind that Marxist philosophy is concluded as confrontation philosophy. It is no accident that it is confrontation philosophy that first comes to people' mind when Marxist dialectics is mentioned. Although we can find some words of identity and unity, words of opposition and conflict are much more. Marxist dialectics is dialectical thinking, which highlights the dialectical relation between identity and non-identity and between unity and opposition, with the emphasis on non-identity and opposition.

The Chinese path, to a certain extent, is a denial to confrontation philosophy. Chinese path has two key words, one is "peaceful development", and the other is "harmonious society". The two key words tell people that choosing peaceful development road and establishing a harmonious society and world are the inherent requirements of socialism with Chinese characteristics. Peaceful development says China's development relies on peaceful long-term self-accumulation, instead of relying on such measures such as aggression and plunder done by some countries when establishing their hegemony. China does not want to seek the so-called shortcut, but to rely on its own long-term self-development. China creatively connect development and peace together, stressing that only peaceful environment could bring smooth development. China aims to re-shape the relation between capitalism and socialism, and puts the overall situation of its own development into the big picture of world development, expecting that China's peaceful efforts would bring world's peaceful development. "Harmonious society" says socialism with Chinese characteristics is socialism pursing world harmony and

22 S*elected Works of Mao Zedong*, Chin. ed., People's Publishing House, Beijing, 1996, Vol. III, p. 316.

common development. Realizing socialist modernization and the great rejuvenation of Chinese nation is the dream of socialism with Chinese characteristics, which represents China's prosperity and the world's peace, stability and development. Face with various social conflicts and class conflicts, Chinese path does not adopt the way of political struggle of the past revolutionary party. Instead, Chinese path applies all means to coordinate the different social interest relations, and stimulate the creativity of all classes and groups, during which conflicts have been resolved, synergy has been formed, and harmonious society has been developed. "Peaceful development" and "harmonious society" have revealed the lofty heights of socialism with Chinese characteristics. The two core concepts reflect that Chinese path closely connects its own development and its promotion of world peace, and closely combine the interests of Chinese people with the interests of people in the world. It is the lofty pursuit of Chinese nation to put its own development into the development of world civilization, and unifies its own progress with the progress of human civilization.

What Chinese path follows is harmonious thought instead of confrontation thought. The key is that Chinese path finds a correct new path to deal with the two contradicting parts, which reveals as the following two aspects. In dealing with international relations, Chinese path seeks to coexist with rather than confront with capitalism, which is the contradicting side of socialism. It tries to treat capitalism with an open and inclusive mind, and tries to find more commonalities with capitalism. The socialism with Chinese characteristics is an open and inclusive socialism, an important symbol of which is that it no longer treats capitalism as enemy, but that it realizes capitalism and socialism in contemporary world can be compatible and interpenetrative. In terms of its relation with capitalism, Chinese path finds not only the difference and conflicts between capitalism and socialism, but also the link and coexistence between them. Chinese leaders, when facing the new world situation, adjusts its relation with capitalism in time and treats common development and peaceful coexistence as a basic long-term strategy rather than a temporary solution. Socialism with Chinese characteristics proactively face all challenges with open and win-win development strategy instead of close and exclusive one.

Inside China, Chinese path cannot be simply defined as recognizing that there still exist class differences, conflicts and even antagonism in our country. Chinese path is aimed to explore new ways to solve class problems based on the such recognition. "New ways" here does not refer to confrontational or violent ways, or "Wudou" in Chinese. Instead, "New ways" refers to peaceful and coordinated ways, or "Wendou" in Chinese. In other words, to solve class differences, conflicts and even antagonism, we should resort to the people, and laws and regulations, instead of adopting confrontational ways in political movements. Such non-violent solution does not only apply to solving intra-class differences and conflicts, but also to resolving group or class differences, conflicts and antagonism. "Non-violent" here refers to solving class problems by improving the democratic and legal system, and cultivating democratic sense and enhancing legal consciousness among the citizens.

When we talk about the success of Chinese path, we cannot ignore a significant factor, which is the basic idea of driving development by coordinating and balancing different aspects of China's issues.

The truth shows that Chinese path transcends and rectifies the "confrontation philosophy", commonly recognized as the universal rule of Marxist dialectics, that upholds "confrontation is absolute while harmony is relative".

III. The Chinese path exposes the flaws of the Marxist "Material Ontology"

The classical Marxist philosophy does not only define the basic problem of philosophy as the logic connection between material and idea, but also make a clear answer to it, which is that material is primary while idea is secondary; the nature of the primacy of the world is material, and idea is a sort of highly-developed material, and the function of human brain is a subjective reflection of objective material; and that the world is united in the form of material, and is a material world that motions and develops to a fixed set of laws in a certain time and space. Some people like to use the term "ontology" to refer to the basic thoughts of Marxist philosophy about the logic connection between matter and idea, and name it "Material Ontology".

Some scholars at home and abroad, represented by the "Western Marxist", did not agree to interpret Marxist philosophy as "Material Ontology", but as "Practice Ontology". We should make it clear that to interpret Marxist philosophy as "Practice Ontology", these scholars altered the definition of "ontology", which was not dilated from *Ludwig Feuerbach and the End of Classical German Philosophy* by F. V. Engels to illustrate the basic problems of philosophy, but a more general explanation. These scholars believed they could find a way that transcended the previous one of defining the world primacy as either material or idea, and only needed to explore something holding a fundamentally important position, and this was "Ontology". But while they also recognized Marxism described something meaningful, which was human's emotional behaviors and practices, they concluded Marxist philosophy as "Practice Ontology".

Marxism indeed considers human's practice as meaningful existences, but does that mean Marxism gives up its basic materialism that sees material as the primacy of the world?

Certainly not. Lenin said: "If the world is material in motion, then we should be able to do limitless research on material according to the manifestation of the motion or the material in motion; and except for material, or a familiar external physical world, the world has nothing".[23]

---

23 *Selected Works of Lenin: in Three Volumes*, Chin. ed., People's Publishing House, 1975, Vol. II, p. 351

"Material is a philosophical concept that marks objective existence, and such objective existence is perceived by human senses. It does not rely on human senses, or in other words, even not being perceived, the existence exists. But it exists for our senses, and is copied, photographed and reflected by our senses".[24] We all know that, in the works of Lenin, especially in the book *Materialism and Empirio-Criticism*, such remarks that the primacy of the world is material are typical.

However, some people think, though Lenin explicitly held the "Material Ontology", it does not necessarily mean that the "Material Ontology" is also held by the Marxism founders.

As a co-founder of Marxism, Engels stated as following: "Though the existence of the world is the prerequisite for its unity, in that the world unites only after it exists, yet the unity of the world does not lie in its existence. Beyond what we can see there exists a problem to be solved. The real unity of the world lies in its materiality. This kind of materiality is in no way proved by simple words, and it should be proved by long-term and sustainable development of philosophy and natural science".[25] "The material and perceptive world where we live, is practical, but our thinking and consciousness is always the outcome of our brain, the material and sensual organ, no matter how pretersensual it seems. Material is not the outcome of spirit, whereas spirit is the high-end outcome of material".[26] These views Engels proposed, like "The real unity of the world lies in its materiality", and "Material is not the outcome of spirit, whereas spirit is the high-end outcome of material" explicitly dilated theories of the "Material Ontology".

Some other people may propose that, the views of Engels and Marx differed actually. Engels held "Material Ontology", while Marx

24 Ibid., 128

25 *Selected Works of Marx and Engels*, Chin. ed., People's Publishing House, 1972, Vol. III, p. 83

26 *Selected Works of Marx and Engels*, Chin. ed., People's Publishing House, 1972, Vol. IV, p. 223

did not agree with. Now, let's take a further look at what Marx said:

> "The law is like the governance method of a country, and we can neither understand it for the sake of itself, nor in terms of general development of human spirit. Actually, it is rooted in the material life...The results that I obtained and applied to my study can be summarized as following: people connect to each other in their life, and the connection is inevitable, necessary and not up to their will, that is, a sort of connection corresponding to their certain development level of material productivity. The sum of these connections constitute the economic structure of society, that is to say, a structure with the legal and political superstructure in position, and also a realistic basis that has corresponding social consciousness. The production pattern in material life limits the social, political and mental life in society. It is not the human's idea that determines human's existence, on the contrary, it is human's social existence that determines human's idea. When the material productivity in society develops to a certain stage, it begins conflicting with existent production and property relations (legal terms in production relations). As a result, these relations develop into the restriction of productivity from a development form of productivity. That is when the social revolution emerges".[27]
>
> "With the change of economic basis, the superstructure also began changing at a slow or rapid pace. My dialectical way is basically different from Hegel's, or rather opposite to Hegel's. From Hegel's perspective, the process of thinking, which he called idea or even saw as an independent subject, was the creator of practical things, and practical things are barely external manifestation of thinking. But I hold different views. Thinking is no more than something material that is instilled into and altered by human's minds".[28]

From the two paragraphs quoted from Marx, we can clearly see that, as for the point that the primacy of the world is material, Marx and Engel shared similar views, nothing basically different.

Having read the elaborations of Marxist writers, we can hardly make it not to link Marxist philosophy and "Material Ontology". Or we can put it in this way, as Marxism-Leninism is a branch of classical

27 *Selected Works of Marx and Engels*, Chin. ed., People's Publishing House, 1995, Vol. II, p. 32-33

28 Capital, Chin. ed., People's Publishing House, 1975, Vol. I, p. 24

Marxism, its philosophy core is undoubtedly "Material Ontology".

In summary, some scholars at home and abroad, represented by the "Western Marxist", who ruthlessly denied the connection between Marxist philosophy and "Material Ontology" were not justified. But we can also see that their re-explanation is based on the flaw of Marxism that the philosophy ignores human's subjective initiative. The criticism they made on "Material Ontology" was partially reasonable, and their mistake lied in that they did not improve or develop Marxist Ontology after they realized the flaws of Marxist philosophy, but imposed newly-built theories on Ontology on Marxism. This gave people an illusion that the original Ontology of Marxism was totally right, and it was just misinterpreted by people. They were not confident enough to "improve" or "renew" Marxist Ontology, only to see their work as "re-discovering" or "re-revealing" Marxist Ontology.

The scholars represented by Western Marxists, had their reason to criticize the "Material Ontology", which was that the theory ignored the dominant position of people. The logic of their criticism was: the point that the primacy of the world is material is nothing wrong, but if people simply regard material as an assemble of purely objective matters, then the world becomes a silent and non-dynamic world, doesn't it? The significance of Ontology lies in that it provides a basic rule for people to learn about and contribute to the world while making an answer to what the world looks like, so what rules can concluding the primacy of the world as material provide? Indisputably, the world belongs to human, but from the perspective of "Material Ontology", is there any position for human? The world that "Material Ontology" describes should be a world without human, but what is the meaning if people still assumes the existence of such a world? We cannot say that the "Material Ontology" totally evades the human issue, but it considers human as barely a component of material motion. Isn't it a philosophy that "misses human existence and only focuses on material"?

Though the criticism on "Material Ontology" raised by these

scholars represented by "Western Marxist" was partially reasonable, yet what truly exposed the flaws of the theory, and what made a breakthrough in and transcended the theory, was the Chinese path, the great practices of Chinese people under the guidance of socialism with Chinese characteristics; it was "people-oriented" practices of China that basically changed the situation in which people were "reluctant to talk about human existence", instead of the criticism of these scholars. A key essence of the Chinese path is upholding the flag of "people-oriented". The concept, to some extent, is tenable and right only when compared to "material-oriented". Obviously, the basic requirement of "people-oriented" is to put human at the first place, instead of material.

It is exactly the under guidance of the "people-oriented" principle that Chinese people have been underlining the primary importance of human throughout the social and historic development, in other words, highlighting the role of human in the process; that Chinese people have been attaching great importance to respecting, emancipating, counting on, considering the interests of, and educating human, paying attention to the living environment of human, and showing long-term concerns for human's livelihood and development. In a way, the success that the Chinese path has achieved over the years can be summarized as the success of implementing the "people-oriented" principle.

Some voices may doubt that the "people-oriented" principle that China has promoted is meaningful in terms of values, but does not contribute to the Ontology theory, that is to say, the perspectives they study the principle are limited to its values and the connection among its values, excluding the perspective of the principle's Ontology meaning. Actually, there is not such a thing as values without Ontology and views of the world as bases, which means that any values have their corresponding Ontology theories, and views of the world. The "people-oriented" principle was proposed, established, and implemented in that it could improve classical "Material Ontology" in philosophy, from there arisen its further value. Chinese Path undoubtedly has its corresponding "Ontology", therefore, if we acknowledge the success of the Chinese path, and acknowledge that the success hinges on the successful implementation of the "people-oriented" principle, then we have to recognize that the Chinese path does rectify the flaws of classical Marxism. However, this kind of rectification does not equal to the "Practice Ontology" raised by scholars represented by "Western Marxist", neither does it equal to an absolute negation of "Material Ontology" in Marxism. Here is a point we have to clarify that, the Chinese path enriches the Marxist Ontology, and develops it from a philosophical theory focusing on "material" yet without subject, to one emphasizing "the subjectivity of human". How to name the new Ontology given birth to by the Chinese path does not matter; what matters is to find a connection point between material and practice.

IV. The Chinese path means a necessary review of the concept that Marxism must rupture with traditional views

The Communist Manifesto explicitly pointed out: "The communist revolution is the most radical rupture with traditional property relations; no wonder that its development involves the most radical rupture with traditional ideas." [29] This is what is called "two ruptures" concept, the core theory of both *the Communist Manifesto* and Marxism.

From the views of Marx and Engels, they took the concept that the communist revolution must "rupture" with "tradition views" as natural. They profoundly pointed out: "The dominant ideology of any era is certainly the ideology of the ruling class."[30] In feudalist society,

29 *Selected Works of Marx and Engels*, People's Publishing House, Chin. ed., 2009, Vol. II, p. 52.

30 Ibid., p. 51.

the ruling class was the feudalist landowners, therefore the dominant ideology of feudalist society was naturally the ideology of feudalist landowners; in capitalist society, the ruling class is the bourgeoisie, therefore the dominant ideology is the ideology of the bourgeoisie. In socialist society, the nature and institution of society determines that we should "eliminate" the feudalist and capitalist ideology while "developing" the proletarian ideology. Marx and Engels said: "People's notion, views or concepts, in a word, people's ideology, changes in accordance with people's life quality, social connection and social[31] existence. Doesn't it require few thinking before getting this point?" In fact, at the very beginning when Marx and Engels established materialist view of history, they already expounded how idea came into being and which social class it was attributed to, why "the capitalist ideology" was an ideology that "occupied a dominant position in whichever era". For instance, they said in *German Ideology*:

> A certain class that enjoys both dominant material and ideological power in society, is in charge of the class of material production and the material for ideological production. As a result, those people without material for ideological production are naturally affiliated to the class. The dominant ideology is no more than the ideological manifestation of dominant material, that is, a reflection of dominant material relations in the form of ideology; in summary, the ideology is the ideological manifestation of what makes a certain class the ruling class, and that's why it is the dominant ideology of the ruling class.

Then, does the concept that the communist revolution must "absolutely rupture" with "traditional views" mean an "absolute rupture" with not only the religious, moral, philosophical, political and legal concepts that "keep changing throughout the course of history", but also the religion, morals, philosophy, politics and laws themselves that "were reserved through the changes in history", and even with the "forever tenable truth shared by all states of society",

31 Ibid., pp. 50-51.

like freedom and justice? Marx and Engels stated that, by then, the history of every society had been proceeding in the dynamic class confrontation, different forms in different times. But no matter in which form, that some people tended to exploit other people was a fact in every century. In this way, it was no wonder that though social ideology differed a lot, different ideologies should have some shared forms of development. If so-called "forever tenable truth" refers to these shared forms, then the communist revolution is destined to "rupture" with the so-called truth, but there is point we have to be aware that, these ideological forms will only disappear after the class confrontation no longer exists.

The creation of the Chinese path required ideological resources, and one was traditional Chinese culture. This proved that the creation of the Chinese path did not "radically rupture" with traditional Chinese culture. On the contrary, it absorbed the prominent and reasonable elements. By looking into a series of "ideological elements" of the Chinese path, we can find that many of these elements derive from traditional Chinese culture, such as, the intellectual pursuit and ideological beliefs.

Chinese people enjoy a traditional and valuable trait in cultivating intellectual pursuit and ideological beliefs, which produced significant influence on the ancient culture and civilization, and even more positive influence on Chinese contemporary reform and socialist modernization. For example, the trait to absorb the essence of old traditions and refresh them. This is a spiritual trait of traditional Chinese culture. The Chinese path was what came into being when the CPC absorbed the essence of traditions of Marxism, the Western culture and the Chinese culture while eliminating the "outdated" planned institution and traditional socialist institution, and building "up-to-date" socialist market economy system and socialism with Chinese characteristics. And another typical trait, progressive attitude and the awareness of Golden Mean. This is another underlying trait of traditional Chinese culture, being progressive, reliable and abiding by Golden Mean. Obviously, the CPC demonstrated such traits when pushing the development of reform and socialist modernization. The reform in China and the "Beijing Consensus" and Chinese Path developed in reform, quite different from the radical or extreme reforms of previously Socialist countries adhering to "Washington Consensus" like Soviet Union, are commonly considered progressive and reasonable, with awareness of abiding by Golden Mean rooted in traditional Chinese culture.

The success of the Chinese path undoubtedly hinges on its absorbing "spiritual elements" from traditional Chinese culture. Today, when studying the success of the Chinese path, many scholars at home and abroad are apt to attribute it to the legacy of traditional Chinese culture, and reveal the implicit connection between the Chinese path and traditional Chinese culture. There are good reasons for the trend. As the Chinese path develops further, the high-level leaders of China have placed increasing emphasis on absorbing traditional Chinese culture, to give new life to traditional Chinese culture in a new time. Besides, this is also a review of the ideology that Marxism must "absolutely rupture with traditional views". The Chinese path has proved to the world with its successful implementation that: the attitude towards traditional Chinese culture should be dialectical, instead of radical. Actually, Chinese path has explored a dialectical attitude towards traditional culture. Firstly, we can see that although Chinese path did not abolish criticism about traditional views, yet it did not agree with the radical idea that criticism on traditional views means abolishing them regardless of its reasonable parts, or have an illusion about tradition's perishing. Contrarily, it emphasized to analyze traditional views from a historic view. Secondly, Chinese path did see traditional views as tenable, and we should distinguish the "essence" from the "dross", so as to absorb the "essence" while eliminating "the dross". In this way, we can "draw lessons from the history to benefit today". In short, criticism on tradition is like bathing a baby, and we cannot pour the baby away with the water.

During the process of exploring a reasonable attitude towards traditional culture, that is, from simply "rupturing" to "dialectically approach", Chinese path found in the theoretical system of Marxism, that except for explicit proposal to "absolutely rupture" with traditional views, there are remarks on "selectively inheriting" traditional views. Some of the remarks were said by the Marxism founders, Marx and Engels, while some said by Lenin and Mao Zedong.

Marx once said: "People do not create their own history, as they please, in an environment they choose, but under the condition that they already encountered, that were already established and inherited from the past. The tradition from previous generations, like a nightmare, keep pestering the mind of people alive."[32] Marx implied that, tradition was definitely negative and like a historic burden, but it would never fade out from the stage of the history, and overcoming tradition was a long-term process. Lenin wrote in *The Heritage We Renounce* that: "When we talk about the heritage of modern people, we should know there are two types: one is the heritage from general torchbearers, which advocates to adopt absolute hostile attitude towards everything before the revolution, and protects the European dream and the interests of the mass; the other is the heritage from the populists."[33] Obviously, Lenin stressed to do specific analysis about "heritage", so he must acknowledge the former heritage and reject the latter one. Mao Zedong pointed out: "China created brilliant ancient culture in feudalist society for thousand years. To develop new culture of and improve confidence in our nation, it is necessary to study the development course of ancient culture, eliminate the feudalist dross and absorb the democratic essence. However, that does not mean absorb everything without selection. We should distinguish the rotten heritage of the ruling class in ancient feudalist society from the

32 *Selected Works of Marx and Engels*, Chin. ed., People's Publishing House, 1965, Vol. VIII, p. 121.

33 *Selected Works of Lenin: in Three Volumes*, Chin. ed., People's Publishing House, 1973, Vol. I, p. 149.

brilliant culture, which was more or less democratic or revolutionary legacy, of the mass."[34]

The problem was that, when people talked about the attitudes of Marxism towards traditional views, the proposal of "absolute rupturing" in *the Communist Manifesto* automatically came into their minds, and they naturally ignored the remarks of Marxism that expected people to adopt a dialectical attitude towards traditional views. In this way, the "absolute rupturing" proposal became a "mainstream" attitude. And looking back on these decades since People's Republic of China was founded, we can see that the attitude has not only been "mainstream" in theory, but also dominated people's practices. What Chinese path has made efforts to change was exactly the "mainstream" attitude. Actually, the process of Chinese path changing and rectifying the "mainstream" attitude, is a process of revealing the remarks made by the founders and successors of Marxism to dialectically analyze traditional views.

There is no doubt that Marxism is still the major source of thoughts for the Chinese path. In the course of adopting a right attitude towards Chinese traditional culture, China realizes that there is common ground between Marxism and Chinese traditional culture despite their differences. Their common ground is embodied in various aspects. First, they both take a dialectical view of the world and perceive the development of history from the perspective of the whole world and all mankind. Second, they surpass state theories in the West by promoting "All man are brothers", "human emancipation" and "communism". Third, they both emphasize the value of human with Chinese traditional culture attaching great importance to "people-oriented thought" and Marxism stressing "human-oriented thought". Fourth, they emphasize communities and advocate "the world is for all" by opposing the overemphasis on individual rights and perpetuity of individual properties. The above similarities make

34 *Selected Works of Mao Zedong*, Chin. ed., People's Publishing House, 1991, Vol. II, p. 707-708.

it necessary and possible for the Chinese path to integrate Marxism into Chinese traditional culture and turn the process of localization of Marxism in China to the one of absorbing excellent Chinese traditional culture.

Chapter Three
The Chinese Path's Development of Marxism

The reason why Marxism is a truth is that it pursues ceaselessly a more advanced level of understanding instead of remaining stagnant. Whether Marxism has vitality depends on whether it could achieve theoretical innovation with the development of the times. To measure whether the Chinese path has contributed to Marxism and how great the contribution is, we need to examine whether the Chinese path has promoted the development of Marxism and how great the development is.

Although it's reasonable to say that the Chinese path was initiated under the guidance of "developing Marxism", the question is how "developing Marxism" came about. The Chinese people certainly didn't think of it randomly but rather it was derived from the Chinese people's practice in the cause of Socialism with Chinese Characteristics. "developing Marxism" guides the Chinese path and meanwhile it's advanced by the Chinese path, which forms a two-way process.

The contribution of the Chinese path to Marxism is that it promotes Marxism in the localization of Marxism in China. After discussing how the Chinese Path verifies and falsifies Marxism, we now focus on the progress of Marxism brought by the Chinese Path. In fact, the verification and falsification of Marxism is closely connected with the development of Marxism as the process of verification and falsification drives the development of Marxism. The development of Marxism brought by the Chinese Path is comprehensive. In other words, the Chinese Path has made remarkable contributions to Marxist philosophy, Marxist political economics, and Marxist scientific socialism, as the three parts constitute Marxism.

I. The Chinese path's influences on Marxist philosophy

The "verification" of Marxist philosophy put forward by the Chinese path is quite obvious. Without the guidance of historical materialism whose core concept is that productivity determines relations of production, we couldn't define the nature of our society as "the primary stage of socialism", nor would we be able to implement a series of strategies consistent with this particular historical period and to take developing productivity as the top priority. Without material epistemology whose core concept is "consciousness is the reflection of material" serving as the ideological foundation, we would not be able to adhere to the ideological line of "freeing our minds and seeking truth from facts" and avoid a closed mind. The process of the Chinese path proves Marxist theory of the basic socialist contradictions and material epistemology great truths. The question is that the development of Marxist philosophy brought by China is not as obvious as the verification of Marxist philosophy, causing the former to be always neglected. In fact, as long as we make an in-depth analysis of the connotation and process of the China path, we will realize that the significance of the development of Marxist philosophy brought by the China path is so great that it couldn't be undervalued.

1. The Chinese path holds high the banner of "putting people first", transforming the Marxist philosophy's "material ontology" into "material-practice ontology"

During the Third Plenary Session of the 16th CPC Central Committee, "putting people first" was written into "Decision of the CPC Central Committee on Several Issues Concerning Perfecting

Socialist Market Economy System". It was of great political significance as it was the first time that "Putting people first" had been written into the official documents of the Communist Party of China. Since then, it has been established as the core concept of Scientific Outlook on Development. The Third Plenary Session of the 16th CPC Central Committee also passed "The CPC Central Committee's Proposals of Amending the Constitution" and decided to submit it to the 10th National People's Congress for deliberation. One of the proposals was about including respecting and protecting human rights in the Constitution, which showed that the Chinese path would take the banner of "putting people first" as a political concept to advance its human rights cause and social progress. In fact, China has addressed the fundamental issue of on whom its development relies and for whom it develops by taking "putting people first" as its stand. It's reasonable for the 17th CPC National Congress and the 18th CPC National Congress to require China to take the stand of "putting people first" more willingly in implementing Scientific Outlook on Development and pushing forward the Chinese path.

There is a profound significance of upholding high the banner of "putting people first".

The great political significance of "putting people first" is premised on its profound theoretical significance. In other words, the former is inspired by the latter.

Apparently, Marxism's "material ontology" is incompatible with "putting people first" as we can't derive it from "material ontology" by any means.

Only the "ontology" of combining "putting material first" with the value of people or the "ontology" of valuing the existence of both "material" and people can be associated with the political concept of "putting people first". When the CPC Central Committee first puts forward the political concept of "putting people first", the Chinese academia was having a discussion about practical materialism to discard the "ontology" of putting material first and the practice of respecting objective laws and depreciating subjective consciousness. Such a discussion could be traced back to the 1980s, when China initiated the reform and opening up and it has been carried on since then. It seems that the discussion was aroused by western philosophies such as Marxism, but actually it was not purely academic but generated by the demand for a theoretical basis of a series of strategies implemented by the CPC in the historical transitional period. The question is why the heated discussion didn't bring forth any theoretic achievements before the CPC puts forward the concept of "putting people first". It indicates that although a new theoretical achievement is a great development for Marxist philosophy, it can't be realized merely through "academic discussion" among the theorists and instead must be based on practical achievements driven by an extensive social campaign. Indeed, if the Third Plenary Session of the 16th CPC Central Committee had not put forward the political concept of "putting people first" and persistently adhered to it, a theoretical breakthrough in Marxist "material ontology" wouldn't have been accomplished, neither would the Chinese academia have reached a consensus on the issue of ontology and made a theoretical achievement based on the long-term discussion about practical materialism. Consequently, a great development for Marxist philosophy's "ontology" couldn't be achieved without the long-term and in-depth discussion among the theorists but such a development mainly benefited from the birth and practice of the political concepts of "putting people first". It is the idea and the practice of "putting people first" on the China path that include people's active practice into "ontology", making practice the top priority.

Certainly, further discussion is needed to choose a proper concept to summarize the great development of Marxist philosophy ontology achieved in China and a proper term to express the Marxist "ontology" that has been developed. The term "practice ontology" is inappropriate as it defies materialism, the basis of Marxist philosophy "ontology". In addition, this term may blur the line between our concepts and idealism concerning "ontology" upheld by "western Marxists". As a result, people may think we share the same idea with the "western Marxists" and duplicate their opinions without making any contributions to "ontology". Let's make a tentative attempt by coining the term "material-practice ontology" to express the development of Marxist philosophy "ontology" achieved in China.

2. China is committed to peaceful development and to building a harmonious socialist society, transforming Marxist philosophy from advocating "struggle" to "identity".

In September, 2004, the Fourth Plenary Session of the 16th CPC National Congress was held in Beijing and passed "Decision of CPC Central Committee on Building up the Party's Governing Capacity". It caught much attention by putting forward "building a harmonious socialist society" and pointing out that "it is a strategic goal set in the overall situation of building a moderately prosperous society in all aspects". From then on, a new concept- "harmonious society" has come into our sight. About six years later, the Sixth Plenary Session of the 16th CPC Central Committee passed "Decision of the CPC Central Committee on Several Issues Concerning Building a Harmonious Socialist Society", thus forming the action policy and the basic framework of a harmonious socialist society. The "Decision" comes straight to the point by pointing out that "social harmony is the essential nature of socialism with Chinese characteristics", which is also the punchline. The "Decision" also explains "a harmonious society" that China aims to build as "a society characterized by democracy and rule of law, fairness and justice, integrity and kindness, vitality, stability and good order and peaceful co-existence of human and nature". Another concept "peaceful development" is consistent with "a harmonious society", but the differences lies in that "peaceful development" came into being the very moment China initiated the Chinese path.

"A harmonious society" and "peaceful development" are more

than ideological concepts. They are also concrete action which can be quite clear if we have a glimpse of China's domestic and foreign policies. Within our country, the Chinese path coordinates the interests of different groups and integrates various social relations to promote positive interaction between different society forces. With respect to diplomatic relations, China works hard to pursue win-win cooperation, a renewed relationship between socialism and capitalism, and adopts an open and inclusive attitude towards capitalism. As "a harmonious society" and "peaceful development" are totally new concepts, the commitment to them is groundbreaking for Marxism. It is groundbreaking not only because of the innovation of governing philosophy and but also the understanding of the relationship between the struggle and identity of contradictions. The struggle and identity of contradictions are interconnected. Traditional Marxist philosophy emphasizes that identity is relative and struggle is absolute with identity embedded in struggle and that development consists the struggle and identity of two opposing sides. Therefore, traditional Marxist philosophy emphasizes that development depends on the struggle rather than the identity of two opposing sides. The concepts of "a harmonious society" and "peaceful development" of the Chinese path successfully show the great strength of the identity of the contradictions. The successful practice of these two concepts has made remarkable achievements, changing the status of identity as being "relative". Since then, Marxist philosophy has shifted from advocating struggle to emphasizing identity.

3. The Chinese Path faces up to and is dealing with complicated matters successfully, highlighting the status of the complexity of the contradictions in Marxist philosophy

An important structural feature of Chinese path is "a unified guiding ideology with coexistence of diverse principles"[1].

[1] *Ouyang Kang: Analysis on Structural Characteristics of Socialism with Chinese Characteristics*, Studies on the Socialism with Chinese Characteristics, 2009 (2) .

The pattern is embodied in the following aspects. First, as a socialist country, China actually upholds "one country, two systems" and the state system is to some extent composite. Second, with the CPC being the ruling party, China upholds its leadership but also emphasizes multi-party cooperation and political consultation system. Third, China's state system means that China must make sure that public ownership remains dominant, but at the same time China allows and encourages economy with diverse forms of ownership develop side by side and proposes establishing mixed ownership. Fourth, as stipulate by China's constitution, China's distribution system must maintain the leading role of distribution according to one's performance, but meanwhile various forms of distribution come into being continuously in China. Fifth, China upholds Marxism as its guiding ideology and works hard to maintains Marxism's leading role, but Chinese people also have a free access to ideologies and culture both from the West and ancient China. A direct result of this pattern- "a unified guiding ideology with coexistence of diverse principles is that "value diversification" has become a "normal" in China. Chinese Path is pushed forward in the midst of knowing and coordinating this complex and diverse social structure. The complexity is truly a great challenge for the those who formulate and implement the Chinese path. Whether the Chinese path could succeed or not is to some extent determined by whether they have enough wisdom and ability to deal with the complexity. The Chinese path learned a lesson from the Soviet Union and China at the period before the reform and opening up. They both ignored complex and diverse truths in pursuit of monism. China realized that it's inevitable for simple and unitary human civilization to transform, as complex and diverse in the end. It's an opportunity as well as a challenge for China who is still at the primary stage of socialism to be complex and diverse.

Consequently, Chinese path embraces such diversity and complexity in hope of generating new development models.

In facing up to and dealing with such diversity and complexity,

China is forming "a complex mode of thinking". A simple, linear and one-dimensional mode of thinking is replaced by complex, non-linear and multidimensional one. With such a complex mode of thinking, Chinese people could make a comprehensive analysis of the problems when facing a complex system composed of various factors, take specific historical conditions into consideration when facing ever-changing, dynamic and irreversible process, put more emphasis on the common ground when facing a conflict between diverse values, and take a holistic approach when facing fragmentary and scattered problems.[2] Determined by the complexity of contradictions, such a complex mode of thinking is making a breakthrough on the basis of Marxist philosophy's view of contradictions. The complexity of contradictions is not highlighted in Marxist philosophy and it is only explained as one aspect of the complexity of contradictions. Chinese Path suddenly brought the complexity of contradictions to an important position, requiring further study of contradictions so as to research the complexity of contradictions. The development of Marxist dialectics theory is continuation of the internal rationale in Hegel's contradiction analysis method. In the analysis of things, contradiction analysis method is used, which is the mind's abstract understanding of the complexity of things themselves. Unfortunately, when people use contradiction analysis method, they have overlooked study on the complexity of things for a long time. Now the Chinese path brings the previous "trivial" and "interference" back to vision, groups regard them as factors in contradictions, and retains them at different levels. This, in fact, highlights the complexity of contradictions, which is continuation as well as improvement of the original contradiction analysis method. The theory of the complexity of contradictions and social practice are truly linked together with the development of The Chinese path, pushing forward a series of reform measures especially the establishment of socialist market economy system, the formation

2 *Ouyang Kang: Complexity and Innovation of Humanities and Social Sciences*, Philosophical Research, 7th in 2003.

of diversified patterns among social interest groups in practice, and the achievement of unity and harmony in a higher level after integration and sublation on the basis of experiencing differences, contradictions and struggles.

4. The Chinese path adheres to incremental reform, giving reform an irreplaceable legal status in the social revolution theory of Marxist philosophy

First of all, in contemporary China, if we want to highlight the characteristics of reform, we may as well call the incremental reform of the Chinese path a sort of "improvement", that is, replacing "continuous revolution" with incremental reform. It can be compared with violent social revolutions as well as improvements in the capitalist society in history. The incremental reform is different from but is still connected with the two. The "improvement" mentioned here is undoubtedly different from the so-called improvement of the capitalist society, which we must treat with caution and criticize the theoretical and systematic reformism. However, if the purpose of reform is the self-improvement of socialist system, it can also be regarded as "improvement" in socialism in terms of its adherence to the fundamental nature of socialism.

Second, as a sort of "improvement", reforms of socialism should highlight the progressiveness, stability and orders in the process, which is a sharp contrast to leap-forward radical changes. Therefore, Chinese path and the Soviet Union's path are different, not only in rejecting capitalism and adhering to the fundamental nature of society, but also in dealing with the relations between reform and stability and in not employing over-radical strategies. In addition to these two insistences, the intensity and magnitude of our reform are significant in term of its long-term and overall effect. In other words, the prominence of its effect is comparable to that of the revolution. Thus, it can be regarded as China's "second revolution".

Third, reforms of capitalism do not affect the fundamental nature of society. In terms of the operation rules of these reforms, the real purpose is only conducive to improving the economic process and order, and enhancing the smoothness and effectiveness in capitalism. Such reforms are not aimed at safeguarding the rights and interests of the people. Rather, they can be means of intensified exploitation and oppression. Reforms of socialism, as a sort of "improvement", closely connects economic growth with social development and human development. In terms of this, "improvement" in socialism and revolution share the same historical goal and both are featured with historical progress.

The historical view of emphasizing incremental reform and orderly development is based on practice ontology and the complex and coherent views of dialectics. This historical view is in line with the theme of China's contemporary practice, that is, the concept of people-oriented, the liberation and development of productivity with incremental reforms and development methods, the completion of China's modernization, and the promotion of Chinese people's free and all-round development. With the aims of moving towards the free and all-round development of human beings, it is necessary for development to obey and serve people's comprehensive needs in political, economic, spiritual and cultural aspects. It is not correct to regard people as animals with pure material needs, or develop economy for the sake of development, or gain material growth at the cost of the survival, development as well as spiritual pursuit of humans. The degree of freedom and comprehensiveness of human development can measure the success or failure of the Chinese path. With continuous actual achievements, the Chinese path is gradually achieving the noble pursuit of Marxism's free and all-round development of mankind.

This historical view of incremental reform and orderly development is also in accordance with China's basic national conditions and the complexity of historical development stage. "China" is a complex country with a particularly large volume, complicated internal structures and their relations. Therefore, on the one hand, carrying out great deeds should begin with taking "China" and "Chinese people" into account. "People-oriented" is needed to ensure that the fundamental interests of Chinese people are well represented. The community needs to support each other and stays united in facing external affairs. On the other hand, we should also objectively face the great differences and imbalances in China, admitting the contradictions and profits gap among people and taking into account the interests of all sides. We cannot do everything by state power under the traditional planned economy model, or penetrate into every micro-level of social functions, or put the intensified central government within the state power system. Rather, we release social vitality and creativity from all aspects of society.

Gradually-advanced reform is the main sign and key of the Chinese path. During the reform, the Chinese path has put forward the social revolution theory of Marxist philosophy. In analyzing the process of social development, the classical theory of Marxism considers class struggle as direct power of development and leverage of social reform, and revolution as the starting point of history. According to the social revolution theory of Marxist philosophy, social reform is necessary in the history and the fundamental reform of social, economic and political system. Social reform transfers social formation from the old one to the new. Traditional Marxist philosophy holds that revolution will drive the society during the time of dramatic changes, and it also plays an important role in the relatively stable period when proletariat became the ruling class. Based on that, the theory of continuing revolution under the dictatorship of the proletariat came into being. Social revolution theory of traditional Marxism does not negate the role of reform in changing society and the necessity of reform in certain historical stages and under certain historical conditions. However, it emphasizes that reform is merely a "byproduct" of the revolution, the "auxiliary means" of the revolution, and it must be "subject to the fundamental task of the revolution". Before the victory of revolution, reform is just a step towards revolution while after the victory of revolution, reform is only "a necessary and reasonable breathing space for the revolution". Sticking to gradually-advanced reform, the Chinese path succeeds "Crossing the river by feeling the stones" demonstrates reform's historical role of making progress in the history. It is not limited to "auxiliary means", "preparation" and "implement" to revolution. Reform does drive the society and make progress in history. The Chinese path has established an irreplaceable yet independent position of reform in the theory of social revolution in Marxist philosophy.

II. The Chinese path toward Marxist political economics

As one of the three components of the Marxist Theory, Marxist Political Economics studies the law of social production and its internal contradictions. Compared with Marxist Philosophy, Marxist Political Economics is more objective and realistic, as its economic dimensions are abstracted from real economic phenomena, economic contradictions and economic relations; it is also more contemporary and hierarchical, which is based on the struggle of the proletariat in different historical stages to determine the main line. Therefore, Marxist Political Economics has to advance with time, which is more urgent than other components of Marxist Theory. The Chinese path's development on Marxism is the development on Marxist Political Economics and its meaning on Marxism is the same as well. The development of Marxist Political Economics driven by the Chinese path is not partial development but an all-round one. Marxist Political Economics consists of capitalism and socialism. As the practice of socialism is still in the process of twisting exploration, Marxist Political Economics has not formed logic and theoretical system. From some point, the practice of Chinese Path has paved the way for Marxist Political Economics especially for the socialism part. From the perspective of the history of political economics, the formation of Chinese Path contains a series of major developments of Marxist Political Economics.

1. The Chinese path established Socialist Market Economy System, combining market with socialism for the first time in the history of Marxist Political Economics

Market economy consists of a non-capitalist market economy and a capitalist market economy. Marxist holds that a non-capitalist market economy is expressed by the former capitalist market economy. He has never thought that socialism could be combined with market economy, but socialism overtakes all forms of market economy, including the non-capitalist market economy and the capitalist economy. Reasons are as follows: the socialism proposed by Marx is the socialism with the first stage of communism where the economy foundation is established on the condition that in the highly developed productive forces, the self-denial happens in the capitalist market economy. Therefore, from the capitalism to the first stage of communism, bourgeois law still exists. However, market economy has disappeared, let alone in the first stage of communism in socialism.

As China's level of productive forces is much lower than developed capitalist countries, market economy is not suitable for China to develop its productive forces, but China has taken detour to realize this. The key lies in the understanding of Marxist. Deng Xiaoping's South Talks has driven the development of socialist market economy, which is a major breakthrough in traditional Marxist Political Economics. It never happens in the history of economy and politics that socialism is combined with market. It is also an achievement made by the Communist Party of China, and a historic leap in the history of socialism. "Market economy", which is considered unique to capitalism, has been written in the report of National Congress of the Communist Party. It is an unprecedented change for Marxist Political Economics. Since then, China has entered a new stage aiming at building a socialist market economy. While providing theoretical guidance for advancing reform and opening up, it has developed Marxist Political Economics more creatively. From household contract responsibility system to the rise of township enterprises, from state-owned enterprises introduced competition mechanism to modern enterprise system, these only strengthen the micro foundation of the development of productive forces, but the establishment of the socialist market economy has promoted the development of collaboration, which opened the way for development of social productive forces in macro level. It has been proved that market economy, "invisible hand", unites all kinds of economic subjects (including state-owned, collective, individual all economic main body, as well as private and foreign capital all, mix all economic entities through collaboration in China and mobilizes production, which greatly promoted the development of the productive forces.

In China, it is a miracle that the market economy has combined with socialism. According to Galbraith, the vitality of micro-basis means that China has absorbed the "conventional wisdom" of neoliberalism, while the avert of financial crisis means that China has absorbed the "conventional wisdom" of Keynesianism. Economic foundation is that public ownership of land and state-owned enterprises are anchor of the market, and political foundation is the Communist Party of China's super control of the realities. All this is tied to the party's grip on ideology. The system shows a vivid picture of market economy and socialism. Marx did not predict that, but China realized this goal.

2. The Chinese path continues to use and develop capital, and the role of capital in value creation is recognized in Marxist Political Economics

The achievement of the Chinese path is linked with the use and development of capital. One important part of "reform" gives capital in China the legality; a key fact of "opening up" is the acceptance of international capital flowing in China. In the deeply civilized process, the driving force must be capital. Chinese people enjoy the civilized society, which means they enjoy the development of capital, either the owners of capital, or the workforce, the opposed to the owners of capital. The Chinese people attribute the great achievements in last three decades to the policy of reform and opening up, which means, to some extent, capital contributes to these achievements. *Capital*, with its historical inevitability, is an important part of China's successful stories. China's socialist market economy system consists of socialist sector economy such as state ownership and collective ownership, and non-socialist sector economy like individual ownership, private ownership and foreign-funded enterprises. Therefore, China's socialist market economy system not only plays the role of market economy, but also that of capital. China's socialist market economy system has widely accepted capital sector, and moreover, capitalist sector. Even in some state-owned enterprises, capital becomes increasingly important.

The practice of the Chinese path has proven that market economy system is compatible with capital principles. Under the system of market economy, there is nothing beyond capital. According to this, introducing market economy mechanism is the introduction of capital principles. There are four basic premises in market economy, namely commodity, currency, exchange, capital, among which the most important one is capital. Since China has chosen market economy, it is bound to use and develop capital.

The way China use and develop capital is based on the recognition of capital theory of Marxist Political Economics. According to Marxist Political Economics, capital is a social category, and a historical category, and the concept of capital contains both the negative effects of human blood, and the "civilized trend" to human. Its theme, however, is a critique of capital that reveals its limits. In the process of history, the ratio of positive effects to negative effects is bound to change, that is, the positive effect is decreasing and the negative effect are increasing. And traditional Marxist Political

Economics, stressed that after human enter the socialist society, the positive effects of capital actually have disappeared, and traditional socialism (here mainly refers to countries represented by the Soviet model of socialism country), tends to be negative on capital in an all-round way. In the traditional socialist countries, they form the concept of state-owned capital. However, some theorists stress state-owned assets when state-owned capital does not have the meaning of capital in Marxist Political Economics. In socialist societies, the Chinese path cannot and should not eliminate capital, for capital plays an irreplaceable role in developing productive forces and drives societies more civilized. More importantly, the practice of the Chinese path has changed the value creating theory in Marxist Political Economics. Traditional Marxist Political Economics neglects the role of capital in value creating, but the Chinese path attaches more attention on it.

3. The Chinese path has established the basic economy system consisting of public ownership as main body and multi ownership economy, and the Marxist Political Economics includes the non-public sector in the category of socialist ownership

In the process of the Chinese path, the political report to the 15th CPC National Congress is equipped with ground-breaking significance, as it breaks through the ownership theory of Marxist Political Economics. Some scholars even regard this as the third time of ideological emancipation since reform and opening up. In the 15th CPC National Congress on Sep. 12, 1997, Jiang Zemin declared that the basic economic system in the primary stage of China's socialism is the public ownership as the main body and the various ownership economy as co-development. "non-public sectors of economy are important components of socialist market economy." It is said that Marx and those scholars do not have that idea. Traditional Marxist Political Economics holds that the form of ownership of socialist society is public ownership, and public ownership is regarded as the main characteristic of socialism. Marx and Engels articulated in *the*

Communist Manifesto as the first program of the Communist Party about 160 years ago that "traditional ownership" is "making the complete break with" private ownership. They also have written saying like "Communists can sum up their theories as one sentence: eliminate private ownership"[3] However, the Communist Party of China in the National Congress declared that they would accept public ownership and non-public ownership and legitimate non-public ownership. This is obviously a breakthrough in the ownership of Marxist Political Economics and a new understanding in Socialism and Marxism. After that, the Communist Party of China has put forward a basic economic system as basic national policy of keeping public ownership as the mainstay of the economy and allowing diverse forms of ownership to develop side by side. The CPC has formed a "two no wavering" basic beliefs, namely, unswervingly uphold the public ownership as the mainstay, and unswervingly encourages a variety of ownership economy. The Third Plenary Session of the 18th CPC Central Committee proposed the concept of "mixed ownership", which means "state-owned capital, collective capital, private capital and cross-shareholding, mutual confluence of the mixed ownership economy" "adhere to the dominant position of public ownership, and further explores the effective implementation of the basic economic system form" effective attempt, and hold they "help state-owned capital amplification function, keep value, and improve competitiveness".

In the process of making breakthrough in the ownership theory of Marxist Political Economics, the Chinese path has found a way toward public ownership under socialism. The 15th CPC National Congress holds that we must have a full understanding of public ownership economy consisting of the state-owned economy and the collective economy and the state-owned components and collective components of the mixed ownership economy. State-owned economy plays a leading role in control. The form of public ownership can

3 *Selected Works of Mark and Engels*, Chin. E. People's Publishing House, Beijing, Vol. II, 1994, p. 45.

be various, that is to say, we can make bold use of all the business methods and organizational forms that reflect the law of social production, and try to find the form of public ownership that can greatly promote productivity. Joint-stock system is a kind of capital organization for modern enterprises, conducive to the separation of ownership and managerial authority, and beneficial to improving the efficiency of enterprise and capital operation. Capitalism and socialism both have an access to apply this system. All those understandings on public ownership under socialism is based on the breakthrough of ownership in Marxist Political Economics. It forms an important part of Marxist Political Economics and sheds light on the economy revolution and social development for China.

4. In face of "Virtual Economy", Chinese path develops and controls "Virtual Economy" for Marxist Political Economics

The definition of capital by Marx is "the value can bring forth the surplus value", or appreciating currency. In his view, capital is converted from currency when labor forces become commodity. Therefore, currency with "fixed as a commodity for universal equivalent" is capital while objects like securities and good titles are qualifies of being capital. However, in the era of highly developed capitalism, with the further development of the division of labor, land market, labor market and even the capital market appeared. In the capital market, securities and good titles, though not capital themselves, can be turned into capital in the market for they can bring stable income. This phenomenon of commercializing, capitated object, is being called "virtual capital" by Marx. However, in the era of Marx, only "virtual capital" existed, and "virtual economy" had not formed. The reason is that there is only virtual capital instead of virtual currency. Before the collapse of the Bretton Woods System which signated that the dollar is pegged to gold, currencies of all nations are pegged to dollar in accordance. Gold is precisely the "commodity that is fixed as a general equivalent", so the currency represents a value entity. With the fall of Bretton Woods System, the dollar is not pegged to gold, and currencies of all nations exchange freely with the dollar. Dollar and other currencies become credit symbols, which realizes "the virtualization of currency". Since then, dollar and other currencies can be traded. Based on that, with "financial innovation" and relaxing financial regulation, "virtual economy" dominated by "virtual capital" comes into being. The disintegration of social welfare in developed capitalism countries and "virtual economy" are two aspects of one body, representing an era of a government retreat and "crazy capital" of market expansion. If "God let him go mad when wants him dead", this kind of "craziness" represents the end of capital. The Chinese path is practicing when "virtual economy" is spreading across the world and resulting to consequences to highly developed capitalist countries. The path is not avoiding but accepting the era of "virtual economy".

The Chinese path has put forward policies dealing with the relationship between the real economy and the "virtual economy" which in order to develop and regulate "virtual economy" as well. More importantly, on one hand, the Chinese path advanced mode of production and productive forces by utilizing market and capital; on the other hand, it strengthens the regulation of market and capital and advances "all-round production" in society, politics, culture and ecology after material production entering "virtual economy". To meet the needs of growing material and culture, the Chinese path must realize the advance of productive forces, and create a good environment for culture. That makes solid a foundation for building a moderately prosperous society in all aspects and the transformation of more advanced social formation. Chinese path has to strike a balance between economy and society, which means understanding society not only from the perspective of "economic form" but also from that of "general communication". The Chinese government must transform from the administrative examination to the market regulation as soon as possible, which regulates not only the traditional real economy but also the emerging market of "virtual economy".

5. Chinese path prioritizes economy development and believes in "development is the absolute principle", and Marxism Political Economics is featured with "focusing on development"

After the completion of the socialist revolution and the establishment of the socialist system, the Communist Party of China has transformed from revolutionary party to the ruling party which focuses on construction. Meanwhile, its historical mission is building socialism with Chinese characteristics converted from the overthrow of the "three mountains". Based on that, the Party has made an important judgement in the 8th National Congress in 1956: the main social contradictions ahead of our country at this stage are the contradictions between the people's need for the rapid development of economy and culture and the situation that the current economic culture cannot meet the needs of the people. According to this, although there are a lot to be done, the CPC should focuses on developing society and economy, meeting the needs of the Chinese people, and building a socialist economy power. However, people have different views on this judgement in a long time. In 1978 The Third Plenary Session of the Eleventh Central Committee reaffirmed that the path of Socialism with Chinese Characteristics is to stick to economic construction. Deng repeatedly stressed that the fundamental task of socialism is to develop the productive forces for development is the key in solving all problems in China and "development is the absolute principle"; in a socialist country, a truly Marxist ruling party must devote itself to the development of productive forces and gradually raise the living standards of the people; only firmly grasping the theme of development can we grasp the people's aspirations and the essence of socialist modernization. In the course of the Chinese path for more than 30 years, the CPC pays special attention to the "development" as its top priority and to the keys to all problems. After the Chinese path has made amazing achievements, thoughts like keeping economic development as its "central task" and developing "the absolute principle" appeared. The 18th National Congress answered: As China is still in the primary stage of socialism and will be in the primary stage of socialism for a long time, the contradictions between the growing material and cultural needs of the people and the backward social production remains the key part of the society. Also, China remains the biggest developing country on the international stage. In the expert seminar on economy, President Xi Jinping stressed that to realize the long-cherished goal of development, we must adhere to the economic construction as the center and insist that development is the party's top priority so as to develop sustainable economy. He also addressed that development and economy is the foundation of "two century goals" and a prosperous nation, harmony society and happiness of people.

The CPC prioritizes developing economy and sticks to "development is the absolute principle". The Party has succeeded in practices and contributed a lot to Marxism Political Economics. The research object of political economics is the social mode of production, the capitalist political economy the capitalist mode of production, and the socialist political economics the social mode of production.

For social production methods being the contradiction with uniformity between social productive forces and production relations, socialist plutonomy should study the same project in the society with socialism. However, the emphasis on "class struggle" and the crisis of "only productive forces theory" lead socialist plutonomy of the traditional Marxism to limit its study subject on production relations only, voluntarily or involuntarily. Beside this, while still ignoring conflicts of interests on the basis of commercial relationships in socialism and blindly regarding production relations of socialism as "a relation in which people treat each other as comrades", the economic rules are ignored and studies on development, especially on economic development, are obliterated. On this condition, the Chinese path takes economic development as the top priority and firmly carries out the principle of "development being the absolute truth", and it virtually has figured out the methods and ways of liberating and improving productive forces in contradictory movement between productive forces and production relations. So in one sense, the socialist plutonomy of the Marxism has become the one which "focuses on the development" and never ignores or gives up studies on the production relations and superstructure, but mainly concentrates on the development of social productive forces.[4]

Based on such socialist plutonomy of the Marxism, which has been developed, the Chinese path creatively puts forward the development model of socialist market economy according to the present need in the primary stage of socialism; deepens the realization of characteristics of economic operation and that of its contradictory movement and its objective laws; and states the principles of scientific development on account of correctly understanding the features of economic operation.

III. The development of scientific socialism theory promoted by Chinese path

Based on the inheritance of basic principles of Scientific Socialism, the Chinese path establishes the new theories of contemporary Scientific Socialism with new and abundant contents. What's the most radical significance of the Chinese path to the world socialist movement is to make innovation and development in this prospect. Besides applying general principles of Scientific Socialism to the reality in contemporary China, the Chinese path also gets rid of rigescent understanding of Scientific Socialism Theory and the Marxism and breaks away from the practice which has transcended the history as well as put forward a series of new theories and principles, many of which has made innovation and development of Scientific Socialism.

4 Xia Jun: "*Scientific Socialism is not Phantasy——About Explorations on some Important Questions of Theoretical System*", shanghai people's publishing house, 2014, pp. 195-197.

The socialist road with Chinese characteristics infuses new blood into it and stimulates it to enter a new stage. Verifying the fundamental judgement that the socialism will eventually win over the capitalism, the Chinese path has made innovative exploration on the process of human society, especially those backward countries, stepping into socialism. To a certain extent, the theoretical system of socialism with Chinese characteristics is the Scientific Theory of today's world, demonstrating that the Scientific Theory has made significant development in contemporary, and also played an important role as the Scientific Theory in the new thesis and situations at present times. Because of the innovation and development of the Scientific Theory promoted by the Chinese path, the basic principles of the Scientific Socialism, as the truth, still exert an indispensable influence at present times and demonstrates the whole trend of human society for people as well as lead them to move forward in this direction. So such innovation and development is comprehensive, what follows in the paragraphs are only five perspectives of it:

1. The Chinese path verified that China is still at the primary stage of socialism, which makes great contribution to the development stage of socialism's theories of the Scientific Theory.

The combination between the Scientific Socialism and China's actual conditions equals to put its socialist establishment on national reality which is considered as standpoint and starting point. After the Third Plenary Session of the 11th Central Committee of the Party, the Communist Party of China rehabilitated the ideological line of emancipating the mind and seeking truth from facts, and the principle of proceeding from actual conditions all the time. The condition revealed by the Communist Party of China is that China is still at "the primary stage of socialism", so is the national reality. In this way, socialism will be deeply and firmly entrenched in China with infinite vigor, invulnerable confronted with various dangers and risks. It is based on the realization of fundamental realities, "the primary stage of socialism", of the country that China formulates the basic line, "to take economic development as basic task" and "to firmly adhere to the four cardinal principles and reform and opening up policy". On same basis, China is able to insist and improve the basic economic system of keeping public ownership as the mainstay of the economy and allowing diverse forms of ownership to develop side by side, and putting up the policy of by helping the minority and some regions to get well-off first to promote the accelerated development of most regions and therefore to achieve common prosperity.[5] The theory of primary stage of socialism indeed has made great contribution to socialist development stage theory of the Scientific Socialism. As the development stage theory of the Scientific Socialism, it must points out that the theory of primary stage of socialism is a complete system, which includes comprehensive explanation of specific contents, social nature, main contradiction and historical tasks, and basic features of the primary stage of socialism.

2. The Chinese path answers comprehensively the nature of socialism and firstly makes the most concise and complete summarize about the most basic question in the development history of the Scientific Socialism, "what is socialism".

The CPC reveals the nature of socialism is "to liberate and to develop productive forces, abolish exploitation and polarization, and reach the state of widespread wealth for all people" on the basis of insisting the basis system of socialism.[6] Firstly, "to liberate and develop productive forces" is the fundamental task of socialism, occupying an prior position in the nature of socialism; Secondly, "to abolish exploitation and polarization" is the fundamental method to achieve the nature of

5 Xu Chongwen:"*Chinese Path has Innovated and Developed Scientific Socialism in the Socialist System*", "Studies on Mao Zedong and Deng Xiaoping Theories", 2012 (1) .

6 *Selected Works of Deng Xiaoping*, Chin. ed., People's Publishing House, Beijing, Vol. III, 1993, p. 373.

socialism; lastly, "to reach the state of widespread wealth for all people" is the value objective of socialism, consisting the core of socialism.

With the successful proceeding of the Chinese path, reform and opening up policy and practice of socialistic modernization drive have been continually deepen, and The Communist Party of China has also deepen and explore the scientific content of the socialist essential theory, such as accepting the social harmony and all-round development of human beings into the nature of socialism.

The success of the Chinese path is attributed to the CPC's correct understanding of socialism nature, and to the party taking the continual improvement of theory on the essence of socialism as the starting point. This theory has firstly made the most concise and complete summarize of the most fundamental question that what is socialism in the development history of the Scientific Socialism. What is socialism? How to build socialism? These are all unsolved questions in world socialist movement. The socialism has been through a process from fantasy to science, from theory to practice, and from single country to various countries. Though the realization of socialism has been deepened gradually, until the middle of 20th century traditional Scientific Theory still simply summarize the nature of socialism as three features: public ownership, labor-based distribution, and planned economy. Obviously, repeated frustration suffered from international socialist movement is closely related to this misunderstanding of socialism nature.[7] The new explanation ,the newest and the most complete, from the Chinese path apparently breaking through conventional Scientific Theory's partial understanding of socialism nature, and for some certain has saved socialist movement in worldwide.

7 Nie Yunnin and other editors: "*Studies on Socialist Theoretical System with Chinese Characteristics*", People's Publishing House, 2011, pp. 167-174.

3. The exploration of the Chinese path to socialist impetus has brought up the sublimation of concepts of the Scientific Theory about development motives.

In the Scientific Theory, the basic contradictions still is the contradiction between production relations and productive forces, and between superstructure and economic base. The continual solution of this contradiction will promote the continual development of socialist society. Then, how to solve it? In a long period, class struggle, a struggle between two lines, and "continuing the revolution under dictatorship of the proletariat" are considered as the radical ways to solve this conflict, which is hence considered as the radical motives of development of socialist society.

The path of socialism with Chinese characteristics breaks through the concept of "Class Struggle being the key" and confirms renovation to be motives of socialist society, which means to solve fundamental contradiction in socialist society with renovation. Deng Xiaoping pointed out that "after the confirmation of basic socialist system, economic system which restricts the development of productive forces should be fundamentally changed in order to build up socialist economic system full of power and vigor, promoting productive forces' improvement. This is the content of reform, so reform also liberates productive forces."[8] Deng's regarding renovation as an impetus of socialist society is theoretical innovation on the problem of socialist development power, and this innovation carves out a way for the development of China's productive forces and of socialist society. On the basis of the correct judgement of " reform being the objective command of basic contradictory movement in socialist society", Deng regarded reform as the impetus of socialism development. In his view, traditional socialist system leads to various shortcomings in society's production relations and superstructure, which impedes the development of productive forces. On this condition, "it is

---

8 *Selected Works of Deng Xiaoping*, Chin. ed., People's Publishing House, Beijing, 1993, Vol. III, p. 370.

inevitably to change production relations, superstructure, and management methods of industrial and agricultural enterprises and that of government applied on them, in order to adapt to the need of modernized large-scale economy.[9] Deng made an all-out effort to promote reforms with a clear purpose which had been explained clearly that "all reforms are made for the only one goal, to eliminate barriers unfavorable to the development of productive forces of society".[10] Deng also demonstrated the principles of reform and pointed out that "it is important to insist on the direction of socialism."[11] He stated that the reform are socialist, and various reform measures are taken on the premise of insisting socialism. As reform is so important in today's China, Deng then put up the meaningful proposition that "reform is China's second revolution". In China, the first revolution refers to that of "overturning the three mountains of imperialism, feudalism, bureaucracy", with Chinese people building up the New China under the leadership of the CPC. This is the revolution that productive forces was liberated and fully developed in order to found politic basis. Comrade Deng Xiaoping calling the reform "the second revolution" is to present that "just like our revolutions, the reform is designed to clear away the obstacles to the development of the productive forces"——[12] The understanding of the reform being the second revolution is based on productive forces liberation, as well as includes the impetus of socialism development.

The continual improvement of the reform is the path to a stronger China with socialism and the historical decisions which will change our fate. The CPC has eventually figured out the real motives of

9 *Selected Works of Deng Xiaoping*, Chin. ed., People's Publishing House, Beijing, 1994, Vol. II, pp. 135-136.

10 *Selected Works of Deng Xiaoping*, Chin. ed., People's Publishing House, Beijing, 1993, Vol. III, p. 134.

11 Ibid., p, 138.

12 Ibid., p. 135.

China's development, and the socialist development drive theory they put forward is one of the most valuable theories contributed by the path of socialism with Chinese characteristics to the Science Socialism theory.

4. The Chinese path continually enhances class basis and expands the mass foundation of the ruling party which has enriched and improved the theory of Party building of the Science Socialism.

Through the enhancement of class basis and the expansion of mass foundation of the ruling party, the important thought of "Three Representatives", put forward by the comrade Jiang Zemin, has enriched and improved the theory of the Party building of the Science Socialism.[13] In February 25th 2000, three months later after delivering "the famous speech in Guangzhou", Jiang held the Symposium on the Party building work in Shanghai, and demonstrated the background of putting up the important thought of "Three Representatives": firstly, the socialism we used to learn commanded to eliminate exploitation and private ownership, but in the practice of new socialist market economy wage labor played a role and private economy became an significant part of it; secondly, while the socialism emphasized the high consistence of interests within people, in reality different groups had different interests and various value views; lastly, the capitalism, used to be considered as dying and decayed, utilized economic globalization and development of technologies to get new vigor in recent decades. In addition, how to treat the development of non-public economy? How to treat the new social class? Does it just as some people say that China has emerged the new bourgeoisie? How to unite and organize people who work in non-public owned enterprises to get close to the party? How to arouse the initiatives of people and all other organizations and institutions

---

13 "*Selections of Important Documents Since 15th NCCPC*", II, People's Publishing House, Beijing, 2001, pp. 1138-1139.

to struggle for a common goal? In view of these new situations, Jiang's opinion is very clear that the CPC, as the ruling party, must strengthen its class base and expand its mass base, or otherwise it will "get outdated" and "take the risk of losing the advancement and leadership".[14]

On July 1, 2001, the CPC ushered in its 80th birthday. In celebration of the anniversary of the founding of the Party, Jiang Zemin delivered the famous "July 1st Speech" In this speech, he clearly pointed out that "The Party should always stick to the vanguard feature of the working class and to maintain its advancement, while continually enhancing its class base and expanding its mass base, and improving its influences on society according to the reality of economic development and social progress."[15]

In China, workers, peasants, intellectuals, cadres and soldiers have been regarded as the most basic social classes, and the most basic power source and class base of the Party. Now with the profound changes in the situation, especially in economy, some new social stratums appeared in China which have brought about changes in the composition of the social stratums. The CPC adjusted its policies to these new stratums timely, and instead of pushing them to the opposition the Party regards them as its important ruling foundation and emphasizes its protection for their interests. The CPC's doing so has theoretically developed the theory of the party building in reality. That it is the vanguard of the proletariat hasn't changed, in the meantime the Party has also become the vanguard of the Chinese people and the Chinese nation. So it is obvious that the understanding of the nature of the CPC deepens, which means that when the Party has been keeping the basic attributions since the foundation, class base and mass base have been profoundly changed after reform and opening up.

14 Team of "Chinese Path" of CCCPC Party Literature Research Office: "*Chinese Path—Classic Works Reviews of Adapting Marxism to China*", Central Party Literature Press, 2011, p. 110.

15 Ibid., p. 114.

5. The Chinese path rebuilds the relations between socialism and capitalism and has changed the opposite thinking of them.

As for "primitivity", socialism is not opposite to capitalism but a replacement for it. When there were theories and campaigns about socialism in the world, it means the end of capitalism. It was known to people in the past that socialism and capitalism could not exist or develop on the same land and the two were contradictory and incompatible. However, the socialism with Chinese characteristics is open and compatible. The Chinese path has contributed significantly in rebuilding the relations between socialism and capitalism in world socialism movements. Instead of blindly considering capitalism as "the natural enemy", the Chinese path treats capitalism openly and tolerantly, which is one of the important symbols of creating the Chinese path, leading to the realization of compatibility and permeability of the two different social systems in today's world with more tolerable attitude. On this question, the Chinese path has noticed both distinctions and contradictions between capitalism and socialism and accepted their coexistence and connections. In face of the capitalistic world, the Chinese path will not adopt measures of "wholesale westernization" or "self-isolation". With attention paid to "peaceful evolution" toward capitalism, the Chinese path will make exchanges with it actively and utilize it to construct socialism.

The Chinese path insists to analyze capitalism with scientific attitude, and endeavors to separate humankind achievements made by capitalism from capitalism itself, which means separating its basic systems from its institutions, mechanisms, methods and other fruits. It emphasizes objections to simply imitating capitalism's basic systems, but actively absorbs and takes in concrete cultural achievements. Thanks to the foundation of the Chinese path, relations between traditional socialism and capitalism are being rebuilt during which a more broad road of civilization development, combining socialism building disciplines with humankind development disciplines together.

Through rebuilding relations with capitalism, the Chinese path actually closely relates the development of China with the development of world civilization. Achieving the value pursuit of socialism is tightly connected with that of human civilization, improving mental shackles of China's building of socialism to a higher level. It is under the background of globalization that the Chinese path tries to find ways to carry out this work. On the premise of scientifically grasping the relations between development of China with the world, especially with the capitalism countries, in this era of economic globalization, designers of the Chinese path put forward the basic strategy of opening up from the overall connections of this world. The so-called opening up policy is to positively and consciously adapt to world historical process and to gain country's own interests in the challenges of economic globalization. Obviously, the key of this strategy is to build relations of mutual communication and mutual benefits with capitalism countries. From the experience of the Chinese path, only by deeply understanding the consistence of value pursuit of socialism and human civilization and by profoundly understanding the humankind achievements had inside the advanced capitalism countries can relations between socialism and capitalism be rebuilt consciously and positively. At the meantime, the experience also shows that creating new relations of coexistence and cooperation with capitalism countries is the only way for socialism countries to achieve its value pursuit.

The Chinese path has formed relatively complete system to handle the relationship between socialism and capitalism in the perspective of theory and practice, achieving the comprehensive development of Scientific Socialism theories of which is about the interaction between socialism and capitalism, in order to provide a successful example for correctly handling the relationship for the international socialist movement

Chapter Four

Inheritance, correction and improvement made by the Chinese Path to Marxism Class Struggle Theory

The foundation of the Chinese path is based on certain ideological resources, the Marxism being the important ones. However, though they admit the formation of the Chinese path is tightly related to the leading of Marxism, some person still endeavors to deny its inner connection with Marxism Class Struggle Theory. In their opinions, even though various relations existing between the Chinese path and other theories of Marxism, the Chinese path will not be established without denying the Marxism Class Struggle Theory while being contradictory to it. For struggle theory being the core of Marxism, how can we say the Chinese path is the inheritance and improvement of Marxism if it is completely adverse to those theories? So, on this condition it is so important to explore the inner relations between the Chinese path and the Marxism Class Struggle Theory. The basic views are: Firstly, the inheritance and improvement of Marxism made by the Chinese path include that of its class struggle theory; Secondly, the Chinese path does not wholly accept Marxism Class Struggle Theory or simply abandon it; Lastly, the Chinese path on the one hand insists and inherits this class struggle theory, on the other hand corrects and promotes it with new historical conditions.

I. On the premise of the confirmation of class struggle still existing in certain regions, the party carries out the policies of denying "class struggle being the core" and insisting "to take economic construction as the central task".

"*The Communist Manifesto*" clearly indicates that "until now all societies' histories are the history of class struggle."[1] Marx and Engels demonstrated general disciplines of class society and pointed out that the oppressed class's resistance to the oppressing class consists of direct motives of class society's development. "The oppressor and the oppressed all along are on contradictory position. They continually fight, covertly or openly, against each other, but all end up with a complete society's renovation or the elimination of all participating classes".[2]

Because of the important role of Class Struggle Theory played in "*The Communist Manifesto*", and in the whole theoretical system of it, the Marxism and Class Struggle Theory have indispensable inner relationships. So Marx and Engels would criticize them without hesitation once some people deny this theory in proletariat movement.

In 1879, Marx and Engels for the trend of abandoning class struggle in proletariat movement issued a statement reiterating that "for nearly 40 years, we repeatedly emphasize class struggle, especially the struggle between the bourgeoisie and the proletariat, and regard it as direct motives of historic development and supporting point of the renovation of modern society; So we definitely cannot agree with those who want to abolish class struggle in movement." [3] They told the proletariat and the mass labour people that "with the elimination of class struggle, then no matter the bourgeoisie or 'all independent

1 *Selected Works of Marx and Engels*, Chin. ed., People's Publishing House, 2009, Vol. II, p. 31.

2 *Selected Works of Marx and Engels*, Chin. ed., People's Publishing House, 2009, Vol. II, p. 31.

3 *Selected Works of Marx and Engels*, Chin. ed., People's Publishing House, 1995, Vol. III, P. 685.

figures' will 'not afraid of moving forward with the proletariat'. This lie only deceives the proletariat."[4]

It is clearly shows that the leaders of the CPC who lead Chinese people to open the Chinese Path does not "follow the steps of those who want to eliminate class struggle in campaigns", because they realized it deeply that "the elimination of class struggle" will only "deceive" "the proletariat". Here let us recall what comrade Deng Xiaoping, the chief designer of the Chinese path, explained about class struggle in the new historical period. On March 30th 1979, Deng clearly pointed out on the forum on the principles for the Party's theoretical work that "class struggle is objective, and it should not be underestimated or exaggerated".

The practice demonstrates that the underestimation or exaggeration of class struggle both will result in catastrophic mistakes."[5] On January 16th 1980, Deng warned those leading cadres on the cadre conference commanded by the Central Committee of CPC again:" some comrades ask that why there still is class struggle without the classes.

Now, we can see that both situations are objective. At present, we fight against counter-revolutionaries, severe subversive enemies, severe criminals and criminal groups, only part of which are class struggle."[6] On December 25th in the same year, on the Working Conference of the CPC Central Committee Deng listed various behaviors breaching the laws and regulations and pointed out that "Depending on their nature, some may be categorized as contradictions between ourselves and the enemy, while others are a form of class struggle reflected, in varying degrees, among the people. This means that even though class struggle is no longer the main contradiction of our society, it

4 *Selected Works of Marx and Engels*, Chin. ed., People's Publishing House, 2009, Vol. III, P. 480.

5 *Selected Works of Deng Xiaoping*, Chin. ed., People's Publishing House, Beijing, 1994, Vol. II, p. 182.

6 Ibid, p. 253.

still exists and exerts significant influences."[7] These speeches from Deng Xiaoping didn't deny the existence of class struggle at all, so dose that of other leaders. For instance, the Comrade Jiang Zemin once said that in building the socialism with Chinese characteristics, we "cannot abandon views and methods of class and class analysis of the Marxism. For these views and methods are always the key for us to observe complicated political situations of fights between socialism and different enemies"[8]. Their insistence on Marxism's leadership to the Chinese path and on "The Four Cardinal Principles" being "two basic points" that the Party must carry out in a sense is to emphasize that CPC should still inherits the Marxism Class Struggle Theory in the new historic period. This inheritance doesn't only reflect in their theories but also in their series of strategies and polices to build the socialism with Chinese characteristics, as well as in their corresponding practice.

For over thirty years, objections to spiritual contamination, the bourgeois liberalism, and penetration of abroad hostile forces have been developed to the movements of quelling the unrest and eliminating corruption, the campaign of "beating the tiger and shooting the flies". In those movements, which one is not the exciting class struggle carried out by Chinese people under their leadership? The fight that between Chinese people and inside and outside enemies who are hostile to our socialist systems and want to destruct them is not exactly class struggle?

Of course the knowledge of the Marxism Class Struggle Theory should not stay knowing that class struggle objectively exists and is the driving force for the development of human's history, what's more important is to grasp how founders of the Marxism revealed the objective necessity of the existence of class struggle. They believe that this objective necessity has roots in contractions between the

7 Ibid, p. 370.

8 *Selected Works of Jiang Zemin*, Chin. ed., People's Publishing House, Beijing, 2006, Vol. III, p. 68.

relations of production and the productive forces and between the superstructure and the economic base in class society. Class struggle originates from the difference in ranks of production system and the occupation relation of means of production of different classes and the irreconcilability in economic benefits caused by them. Marx and Engels exposed the mystery of social phenomena by pointing out that the relations of production must be suitable for conditions of productive forces and that the superstructure must be suitable for the economic base. According to their explanation, in some situation, class struggle is needed to achieve that goal.

To master the Marxism Class Struggle Theory for real, what should be kept in mind is the important explanation of Marx on this theory, which was proposed in the letter of Marx to Jose Pheydemeyer in 1852: "Before me, some bourgeois historians specialized in historical compilation have narrated the historical development of class struggle, meanwhile, some bourgeois economists have also analyzed each class from the perspective of economy. The new contents I added is to prove the following points",[9] the first point he put forward was "the existence of class is merely related to a certain historical period". Marx emphasized that the class was not born but closely related to the development of social division of labor and the corresponding appearance of the suitable private ownership of the means of production. A rapid development of productive forces is the premise of the elimination of classes. Indeed, it's significantly initiative that the founders of the Marxism connected the existence of classes with some historical period of the development of production.

Like the Marxism Class Struggle Theory said, class struggle originates from the differences in ranks of production system and the occupation relation of means of production of different classes, then through analyzing the conditions of ownership and the situations between the relations of production and the productive forces in a

9 *Selected Works of Marx and Engels*, Chin. ed., People's Publishing House, Beijing, Vol. X, 1994, p. 190.

certain period, we should have a clear idea of not only the objective necessity but also the correspondent particularity of the class struggle there. As Marx emphasized that the existence of class was only associated with the historical period of the development of production, it's been proved that the existence of the class struggle is historical so that the existence form of class struggle can be different regarding the different levels of the development of production in different historical periods. The valuable point of the communist leadership represented by Deng Xiaoping lies in the clear acknowledge of class struggle still existing and the reasonable analysis of the concrete particular forms of class struggle in this period according to the conditions of ownership and the situations between the relations of production and the productive forces in some specified period. They insisted on viewing the class through the development of production and the productive forces in some specified period, which means that they insisted on analyzing the class struggle in a historical way, so they can realize the universality that the class struggle still exists and the particularity reflected by the class struggle in the new historical period.

To be specific, under the premise of the emphasis on "the class struggle exists" of the communist leaders in the new historical period, a statement was proposed that class struggle was no longer the principal contradiction so that the economic construction rather than the class should be taken as the core. The unification of "universality" and "particularity" of contradiction was fully indicated here: the "universality" is that the class struggle will never "die out" and still exist as the driving force of social development; Meanwhile, the "particularity" was that the class struggle was no longer the principal contradiction and the "core", neither constituted the driving force of social development.

The following quoted speech of Deng Xiaoping was the vivid manifestation of the dialectical unification of universality and particularity. In the speech of the forum on the principles for the Party's theoretical work on March 30th 1979, on the one hand, he emphasized that the class struggle exists objectively, on the other hand, he proposed that the class struggle "should be neither underestimated nor exaggerated", that's to say, the class struggle in the new socialist modern construction period should be accurately located and should be recognized that it's obviously different from that in historical class societies. He pointed out clearly that to understand the new characteristics in the socialist modern construction period "involves many complicated and difficult questions both of theory and practice, and they cannot be answered merely by quoting from books by our predecessors"[10]. On January 16th 1980, in the speech at a meeting of cadres called by the Central Committee of the CPC Deng Xiaoping's emphasis was that the exploiting classes and the class struggle had been abolished, "both these things are objective facts", in this case, "a clear distinction between the two different types of contradictions must be made"[11].

In the speech at the Central Working Conference on December 25th 1980, while Deng emphasized that "the class struggle still exists and cannot be neglected", he also pointed out that "it is no longer the principal contradiction in our society" and "must be handled promptly and unhesitatingly as required in each individual case"[12].

From these speeches of Deng Xiaoping, we can fully understand how THE central communist leaders represented by Deng saw problem of the class struggle, they did not "merely quoting from books by the predecessors", instead, on the basis of the Marxism Class Struggle Theory which was applied and developed creatively, making clear that "the class struggle will exist for a long time in a certain area and may be stimulated under some situation", they emphasized that "the class struggle is no longer the principal contradiction" and the focus of work should be turned to economic construction. Chinese

10 *Selected Works of Deng Xiaoping*, Eng. ed., Foreign Language Press, Beijing, 1995, Vol. II, p. 190.

11 Ibid., p. 253.

12 Ibid., p. 370.

people can carve out an unique developing path just for the process of inheriting, improving and developing the Marxism Class Struggle Theory.

II. Under the premise of the class differences and opposition confirmed existing, peaceful means or non-violent means are applied to solve the difference and opposition.

As the pioneer of the Chinese path considered that class struggle still exists in China, then it's with no doubt that class differences, contradictions and even opposition also exist. In today's China, the occupation of means of production of different people is different. Correspondently, the ranks of production system of different people are also different. Therefore, it's very natural to see difference, contradictions and opposition forming among those "different people". They share common interests and special interests of their own which are related but also conflicted with each other. Although such differences among them is less like that "forming a public and complete class" under capitalism, which's, "producing a bourgeoisie class or exploiting class", it does bring differences, contradictions and opposition between person to person. Some of the differences, contradictions and opposition are within the class, that's to say, they happened in the same class; others belong to class against class, happening between different classes. The conflicts originate from the later one of course wear the characteristics of the class struggle. To put it clear, Deng Xiaoping said, "We are opposed to broadening the scope of the class struggle. We do not believe that there is a bourgeoisie within the Party, nor do we believe that under the socialist system a bourgeoisie or any other exploiting class will re-emerge after exploiting classes and the conditions of exploitation have really been eliminated".[13] However, the class struggle remains existing. It "is different from the struggle of one class against another, which occurred in the past (these individuals cannot form a cohesive and overt class). But it is still a special form of the leftover, under socialist conditions, of the class struggles of past history". Obviously, the recognition of class struggle still existing is completely consistent with that of class differences, contradictions and even opposition remaining existing.

Although currently public analysis of class differences, contradictions and even opposition objectively existing is hard to see in domestic newspapers and magazines, we can find pieces of articles on so called "analysis of stratums" from time to time. The most influential one divides our people into various stratums and makes a strict differentiating of the bound between different stratums. In fact, stratum analysis is a part of the Marxism class analysis, which is, indeed, class analysis. Class analysis involves stratum analysis. The acknowledgement of differences still existing in social classes in China at present, to some degree, equals to the admission of differences between classes existing at this stage of China.

The class differences in current China reveals at most in the differences between labor and capital, or it could be said that the origin of the class differences existing in China now lies in the differences between labor and capital. In accordance with the Marxism Theory, under the situation of socialism, labor is no longer wage labor, neither is labor force the product, so the means of production and currency can't be capital, the traditional relations between labor and capital also lost the premise and foundation of existence, that's to say, similar relations between labor and capital of capitalist society can never exist in socialist society. However, the reality is that since we are at the primary stage, we are implementing the socialist market economy suitable to this historical period. And if we carry out the

13 *Selected Works of Deng Xiaoping*, Eng. ed., Foreign Language Press, Beijing, 1995, Vol. II, p. 177.

socialist market economy system, the basic regulatory role of market in labor resource allocation, salary determination and labor mobility should be realized, which means labor force becomes products, at the same time the means of production and currency become capital. Isn't the formation of labor market and the systematization and contractual relationship of employment making the traditional employment relations between labor and capital form again?

We must have a clear idea that the relation of labor and capital at the present stage of China, which under the socialist market economy system, is essentially different from that studied by Marx before. The relation of labor and capital studied by Marx was based on the private ownership of productive means, which represented an adversarial class relation of being exploited and exploiting between the proletariat and the bourgeoisie. However, the relation of labor and capital we face now is more like an appeal of the interests between labor and capital, which is the relation of conflict and unity formed in the process of realizing socialist ownership of labor force and ownership of capital. Anyhow it is a fact without disputes that the relation of labor and capital still exists in China at present. Therefore, it provides experience of reference and enlightenment for exploring the basic thoughts of class opposition in the light of the way that Marx used to think about the relation of labor and capital. Then it's reasonable to see the owner of production means and the seller of labor force be exclusive and opposed against each other in sharing fruits of labor.

The reason why Chinese statesmen pay so much attention to improving people's livelihood, protecting labors and the rights of labors is for the premise of the acknowledgement of the difference between labor and capital and above it the differences in class still existing in China. Even in dealing with some routine work, Chinese statesmen are concerned with such differences and aiming at removing them. At a forum Deng said:

"Recently, I have spoken twice about the four guarantees of our adherence to the socialist system and of our success in the modernization drive. The first guarantee is to undertake structural reform, including the organizational streamlining we are now carrying out. The second is to build a socialist civilization with a high cultural and ideological level…The third guarantee is a firm crackdown on economic crime. The fourth is Party building, the consolidation of the Party's organization and the rectification of its work style…In sum, we cannot attain the four guarantees all at once; We must keep working for them for a long time. We won't launch any mass movements, but we must continue our efforts in this regard throughout the course of the four modernizations. We must not forget the four guarantees for a single day. We must make their realization part of our daily work and struggle. Not all the problems related to the four guarantees are in the nature of class struggle, but there is class struggle in some cases."[14]

The four "daily works and struggle" mentioned above, to Deng, is to be engaged in that daily works and do not forget to associate it with the class struggle.

He believed that they can help improving and removing class differences and contradictions.

The preciousness of pioneers of the Chinese path lies in that they don't simply admit that class differences, contradictions and even opposition remain exist in China, what's more, they devote themselves to exploring a new path to solve those problems. As a new way of constructing socialism, an important aspect of the "new" of the Chinese path is to work out a successful way to solve class differences, contradictions and opposition. The new way here is not about fights or violent means, which is to remove class differences, contradictions and opposition by "a resort to violence". Instead, it's about peaceful means and coordination, which is to relieve class differences, contradictions and opposition by "verbal struggle". That's to say, the class differences, contradictions and opposition are solved by the strength of the masses and legal arms rather than by political movement like the struggle

14 *Selected Works of Deng Xiaoping*, Eng. ed., Foreign Language Press, Beijing, 1995, Vol. II, p. 365.

of the mass. Not only within class, differences, contradictions and opposition between different groups or classes can also be settled by "non-violent means". The "non-violent means" mentioned here refer to the complement and improvement of democracy and legal systems, the enhancing of the democracy and law consciousness of citizens in resolving difference, contradictions and opposition between different classes. In the period of "the class struggle being the core", mistakes made in the class struggle mainly are reflected in two aspects. On the one hand, they are manifested in overusing the Class Struggle Theory where the class struggle was emphasized repeatedly in every day, every month and every year, believing in the idea that "the class struggle is grasped, all problems can be solved", which exaggerates the extent of the class struggle existing in a certain area during socialist times; on the other hand, they are revealed in regarding the class struggle one-sidedly as violence and dictatorship, that's to say, solving class differences, contradictions and opposition blindly by bloody means like violence and deprivation. In the new historical period, the pioneers of the Chinese path have corrected those mistakes on the class struggle in time. Based on the specific situation that China is still in the primary stage of socialism, the leaders believe that contradictions in China currently are not all about the class struggle and the class struggle is not all about adversarial contradictions, and even if it is, those adversarial contradictions cannot be solved by rivalry or violent means. As the Chinese path opens up, China farewells the time when social contradictions were settled by the struggle of the mass and starts resolving social contradictions with laws as the basis and within the legal system. Deng Xiaoping makes it clear that developing the class struggle in the new historical period, "We should not mount a political movement to accomplish this, as we have done in the past. We should abide by the principles of socialist legality"[15]. And he noted particularly: "In fighting anti-Party and anti-socialist

15 *Selected Works of Deng Xiaoping*, Eng. ed., Foreign Language Press, Beijing, 1995, Vol. II, p. 365.

forces and miscellaneous criminals all Party members and cadres should act according to the Constitution and within the bounds of laws and decrees. They should learn to use legal means(including economic penalties such as fines and heavy taxation). This is a new method that we must learn as quickly as possible in order to develop socialist democracy and improve the socialist legal system[16]".

It is indeed a great development of the Marxism Class Struggle Theory under the new historical conditions to associate problems of solving the class struggle and contradictions with the complement and perfection of socialist legal system by law arms, which becomes a basic principle to extend national political life.

III. Under the premise of adhering to the people's democratic dictatorship, specifying the target and main scope of dictatorship in a scientific way.

About the class struggle theory that Marx once talked about, as mentioned above, in which he only added three "new points" based on previous study, the second and the third point are:

"The class struggle is bound to lead to the dictatorship of the proletariat" and "this dictatorship is nothing but a transition of the realization of eliminating all classes and entering into a non-class society".[17] The dictatorship of the proletariat is, indeed, the core of the Marxism Class Struggle Theory. Lenin proposed later that only those who accept class struggle theory and agree on the dictatorship of proletariat can be called Marxists.

The pioneers of the Chinese path admit that to some extent class struggle still exists in current China, which calls for the necessity of adhering to the dictatorship of the proletariat. However, in some situation, the dictatorship of the proletariat is described as "people's

16 Ibid., p. 366.

17 *Selected Works of Marx and Engels*, Chin. E. People's Publishing House, Beijing, Vol. X, 1994, p. 106.

democratic dictatorship", which is the same. Deng Xiaoping once explained it : "Comrade Mao Zedong once said that people's democratic dictatorship" means the combination of democracy among the people with dictatorship over reactionaries. This, in essence, is the dictatorship of the proletariat. But in our country the term 'people's democratic dictatorship' is more suited to the reality"[18].

The frontiers of the Chinese path put adhering to people's democratic dictatorship as one of the four cardinal principles that must be upheld. The four cardinal principles were put forward by Deng Xiaoping, in which he emphasized that "the principle of adhering to people's democratic dictatorship should not be lower than the other three". In the speech of the forum on the principles for the Party's theoretical work on March 30th 1979, he pointed out:

> "We have conducted a lot of propaganda explaining that the dictatorship of the proletariat means socialist democracy for the people, democracy enjoyed by the workers, peasants, intellectuals and other working people, the broadest democracy that has ever existed in history...Therefore, so long as class struggle exists and so long as imperialism and hegemonism exist, it is inconceivable that the dictatorial function of the state should wither away, that the standing army, public security organs, courts and prisons should wither away. Their existence is not in contradiction with the democratization of the socialist state, for their correct and effective work ensures , rather than hampers, such democratization. The fact of the matter is that socialism cannot be defended or built up without the dictatorship of the proletariat."[19]

Ten years later, he further stated it in a speech when he visited the South of China in 1992:

> "One of the basic concepts of Marxism is that the socialist system must be defended by the dictatorship of the proletariat...History has proved that a new, rising class that has just taken power is, generally speaking,

18 *Selected Works of Deng Xiaoping*, Eng. ed., Foreign Language Press, Beijing, 1995, Vol. II, p. 367.

19 Ibid., pp. 177-178.

> weaker than the opposing classes. It must therefore resort to dictatorship to consolidate its power. Democracy is practiced within the ranks of the people and dictatorship over the enemy. This is the people's democratic dictatorship. It is right to consolidate the people's power by employing the force of the people's democratic dictatorship. There is nothing wrong in that."[20]

Adhering to people's democratic dictatorship has been written into the Constitution of China. According to our Constitution:

The People's Republic of China is a socialist country under the people's democratic dictatorship, led by the working class and based on the alliance of workers and peasants. In accordance to the Constitution of People's Republic of China, people's democratic dictatorship mainly contains the following five aspects of meanings: (1)the working class is under the lead of the Communist Party of China but not led by any other classes, parties or multi-parties, neither in any multi-party system; (2)basing on the alliance of workers and peasants is not equal to developing pluralism; (3)people's democratic dictatorship means that all rights belong to people including all socialist laborers and constructors and patriots who support socialism and the reunification of the motherland rather than some interest groups or any foreigners; (4)the dictatorship is practiced to all anti-socialists and anyone who attempts to split the motherland and the government will never apply "a policy of benevolence"; (5)socialist system is the fundamental political system of People's Republic of China, which forbids any organization or person to destroy.

In the new historical period, the pioneers of the Chinese path organically unify the persistence of people's democratic dictatorship with the persistence of opening up policy. On one hand, our state system can stand firmly on the basis of the strong development in society and economy by persisting opening up policy which lays a solid material foundation for people's democratic dictatorship; on another

20 *Selected Works of Deng Xiaoping*, Eng. ed., Foreign Language Press, Beijing, 1995, Vol. III, p. 367.

hand, socialism with Chinese characteristics can move forward in the right direction and road by persisting people's democratic dictatorship which secures the policy of reform and opening up. They creatively and organically unify these two into the socialism with Chinese characteristics and the historical progress of realizing the Chinese dream of great national rejuvenation.

Adhering to people's democratic dictatorship and adhering to opening up are important parts of the Party's basic line in the elementary stage of socialism as well as of socialism with Chinese characteristics. Looking back to the speeches of leaders of the CPC from Deng Xiaoping to Xi Jinping, we can find that they always emphasize the importance of reform and opening up, meanwhile, lay great stress on adhering to people's democratic dictatorship, paralleling "no opening up no way out" with "never give up people's democratic dictatorship" all the time. At the end of 1970s and the beginning of 1980s, China practiced like that when stepping into socialism with Chinese characteristics; When socialism with Chinese characteristics has achieved great success and China has entered into the new developing era of 21st century, it still performs in the same way.

There is no doubt that the socialism with Chinese characteristics is upholding people's democratic dictatorship, which is to practice democracy to the people and dictatorship to the enemy, to develop its road. This, from another aspect, fully proves that the pioneers of Chinese Path have inherited the Marxism Class Struggle Theory. The development and innovation of the Marxism Class Struggle Theory by them on the problem of upholding people's democratic dictatorship represent in ensuring and adjusting constantly the range of "people", as the subject of dictatorship, and of "enemy", as the target of dictatorship, according to the reality in the new historical period of China, maximizing the range of "people" while minimizing the range of "enemy" to help more people to enjoy socialist democracy and to list the least one to the opposite of "people" at best.

Mao Zedong once said that the initial problem of revolution is to figure out who our friends are and who our enemies are, which is also the initial problem of realizing the great national rejuvenation of Chinese people and constructing socialism with Chinese characteristics. The pioneers of the Chinese path did not distinguish them by "books". Reading theories of Deng Xiaoping and other Chinese statesmen, the most impressive point is that on the one hand anytime they put questions that who the Chinese can rely on, who they represent for, who the Party to serve and who to hit and seclude at the first place, on the other hand, they always distinguish friends and enemies based on the social reality of China. According to the statements of these leaders, the meaning of people and enemy seems to be very complicated, but is simple in essence. Those who advocate the system of socialism with Chinese characteristics and people's democratic dictatorship, those who advocate the legal system formed by the system of socialism with Chinese characteristics and people's democratic dictatorship, those who love our country and nations and those who abide by our spiritual and moral civilization belong to the group of "people", otherwise, they are the opposite. By this standard, currently, "people" do take up the majority of the total population in China while the opposite are the minority, at the same time showing a tendency of the former one increasing and the later one decreasing.

When talked about the target of dictatorship, Deng Xiaoping pointed out:

> "But we must recognize that in our socialist society there are still counter-revolutionaries, enemy agents, criminals and other bad elements of all kinds who undermine socialist public order, as well as new exploiters who engage in corruption, embezzlement, speculation and profiteering. And we must also recognize that such phenomena cannot be all eliminated for a long time to come. ......It is still necessary to exercise dictatorship over all these anti-socialist elements, and socialist democracy is impossible without it. This dictatorship is an internal struggle and in some cases an international

struggle as well; in fact, the two aspects are inseparable."[21]

Here Deng clearly cataloged counter-revolutionaries, enemy agents, criminals and other bad elements of all kinds who undermine socialist public order, as well as new exploiters as the target of dictatorship. Jiang Zemin also proposed:

"We must lawfully and resolutely work to prevent and combat infiltration and sabotage by international hostile forces, political conspiracies by hostile elements attempting to subvert the CPC's leadership and China's socialist system, separatist activities of ethnic separatist forces, violent terrorist activities, serious crimes that present a grave threat to the lives and property of the people, cults that harm lives and endanger state power, and corruption that seriously harms the interests of the country and the people. We must use the people's democratic dictatorship to protect the political power of the people and their fundamental interests. On this issue, we must be bold and confident. Not only can we not allow the dictatorship of socialist political power to be weakened, but we must strengthen it. On this issue, we cannot be bookish or naïve."[22]

The identities of enemy need to be under dictatorship that mentioned by Jiang Zemin were almost the same as that of Deng Xiaoping, which only further emphasized that we must practice dictatorship over ethnic separatists, terrorists and cults that harm lives and endanger state power.

As for "people", the leaders of the CPC are extending its range by the change of current economic structure in China. Deng Xiaoping had already stated in 1979:

"During the three decades, the class situation in Chinese society has changed fundamentally. The position of our working class has been enormously strengthened, and our peasants have been members of collectives for more than 20 years...Chinese intellectuals, including the overwhelming majority of the old intellectuals from pre-Liberation society,

---

21 *Selected Works of Deng Xiaoping*, Eng. ed., Foreign Language Press, Beijing, 1995, Vol. II, p. 178.

22 *Selected Works of Jiang Zemin*, Eng. ed., People's Publishing House, Beijing, Vol. III, 2006, p. 218.

> have become part of the working class and now serve the cause of socialism consciously and actively...The means of production formerly owned by the Chinese capitalist class came under state control long ago, and the payment of a fixed rate of interest ended 13 years ago. The overwhelming majority of the capitalists with the capacity to work have transformed themselves into working people who earn their own living in our socialist society...and because most members of the capitalist class, especially the progressives among them, played a positive, co-operative role in accepting this transformation. Today, as working people, they are contributing their share to our socialist modernization."[23]

Here Deng not only profoundly explained that the majority of the old intellectuals from pre-Liberation society have become parts of the working class and serve the important cause of socialism, he also persuasively stated the reasons why overall capitalist class can be listed into the range of "people".

With the development of opening up, the structure of Chinese social stratums has some new changes. This mainly reveals in the appearance of groups of personnel doing pioneering work and technical work in privately-owned science enterprises, private entrepreneurs, individual entrepreneurs, many managerial and technical staff employed by foreign companies, employees in intermediaries, free-lance professionals and so on. How to view these new class stratums? Can we view them as the same as workers, peasants and intellectuals as "people" and the constructors of socialism with Chinese characteristics?[24]

Jiang Zemin analyzed this in time: "In view of this, we cannot simply judge people's political orientation simply by whether they own property or how much they own. Rather, we should judge them mainly by their ideological and political awareness and their actual performance by how they acquire property and by how they allocate and utilize it, and by how much their labor contributes to the cause of

23 *Selected Works of Deng Xiaoping*, Eng. ed., Foreign Language Press, Beijing, 1995, Vol. II, p. 192.

24 Xu Donghai and others: *From Organizing Class Struggle to Developing Harmonious Socialist Society*, Scientific Socialism, 2008 (5) .

building socialism with Chinese characteristics".[25] Actually Jiang had clearly said here that all such persons are parts of "people". It is not by the own property to define whether they belong to "people" or not, whether they belong to the subject of dictatorship or the target. This is indeed great development of the Marxism Class Struggle Theory under the new historical conditions. It has remarkably extended the range of "people" and shrunk the range of "enemy" in China for not blindly regarding property-owners as exploiting class or who must stand opposite to the major labors.

25 *Selected Works of Jiang Zemin*, Eng. ed., People's Publishing House, Beijing, Vol. III, 2006, p. 287.

References

I. Classics

1. *Complete Works of Marx and Engels* (Vol. II~X), People's Publishing House, 2009.

2. *Selected Works of Marx and Engels* (Vol. I~IV), People's Publishing House, 1972, 1995, 2009.

3. *Capital* (Vol. I), People's Publishing House, 2004.

4. *Collected Works of Lenin*, People's Publishing House, 2009.

5. *Selected Works of Stalin* (Vol. II), People's Publishing House, 1979.

6. *Collected Works of Mao Tse-Tung* (Vol. VII), People's Publishing House, 1999.

7. *Selected Works of Mao Tse-Tung* (Vol. I), People's Publishing House, 1999.

8. *Selected Readings of Mao Tse-Tung* (Vol. II), People's Publishing House, 1986.

9. *Selected Works of Deng Xiaoping* (Vol. II, Vol. III), People's Publishing House, 1993, 1994.

10. *Selected Works of Jiang Zemin* (Vol. I, Vol. III), People's Publishing House, 2006.

II. Chinese Originals

1. *Selections of Important Documents Since 16th NCCP* (Vol. II), People's Publishing House, 2008.

2. *Selections of Important Documents Since 17th NCCP* (Vol. I), People's Publishing House, 2009.

3. *Selections of Important Documents Since 13th NCCP* (Vol. I , Vol. II), People's Publishing House, 1991.

4. *Selections of Important Documents Since 15th NCCP* (Vol. II), People's Publishing House, 2001.

5. *Decision of the CPC Central Committee on Several Issues Concerning Perfecting Socialist Market Economy System*, People's Publishing House, 2003.

6. *Zhu Rongji Meets the Press*, People's Publishing House, 2009.

7. Chen Jiagang edited: *Crisis and Future, Francies Fukuyama's Speeches in China*, Central Compilation&Translation Press, 2012.

8. Chen Xueming and others: *Why Does China Still Needs Marxism-To Answer 10 questions About Marxism*, Tianjin People's Publishing House, 2013.

9. Ding Xueliang: *Debating the Chinese Model*, Social Sciences Academic Press, 2011.

10. Guo Liancheng: *Russia's Economic Shift and the Theory of this Period*, The Commercial Press, 2005.

11. Hu Jintao: *Firmly March on the Path of Socialism with Chinese Characteristics and Strive to Complete the Building of a Moderately Prosperous Society in all Respects-Report to the Eighteenth National Congress of the Communist Party of China*, People's Publishing House,2012.

12. Jiang Zemin: *On Socialism with Chinese Characteristics (Special Excerpts)*, Central Party Literature Press, 2002.

13. Nie Yunlin and others edited: *Study on the Theoretical System of Socialism with Chinese Characteristics*, Chin. ed., People's Publishing House, 2011.

14. Pang Yuanzheng edited: *Contemporary China's Scientific*

Development View, The Central Party School Publishing Press, 2004.

15. Tong Shijun: *On Modernity Between China and the West*, Xuelin Publishing House, 2010.

16. Xia Jun edited: *Scientific Socialism is not Phantasy——About Explorations on some Important Questions of Theoretical System*, Shanghai people's publishing house, 2014.

17. Yang Yongzhi and others: *Socialism with Chinese Characteristics and Scientific Socialism*, Nankai University Press, 2010.

18. Yu Wenlie and others: *Socialist Market Economy*, Economy Daily Press, 2008.

19. Yu Keping edited: *"Socialism" of Globalizational Times*, Central Compilation & Translation Press, 1998.

20. Zhang Weiwei: *Chinese Shock-the Rise of a 'Civilisational State'*, Shanghai People's Publishing House, 2011.

21. Central Party Literature Research Office edited: *Biological Chronology of Deng Xiaoping* (1975-97) (Vol. II), Central Party Literature Publishing House, 2004.

22. Central Party Literature Research Office edited: *Chronicle of Events in Foundation and Development of the Theoretical System of Socialism with Chinese Characteristics*(1978-2008), Central Party Literature Publishing House, 2008.

23. Team of "China Road" of CCCPC Party Literature Research Office: *China Road—Classic Works Reviews of Adapting Marxism to China*", Central Party Literature Press, 2011.

III. Translations of Foreign Works

1. [German] Hegel wrote: *Philosophy of Right*, Zhang Qitai, Fan Yang translated, Commercial Press, 1996.

2. [Russia] Mi Leo Titarenko wrote: *Russia and Its Asian Partners*

under the Framework of Globalization, Li Yanlin, Li Qiangwei, Li Fang,etc. translated, China Social Sciences Press, 2014.

3. [Russia] Lekhanov wrote: *A Year in Motherland*, Wang Yinting, Yang Yong translated, SDX Joint Publishing Company, 1980.

4. [France] Thomas Piketty wrote: *Capital in the Twenty-First Century*, Ba Shusong translated, China Citic Press, 2014.

5. [U.S.] David Kotz, Fred Weir wrote: *Revolution from Above*, Cao Rongxiang and others translated, China Renmin University Press, 2008.

6. [U.S.] Francies Fukuyama wrote: *The End of History and the Last Man*, Huang Shengqiang, Xu Mingyuan translated, Distance Press, 1998.

7. [U.S.] Francies Fukuyama wrote: *Trust: the Social Virtues and the Creation of Prosperity*, Peng Zhihua translated, Hainan Publishing House, 2001.

8. [U.S.] Herbert Marcuse wrote: *Reason and Revolution: Hegel and the Rise of Social Theory*, Cheng Zhimin and others translated, Chongqing Publishing House, 1993.

9. [U.S] Robert Mangold edited: *Biographical Dictionary of "New Marxism"*, Zhao Peijie and others translated, Chongqing Publishing House, 1990.

10. [U.S] Jonathan Anderson wrote: *How to Think about China*, Yu Jiang and others translated, China Citic Press, 2006.

11. [U.S] John Naisbitt, [Australia] Doris Naisbitt wrote: *How the Global Southern Belt Will Reshape Our World*, Zhang Yan, Liang Jifeng, Chi Zhijuan and others translated, Jilin Publishing Company, Chinese Industry and Commerce Publishing House, 2015.

12. [U.S] John Naisbitt, [Australia] Doris Naisbitt wrote: *China's Magatrends*, Wei Ping translated, Jilin Publishing Company, Chinese Industry and Commerce Publishing House, 2009.

13. [U.S] Zbigniew Brzezinski wrote: *Global Turmoil on the Eve of the 21st Century*, Pan Jiafen, Liu Ruixiang translated, China Social Sciences Publishing House, 1995.

14. [Italy] Giovanni Arrighi wrote: *Adam Smith in Beijing*, Lu Aiguo, Huang Ping, Xu Anjie translated, Social Sciences Academic Press, 2009.

15.[England] Martin Jacques wrote: *When China Rules the World: The Rise of the Middle Kingdom and the End of the Western World*, Zhang Li, Liu Qu translated, China Citic Press, 2010.

IV. Journal Articles

1. [France] Jacques Derrida: *Specters of Marx*, New Left Review, 205th in 1994.

2. Chang Zongyao: *"About the World Significance of Socialism with Chinese Characteristics"*, Theoretical Exploration, 4th in 2008.

3. Chen Bao: *Analysis of the Position of Socialism with Chinese Characteristics in World Socialist Movement*, Study and Practice, 4th in 2011.

4. Chen Xueming: *"Misinterpretation" of What China Has Achieved Over the Last 30 Years In Commemoration of the 90th Anniversary of CPC*, Journal of Shanghai Normal University(Philosophy & Social Sciences Edition), 4th in 2011.

5. Guo Wanchao: *Science Positioning of Socialism with Chinese Characteristics*, New Horizon College English, 1st in 2009.

6. Guo Zhipeng: *Socialism Replaces Capitalism: a Revolution of Fairness and Efficiency Concept*, Studies on Marxism, 5th in 2001.

7. Hu Zhenliang: *On Socialism with Chinese Characteristics and Contemporary World Socialism*, Scientific Socialism, 3rd in 2010.

8. Li Bailing: *Arif Dirlik's View on Global Modernity and Capitalism with Chinese Characteristics*, Studies on the Socialism With Chinese

Characteristics, 6th in 2008.

9. Li Qiqing: *Criticism of Two Negation of Socialism with Chinese Characteristics*, Contemporary World & Socialism, 4th in 2005.

10. Liu Zie: *On Great Contribution of Developing Socialism with Chinese Characteristics to World Socialism*, Theory Journal, 3rd in 1996.

11. Lu Ming: *Appropriate Institution, Economic Growth and Balanced Development - Development Path of China as a Big Country and Its Implication for the World*, Academic Monthly, 6th in 2008.

12. Luo Huide: *The Historic Position and Era Features of the Development of Socialism with Chinese Characteristics in the light of Globalization*, Contemporary World and Socialism, 1st in 2013.

13. Ouyang Kang: *Complexity and Innovation of Humanities and Social Sciences*, Philosophical Research, 7th in 2003.

14. Ouyang Kang and others: *Analysis on Structural Characteristics of Socialism with Chinese Characteristics*, Studies on the Socialism with Chinese Characteristics, 2nd in 2009.

15. Pu Guoliang: *Socialism with Chinese Characteristics in the View of World Socialism*, Teaching and Research, 8th in 2008.

16. Qin Xuan: *International Perspective of the Chinese Model - Also on the Socialism with Chinese Characteristics and its International Influence*, Journal of Renmin University of China, 4th in 2008.

17. Sun Daiyao: *The Development of Contemporary Chinese Society in the View of World History*, Wuhan University Journal of Humanities and Sciences, 5th in 2002.

18. Sun Zhongliang: *The Meaning of Chinese Model in Post-Crisis Era*, Scientific Socialism, 1st in 2012.

19. Tang Guanghong: *The International Significance of Socialism with Chinese Characteristics-Also on the so-called Ideological Threat of Chinese Development Model*, Journal of Yangzhou University, 1st in 2008.

20. Tao Wenzhao: *The African Effect of Chinese Model*, International

Studies, 1st in 2009.

21. Wu Bo: *Research summary of these years on Chinese Model*, Shan Dong Social Science, 1st in 2011.

22. Wu Xiaoming: *On the Peaceful Development of China and its World Historical Significance*, Social Sciences in China, 5th in 2009.

23. Xie Yongkuan and others: *A Multidimensional Perspective on the Advantages of the Socialism System with Chinese Characteristics under the Background of International Economic Crisis*, Theoretical Exploration, 2nd in 2012.

24. Xu Chongwen: *Socialism with Chinese Characteristics is a Great Creation in the History of Human Civilization*, The Journal of CPC Yunnan Provincial Committee School, 5th in 2012.

25. Xu Donghai and others: *From Organizing Class Struggle to Building Socialist Harmonious Society*, Scientific Socialism, 5th in 2008.

26. Xu Juezai: *View of Foreign Scholars on Socialism with Chinese Characteristics*, Studies on the socialism with Chinese characteristics, 3rd in 2008.

27. Xu Jinyun: *The Theory of Types of Civilization and Socialism with Chinese Characteristics*, Probe, 1st in 2011.

28. Yan Xu: *The Full knowledge of the Significance of Socialism with Chinese Characteristics to the Evolution of World Civilization*, Party Construction, 4th in 2012.

29. Yang Genqiao: *The Global Significance of the Theoretical System of Socialism with Chinese Characteristics*, Journal of Anhui Administration Institute, 1st in 2010.

30. Yao Yang: *The Global and Historical Significance of China Road*, International Economic Review, 1st in 2010.

31. Zhang Aiwu: *On the World Significance of the Theoretical System of Socialism with Chinese Characteristics*, Marxism & Reality, 3rd in 2009.

32. Zhang Shujun: *A Scientific Answer to the "World Question" of*

humans – The Global Value of Socialism with Chinese Characteristics, Studies in Ideological Education, 2nd in 2013.

33. Zheng Derong: *On Basic Problems of Socialism with Chinese Characteristics*, Social Sciences in Chinese Higher Education Institutions, 3rd in 2011.

34. Zheng Jie and others: *The Historical World Significance of Socialism with Chinese Characteristics*, Shangdong Social Science, 5th in 2010.

35. Zhou Jianjun and others: *The meaning of China's Transformation: From Washington Consensus to Beijing Consensus*, Forum of World Economy and Politics, 1st in 2005.

36. Zhou Yuyun: *The Theory of Building Socialism with Chinese Characteristics and World Socialist Movement*, The Journal of International Studies, 2nd in 1996.

Afterword

In 2015, with other scholars, I wrote *The Global Significance of China Road*, which was published by Tianjin People's Publishing House. It's the final outcome of the major project of the National Social Science Foundation of China, "The Global Significance of Socialism with Chinese Characteristics" (Grant No. 11&ZD065).

This book is selected into the "Publishing Project of Studying Deeply and Carrying Out the Spirit in Important Speeches of Xi Jinping" and is subsidized by National Press Fund. In 2016, it had the honor to win the "Sixth Chinese Excellent Publication Award" which is one of the "Three Big Awards" in Chinese books. As one of the major authors, I feel gratified at the recognition and acknowledge of our state and scholars on this book for its interpretation of the global significance of China Road, which has been fully proved by its selection into the project and gaining one of the "Three Big Awards".

The Global Significance of China Road is a thick book of more than 500 thousands of words. Even the relevant research learners find it difficult to read, so I deleted and revised the original book for the most readers' convenience. With the idea of streaming the structure and refining words, the original book of four parts is simplifying into 12 chapters from 33 chapters, deleting all appendixes and becoming this new book – *The Chinese Path: What Has the Rise of China Contributed to the World?*. Through "slimming", I hope this book can be easier for most readers and help more people to know about socialism with Chinese Characteristics explored and developed by China itself. When China Road has brought earth-shaking changes to China, what kind of meaningful developing pattern it will provide for the world?

Although *The Chinese Path: What Has the Rise of China Contributed to the World* is deleted and finalized on the basis of the original book, the editors in Tianjin People's Publishing House have finished the redaction process responsibly, correcting few missing mistakes in the original book and increasing the quality of the book. I want to express my sincere appreciation to the executives and editors in Tianjin People's Publishing House for publishing this book with high quality once again!

For the views in the original book, I didn't make any amendment. Advice or suggestions from scholars and readers are highly appreciated.

Chen Xueming March 7th, 2017.